Zed Titles on Poverty

Many Zed Books titles on international and Third World issues deal, one way or another, with the question of poverty. The following titles, however, deal with the question specifically.

Brian C. Aldrich and Ravinder S. Sandhu (eds), *Housing the Urban Poor: A Guide to Policy and Practice in the South*

Michel Chossudovsky, *The Globalization of Poverty: Impacts of IMF and World Bank Reforms*

Siddharth Dube, *In the Land of Poverty: Memoirs of an Indian Family, 1947–97*

Neil Webster and Lars Engberg-Pedersen (eds), *In the Name of the Poor: Contesting Political Space for Poverty Reduction*

David Gordon and Paul Spicker (eds), *The International Glossary on Poverty*

Rajni Kothari, *Poverty: Human Consciousness and the Amnesia of Development*

John Madeley, *Big Business, Poor Peoples: The Impact of Transnational Corporations on the World's Poor*

Suzanne Thorbek, *Gender and Slum Culture in Urban Asia*

Willem Van Genugten and Camillo Perez-Bustillo (eds), *The Poverty of Rights: Human Rights and the Eradication of Poverty*

Francis Wilson et al. (eds), *Poverty Reduction: What Role for the State in Today's Globalized Economy?*

For full details of this list and Zed's other subject and general catalogues, please write to: The Marketing Department, Zed Books, 7 Cynthia Street, London N1 9JF, UK or e-mail: sales@zedbooks.demon.co.uk

Visit our website at: http://www.zedbooks.demon.co.uk

In the Name of the Poor: Contesting Political Space for Poverty Reduction

edited by Neil Webster and Lars Engberg-Pedersen

Zed Books

LONDON · NEW YORK

In the Name of the Poor: Contesting Political Space for Poverty Reduction
was first published by Zed Books Ltd, 7 Cynthia Street, London N1 9JF,
UK and Room 400, 175 Fifth Avenue, New York, NY 10010, USA in 2002

Distributed in the USA exclusively by Palgrave, a division of St Martin's
Press, LLC, 175 Fifth Avenue, New York, NY 10010, USA

Cover designed by Andrew Corbett
Set in Monotype Ehrhardt and Franklin Gothic by Ewan Smith
Printed and bound in Malaysia

A catalogue record for this book is available from the British Library

Library of Congress Cataloging-in-Publication Data: available

ISBN 1 85649 958 8 cased
ISBN 1 85649 959 6 limp

Contents

Preface

In 1996 the Centre for Development Research (CDR) established a research programme with the title Local Organisations and Rural Poverty Alleviation (LORPA), with Neil Webster as its coordinator. Of the nine researchers attached to the programme, two are permanently employed at CDR and the other seven are from universities and research centres in Denmark, Mexico and India. All were based for various periods at CDR between 1996 and 2000. This book is one of the publications to emerge from the research programme.

The focus on poverty and poverty reduction in development studies and development policy has increased quite dramatically just in the four years of the programme. While carrying out the field research for the various case studies within the programme, it has at times been difficult not to be swept up with the emerging trends and fashions that have returned poverty to the centre foreground in development.

On the one hand are the many conferences and workshops in which seemingly new theoretical, conceptual and methodological concerns with the subject have been presented and explored; on the other hand is the growing demand for 'poverty experts' as donor agencies and development practitioners sought to raise the poverty objective in their programmes and projects, often as part of the broader project of developing aid programmes and intervention strategies for the new millennium.

Where LORPA has perhaps retained a degree of distance from other work is in its focus upon detailed research into the local politics of poverty, into the processes through which external interventions directed towards poverty reduction have impacted upon the local and into how groups of the poor have pursued their own strategies for poverty reduction. At the same time LORPA has sought to draw upon much of the new thinking around poverty reduction: its multi-dimensionality, its diversity and complexity, and not least the importance of recognizing the agency of the poor as a central factor in contesting poverty. The result is a critical and grounded approach to the politics of poverty in local contexts around the world. It is designed both to fill a gap in resent research, and to indicate an important direction for future research.

Core funding for the LORPA programme came in the form of support from CDR and research grants to individual researchers from the Danish Council for Research Development. In India, financial support was also provided by GTZ Self-Help Project and by the Institute of Social and Economic Change in Bangalore. Without this support, the research programme and this book would not have been possible. The wider debts incurred in undertaking the research and in the preparation of this book are considerable. Our first thanks are to all those who permitted LORPA's researchers and its research to enter their lives in so many ways during the course of the fieldwork. The book is about them and for them. We must also thank all the families and friends of the researchers who supported the work with such help and understanding. Our many colleagues at CDR have provided many forms of support, both intellectual and practical. We would single you all out for our special thanks and appreciation for the working environment that you have provided us with. Beyond the walls of CDR we wish to thank Narayan Banerjee, Diana Conyers, Ben Cousins, Preben Kaarsholm, Steffan Lindberg, Monique Nuijten, Rajni Palriwala, Ben Rogaly, Brian Smith, Olle Törnquist and Peter Uvin for their comments to various drafts of the papers that provided the basis for this book. Finally we wish especially to thank Ane Toubro, who, as secretary to the programme, has demonstrated immense patience and tremendous good sense.

Neil Webster
Lars Engberg-Pedersen

Contributors

Astrid Blom is a Ph.D. researcher at the Centre for Development Research, Copenhagen, affiliated to the Researcher School at International Development Studies, Roskilde University. She holds a master's degree in international development studies and geography and has carried out fieldwork and held consultancies in Mozambique since 1994.

Lars Engberg-Pedersen is a former research fellow at the Centre for Development Research in Copenhagen. In June 2000 he became head of the International Department in the Danish Association of International Cooperation (MS). He has carried out fieldwork and other longer-term assignments in Burkina Faso, Nicaragua, Indonesia and Karnataka, India. His publications include work on institutional change, rural development and natural resource management.

Anne Marie Ejdesgaard Jeppesen is an associate professor at the Department of Romance Languages, University of Copenhagen. She has been attached to the Centre for Development Research as a project senior researcher. At the moment she is working on labour movements and peasants' organizations and their role in Bolivian democracy. She has previously worked on Peronist unions and changes in the culture and perceptions of economic development in Argentina.

Amanda Hammar is a Zimbabwean researcher, currently based at the Centre for Development Research in Copenhagen, where she is completing work on her Ph.D. on the politics of land, place and displacement in the communal areas of Zimbabwe. Prior to this, she worked as a rural development practitioner and consultant for some fourteen years. Her most recent work in this field focused on processes of decentralization and local government reform.

Abul Hossain has an M.Phil. in sociology from Dhaka University. He is a research fellow at the Power and Participation Research Center in Dhaka, Bangladesh. Mr Hossain has collaborated on a number of research projects in rural Bangladesh, and has worked as a consultant for the British Department for International Development (DFID). Since 2000 he has been studying sociology as a Ph.D. student at the University of Pune, India.

Karsten Paerregaard is a senior lecturer at the Department of Anthropology, University of Copenhagen. He is currently working on a comparative study of Peruvian migration and immigration policies in Europe, the USA, Japan and Argentina. He has published several books, including *Linking Separate Worlds: Urban Migrants and Rural Lives in Peru*, Oxford: Berg, 1997, and articles including 'The dark side of the moon', *American Anthropologist*, vol. C, no. 2, 1998.

D. Rajasekhar is a development economist based at the Institute for Social and Economic Change, Bangalore, India. He has published seven books and numerous articles in Indian and international journals on rural credit, NGO savings and credit programmes, NGOs and decentralized government, agrarian change, irrigation and rural development.

Magdalena Villarreal is a lecturer and researcher at the Centre for Research and Advanced Studies in Social Anthropology (CIESAS) based in Guadalajara, Mexico. Her publications include: 'The poverty of practice', in Norman Long and Ann Long, *Battlefields of Knowledge: The Interlocking of Theory and Practice in Social Research and Development*, London: Routledge, 1992 and 'Small product, big issues: value contestations and cultural identities in cross-border commodity networks', with Norman Long in Birgit Meyer and Peter Geschiere (eds), *Development and Change*, vol. 29, no. 4.

Neil Webster is a senior research fellow at the Centre for Development Research and coordinator for the programme Local Organisations and Rural Poverty Alleviation (LORPA). He has undertaken research on rural development in India for more than twenty years. His publications include: *Do the Poor Matter? A Comparative Study of European Aid for Poverty Reduction in India*, co-authored with Aidan Cox, Steen Folke and Lau Schulpen, London: ODI, 2000 and 'Democracy, development and the institutionalised participation of the poor for poverty reduction', in Paul Collins, *Applying Public Administration in Development: Signposts for the Future*, London: John Wiley, 2000.

Kirsten Westergaard is a senior research fellow at the Centre for Development Research in Copenhagen. Dr Westergaard has undertaken a number of research projects in India and Bangladesh focusing on gender and various aspects of state–society relations, including local power structures, local government and NGOs. Her publications include 'Local government in Bangladesh: past experiences and yet another try', *World Development*, vol. 23, no. 4, 1995, and 'People's empowerment in Bangladesh. NGO strategies', *Journal of Social Studies* (Dhaka), no. 72, 1996.

Introduction to Political Space

Lars Engberg-Pedersen and Neil Webster

Tackling poverty has long been the raison d'être for development studies and aid policy, if not always the guiding principle. Today, despite improving conditions in many countries, about 1.3 billion people still subsist on incomes of less than US$1 a day (UNDP 1997) – that is, nearly one-quarter of the world's population. Even where one finds a relative decline in the proportion of poor, population growth has ensured an absolute increase. India, the country possessing the greatest number of poor, saw a relative decline from over 50 per cent to 35 per cent between 1953 and 1994 while at the same time experiencing an increase of more than 170 million in absolute terms.

At first sight, the scale and persistence of the 'poverty problem' suggest that attempts to reduce poverty have not been particularly successful. To some extent this is true. Yet today the attention given to poverty as a problem of development has never been greater. One reason for this can be found in the end of the Cold War and the retreat from the logic of *realpolitik* that dominated international politics for nearly four decades. Another reason must lie in the sheer scale and extent of poverty in the world today, which have become morally and politically unacceptable. However, a third and perhaps more optimistic reason lies in the advances made in the theoretical and methodological approaches to the study and analysis of poverty. While it can be said that poverty has never been such a problem, never has more been known about poverty, its dynamics and its dimensions.

Improvements in our knowledge and understanding of poverty must serve as a basis for better policies and programmes designed to reduce and alleviate poverty. For example, improvements in quantitative data have revealed that not only has the distribution of populations between rich and poor become more skewed, so too has the distribution of the poor beneath the poverty line (UNDP 1998). The absolute poor are becoming locked into an increasingly desperate situation in which much that is undertaken for purposes of poverty reduction fails or merely passes them by. Similarly, developments in qualitative methodologies enable us to identify and research poverty dynamics and dimensions that sustain marginalization and exclusion in ways previously unknown or ignored. This has facilitated a major reassessment of existing and alternative approaches towards poverty reduction (Baulch 1996; Chambers 1995).

It is now clear that while economic growth and better access to markets are crucial requirements in reducing the number of people in economic poverty, they are not sufficient. Nor, as attempts at state-led development have revealed, is it sufficient to leave poverty reduction to the state. In the contemporary world, with the vagaries of fluctuating world markets rendering national economies fragile and their institutional structures often in crisis, poverty reduction is not likely to take place in a sustained manner without the involvement of the poor. Today poverty reduction requires the generation and facilitation of opportunities for the poor and organizations working on their behalf to exert an influence on political and economic processes. This is so whether it is a case of poverty firmly rooted in structures of exploitation and social inequality or a matter of the poor simply not being able to benefit from social policies and economic opportunities in their immediate vicinity.

The reduction of poverty therefore requires that we begin by understanding processes of impoverishment. Here we should take as our point of departure the actions and strategies of poor people themselves. Taking this step leads to the immediate recognition of the complexity and diversity of poverty. That the poor are no homogeneous group, that the particular conditions of impoverishment differ substantially, and that the needs and ambitions of poor people vary even more are well documented. There is accordingly a need for studies that are based on these particularities, that focus upon the specificities of diverse forms of poverty, the groups of poor that social change has given rise to, and not least their actions and strategies.

In setting out to undertake such studies, the researchers represented in this volume have first sought to establish a conceptual framework from which to approach poverty and poor people. The point of departure is a recognition of the fact that what may be labelled poverty covers a very wide and diverse range of experiences and processes of marginalization, which are excluded if one only considers economic issues such as lack of income and consumption. Vulnerability, isolation and humiliation are dimensions that might capture the hardship endured by specific groups better than the lack of income. The diversity in experiences of poverty also suggests that generalizations about it or about the interests of the poor will always be prone to being a reflection of the ideas of the observer more than the realities of the observed. In this sense, the concept of 'the poor' is problematic because it has become an outsider's concept. In many societies no one would like to describe oneself or be designated as poor and thus having one's own hardship made public. To be poor is often to be associated with low social status, laziness and irresponsibility. The fact of poverty must therefore always be weighed against the experience and perception of poverty in a specific context. Furthermore, some would question whether the observer should herself or himself use the terms 'poverty' or 'the poor' when these are not recognized by those categorized as such. The diversity in the use of the poverty concept in the literature and the problems associated with identifying the poor are reflected in the chapters in this book, not least in the reluctance of some authors to use the general term 'the poor' in the context of their studies.

Conceptually, one crucial aspect of poverty has to do with structural inequalities and the power struggles these give rise to. This is the relational dimension of poverty. In many situations particular groups of people are politically excluded and economically exploited by others who are seeking to maintain a relation of dependence. Such relations range from those within the household through to inter-sectoral relations involving substantial populations. Examples range from gender relations or those between landowner and sharecropper through to the impersonal relations based upon prices between urban consumers and rural producers. The relational dimension of poverty is concerned with the processes by which poverty emerges. Poverty is manifested in a lack of resources and opportunities compared to others, reflecting a condition of relative deprivation. Here, poverty is seen as the comparative lack of a good livelihood, assets, information and knowledge, rights, and so forth. To raise questions concerning the equity of the prevailing distribution is often the first step towards an exploration of the processes that have given rise to it. In situations where deprivation involves a lack of the necessities required to maintain a basic standard of living, one approaches the condition of absolute poverty. Here it is not so much the condition relative to others' condition that matters so much as the need to survive at an acceptable level. Society's role in setting standards and expectations is a recurrent theme, and context remains a central factor in discussions of poverty.

A common feature of the contributions to this book is the emphasis upon marginalized people as social actors seeking to cope with their conditions and to develop strategies to exploit emerging opportunities (Beck 1994; Chambers 1989; Swift 1989; Thompson 1993). Vulnerable and excluded people tend not to be passive victims of an unjust world. In that they face poverty on a daily basis, their actions and strategies provide a rich source of material for understanding poverty and for work towards poverty reduction. The failure to recognize the importance of these activities and the motivations and constraints faced by the poor are central reasons as to why poverty-reduction policies and programmes are often of little use or serve simply to reinforce the problems of poverty.

However, to place emphasis upon the agency of the deprived does not have to imply that, given the opportunity, they can pull themselves up by their own bootstraps and overcome impoverishment. When opportunities emerge they may sometimes be able to improve their lot, but in the face of deteriorating or static conditions, people characterized by few resources, subordination and exclusion do not face a promising future. Sometimes optimistic expectations are very difficult to entertain, as the following description of the poorest households in two Tanzanian villages suggests:

> Equipped with one instrument, the hoe, and two resources, land and labour, but often physically weak, lacking food, in dependent relationships with other households, and often lacking time at the right moment, not to speak of inputs, to cultivate their own farms, it is difficult to associate them with agency. They cope, but are mostly without surplus to make choices, to devise strategies, and to find ways to manage their resources in a sustainable manner. (Sano 1996: 23)

In the face of such severe constraints, to cope is in itself a triumph and an outcome that many others outside this situation would not consider possible.

Local Organizations and Poor People

In connection with poverty reduction, local organizations have emerged in recent years as an important focus for development studies. People's associations, decentralized governments, the local offices of ministries and NGOs are the sorts of organization that policy-makers and aid practitioners have increasingly come to involve when seeking to address conditions of poverty. To the external observer, the range of local organizations divides itself into fairly standard categories based upon relationship to the state, type of activity and relationship to the 'local' population. Yet seen from the perspective of marginalized people, the institutional landscape may look somewhat different and be viewed in terms of quite different criteria. Depending upon one's position and condition, the roles and activities of the different organizations can lead not only to very different outcomes, but often to outcomes that are unintended on the part of the policy-makers. Despite this being dangerous terrain, through both choice and necessity poor groups must often seek to negotiate it and to attempt to exploit the opportunities arising from the various interventions. In conflict with those who are better endowed, they might well seek to go beyond contesting the actions of local organizations and seek instead to 'open up' the activities of the organizations and to re-orient their natures (Berry 1993; Olivier de Sardan 1995).

The way in which this takes place depends very much upon the nature of the deprivation that people experience, on the history and character of the organizations working in the area, and on the broader political context. In a situation in which relative deprivation is of central concern, organizations providing social services will be of importance. However, educational opportunities will not, in the short term, change a relationship of dependency that forces one group to undertake work that systematically undervalues their contribution and thereby their entitlement. In fact it might well be that such a relationship denies access to those very opportunities that are being made 'available' to them. Here, organizations trying to empower these groups and to advocate their cause may be more valuable to the poor. If such empowerment seeks to draw upon existing organizational experiences, they may be able to exploit local organizations and provide access to political arenas. To work towards poverty reduction it is therefore essential to explore the historical processes of impoverishment and enrichment that lie behind the marginalization of specific groups and to search out the practices or coping strategies utilized in the face of such marginalization.

Turning to the history and character of different local organizations, clearly these differ immensely. To understand their respective histories requires that the context for their emergence and activities be studied. In this way one can avoid the dangers of a simple comparative assessment of local organizations and their capacities. This has, however, been a tendency when discussing local organizations in terms of their respective comparative advantages in poverty reduction. Local organizations are heterogeneous entities pursuing a wide range of interests often in conflict with one another. In that it is more often than not the better educated and the wealthy who constitute the leadership in these organizations, the interests of the poor are not an automatic concern.

It is also clear that while a particular type of organization might be successful in pursuing poverty reduction in one society or country, the same type of organization with similar strategies might not be successful elsewhere. In Bangladesh there are examples of local NGOs supporting the organization of marginalized social groups and successfully advocating their cause to local government and the state (see Chapter 9). In Bolivia, however, 'people's organizations' such as the *sindicatos* are quite critical of many local NGOs, as they are competing for the same funds (see Chapter 2). Similarly, the relationship between and work of local governments and ministries' local offices differs substantially both between and within countries. These differences have to do with the histories of the particular organizations, and the local socially and economically marginalized groups are often well aware of these histories. The interaction of local organizations and the poor therefore needs to be seen in the light of the specific context and the historical relationship between different local organizations and the different groups of the poor found there.

The political context of the interaction between the poor, local organizations and the state is the subject of this book. Political processes at national and local levels not only frame the working conditions of local organizations and their objectives and activities, but directly confront or sustain the causes of impoverishment and social exclusion. This is why political struggle to influence the actions and policies of the state in policy design and implementation is a fundamental part of the poverty-reduction agenda. Agency by the poor or on their behalf is essential in this respect.

In many contexts, however, apart from foot-dragging and other forms of low-intensity resistance, the poor are reluctant to influence processes of policy-making affecting broader social groupings. From the perspective of the poor there are several problems with political endeavours: they tend not to deliver immediate material gains; they are often dangerous, in that they exacerbate the vulnerability of the poor; and they require resources that the poor seldom possess. Thus attempts to influence policies and decisions affecting the conditions of the poor are typically, but not exclusively, undertaken by various kinds of organization on their behalf. Naturally this creates significant problems of representation, first because the interests and concerns of the poor must pass through intermediaries who must identify these interests and concerns, and second because these same intermediaries have their own concerns and interests. Sustained poverty reduction is therefore strongly dependent on the organizational landscape, and not least its pro-poor orientation.

In the first instance, the political context of processes of impoverishment and enrichment is national, in that the state and its policies, together with the processes and contests these involve, are of central importance. But the international or transnational dimension plays a constituting role, in that many organizational actors working with the poor are financially and administratively based outside the national state and can often be seen as located in global discourses on development. Moreover, during the last couple of decades international organizations and bilateral aid agencies have increasingly prescribed the policies to be implemented by recipient governments as a condition of development assistance.

The political space for poverty reduction is therefore influenced, directly and indirectly, by a very diverse range of actors. If we then argue that political space for the poor is necessary for effective and sustainable poverty reduction, then the latter becomes linked to a more complex set of political, economic and social factors than is generally accepted on the part of development practitioners.

This book seeks to explore dimensions of the political space for poverty reduction in different countries by applying different analytical approaches. The ambition is to investigate the ways in which political space is shaped, its implications for processes of impoverishment and enrichment, and the strategies of the poor and of organizations to manoeuvre and create opportunities for poverty reduction.

The Concept of Political Space

In referring to the concept of political space, we are proposing an analytical tool with which to explore the role of the poor in poverty reduction. Our research suggests that there are two main groups of strategies through which the poor can achieve a change in their conditions of poverty. First, there are strategies that are carried out by the poor in an attempt to change their poverty in terms of their resources and assets. Second, there are strategies through which the poor, or those representing the poor, seek to secure their interests by effecting change in the actions and policies of others and, in particular, bringing about change in public policy and in its implementation.

The former is often analysed in terms of the coping strategies of the poor. It is usually based upon individual or local groups of poor seeking ways to offset the economic disadvantages they face by exploiting opportunities to utilize the resources and assets they possess or can access. Migration, grassroots production cooperatives, loans from relatives or credit associations, diversification of production and entering new labour markets are some examples.

The second group of strategies is characterized by the need to change the policies and practices of others in order to bring about change. In particular it is directed at achieving a redistribution of resources in order to change the poverty condition. Here an important focus is upon effecting institutional change in terms of the formulation and implementation of policies. In terms of resources, this represents an attempt to change the basis upon which existing resources are distributed and utilized within the locality, and upon which new resources might be introduced into the locality and distributed. The discussion of poverty reduction thereby becomes one of mobilization, organization, representation and empowerment.

These two groups of strategies are contingent upon the political space. Here the concept of political space seeks to address two weaknesses of contemporary discussions of marginalized groups and local organizations with respect to poverty reduction. One weakness has to do with the widespread concern with participation and the 'comparative advantages' of local organizations in achieving participation. There is a tendency on the part of both donors and governments to regard poor people's participation in projects and policy-making as essential in poverty reduction; to see local organizations as being closer to the poor and therefore good at poverty reduction; and to suggest that local NGOs have specific characteristics that make them more poverty-oriented than local state organizations. Furthermore, the case for local organizations is often argued irrespective of the political context in which the organizations themselves are situated.

The second weakness is that when the political context is considered, it tends to be in a somewhat superficial and often ambiguous way. Reference is either made to a conducive political environment, typically meaning 'pro-poor' policies and a government commitment to poverty reduction, or else the political context is used as a general term embracing, among other things, state policies, the political system, civil society, political culture, and so on. While the former remains limited to the formal institutions of the state, the latter fails to bring any conceptual incisiveness to the analysis.

Given these problems, a concept of political space is elaborated below in which the perspective is that of those in poverty. Here political space is understood as the types and range of possibilities present for pursuing poverty reduction by the poor or on behalf of the poor by local organizations. On the basis of this understanding, political space for poverty reduction based upon the participation of the poor can be said to be constituted by:

- institutional channels through which policy formulation and implementation can be accessed, controlled or contested by the poor;
- political discourses in which poverty and poverty reduction are significant issues; and
- social and political practices of the poor which may be a basis for influencing decision-making, agendas, policy and programme implementation, etc.

First, institutional channels should include formal procedures for affecting policy formulation and implementation. These include regular elections, hearing procedures, general assemblies and coordination meetings. Processes of democratization and decentralization often concentrate upon these procedures. The problem is that the processes may not match the spirit behind the procedures, and they can also be circumscribed or obstructed by particular interested parties, including the state, safe in the legitimacy accorded to them by their apparent democratic status.

Second, political discourses are not only important in shaping approaches towards policy formulation and implementation, they are also central to the formation of popular culture, not least in ideas concerning rights, responsibility and culpability with respect to poverty. Issues concerning culpability for the condition of the poor, responsibility for poverty reduction and the rights the poor possess with regard to other members of society and the state have long reflected broader political values and social thinking in societies. The nature and location of these discourses on poverty have been central to the manner in which poverty reduction has been approached, from revolution to welfarism.

Since the early 1980s, a powerful global discourse on poverty and development has emerged, in which the economic liberalization of markets has been increasingly linked to a political liberalization that advocates a range of reforms. These include a shift away from state-led development, the strengthening of civil society, the democratization of the political system, the decentralization of government, the strengthening of associational activities in communities, and so on. It is a discourse that is shared by academics and policy-makers, but it has increasingly come to shape donor agency policies as well as those of recipient governments too, though perhaps not always with the conviction hoped for. The overarching priority given by many bilateral and multilateral donor agencies to poverty reduction in the 1990s has served further to enhance and to legitimate the view that poverty is not the poor's own fault and that poverty reduction is a priority development objective.

At the local level in society, such a view of poverty and the title of 'poor' remain in some places something of an anachronism, where poverty is associated with failure and shame, and may even be a word simply missing from the local language, as in Burkina Faso, where poverty is an 'outsiders'' concept (see Chapter 7). Elsewhere it has emerged as a term of accusation against the non-poor and a demand on the state to act, as in West Bengal, where social movements of the poor resulted in the Left Front government coming to power in 1977 (see Chapter 10). In the light of commonalities and diversities in the discourses on poverty, it is important to analyse the particular discourses prevailing nationally and locally in a society in order to comprehend the political space for articulating the interests, needs and concerns of different marginalized groups, which also have to be explored in order to assess whose understanding of poverty is being promoted.

More perhaps than on industrial and technological might, the nascent order of capitalism and modernity relied on a politics of poverty the aim of which was not only to create consumers, but to transform society by turning the poor into objects of knowledge and management. What was involved in this operation was 'a techno–discursive instrument that made possible the conquest of pauperism and the invention of a politics of poverty'. (Escobar 1995: 23; quoting Procacci 1991: 157)

Third, social and political practices that influence politics constitute a further dimension of political space. Such practices form a more or less collective memory of historical attempts to access and contest political processes, and they can be drawn upon in relation to new issues and constraints. These practices might involve quite limited social groups and their specific ways of attempting to exercise influence, or they might involve broad social movements seeking to draw upon a range of political means and tactics to effect their aims and objectives. Such practices are not limited to the realm of policy formulation but also extend to the implementation of policy, which in some instances can be more significant for poverty reduction than influencing policy.

The reason for emphasizing this aspect of political space is not least that it conveys the point that political space cannot be straightforwardly created through government intervention. It also depends on the organizational practices and political experiences of the different social groups, and it involves the discourses and ideas concerning rights and responsibilities present at different societal and institutional levels. A favourable policy environment and committed government may achieve little in poverty reduction if marginalized groups are unorganized, poverty is internalized, and if the interests and views of the marginalized remain excluded from the process of governance.

On the basis of the above it is possible to see that political space is constantly being contested and challenged. Social actors who do not subscribe to its orientation seek to change institutional channels, to modify discourses and to reconstruct social and political practices. Thus political space is not just an abstract frame within which marginalized groups and local organizations manoeuvre. If possible, they actively seek to address the different dimensions of political space, and power to do so is clearly of crucial importance. Although generally characterized by powerlessness, marginalized groups may be able to profit from temporary or long-term changes and to gain leverage in various areas of social life.

From the perspective of the poor, the emergence of political space is tied to the possibility of moving from a situation of political exclusion to one of political inclusion. This is not just a question of political opportunity, however. From the above, one can see that political space also assumes the possibility of political agency on the part of marginalized groups. It is not sufficient for a political system to introduce institutions designed to offer opportunities for political participation if the poor are not in a position to utilize it. Nor is it likely that a state would introduce such institutional innovations without pressure from below.

At the local level such agency is likely to require a weakening of the economic, social and political powers held by local patrons. It also requires a local discourse on poverty that removes from it the veil of shame, denial and fate. It must be possible to question poverty and its constitution. It must also be possible for marginalized groups to organize and to be willing to be organized by others.

At the macro level political space is more likely when there has been a transition towards some form of democracy, whether from feudalism or from one of the more recent forms of authoritarian government. An elected government, a professional bureaucracy and an independent judiciary are only some of the prerequisites. An opening up of the relationship of the poor to the state through popular participation and representation is central to the process. This can be as individuals via citizenship and the rights associated with it, or through organizations such as political parties, trade unions, different types of informal association, and so on. Finally, securing such inclusion in politics also requires knowledge and information through the media, access to education, and similar resources.

In this way political space is linked to democratization and the broad range of structural and institutional reforms associated with the transition to democracy. This is not to say that liberal democracy is a condition in providing political space for poverty reduction. Other forms of democratization may be just as relevant or more so. Land reform, human rights, civil service reform, freedom of association and minority and gender rights are all examples of changes associated with redefining and enlarging political space. Given the vested interests involved, these are not given but have to be fought for. Such change is about struggles for rights, representation, etc. Political space is therefore about the outcome of contests and is rooted in specific political histories. It will vary considerably from arena to arena within a political system and from country to country. If we talk in terms of important and insignificant political spaces, what might be important for small farmers and industrial labourers on the basis of land and trade union rights, can be insignificant for women and minority ethnic groups due to a lack of rights, representation and social recognition. Between countries it might be considerable in India on the basis of its democratic constitution, decentralized government and an active voluntary sector, but insignificant in Burkina Faso, due to the presence of an authoritarian state and political exclusion.

The notion that there can be differences in the political space within a system is important because it demands a focus upon not just the institutional structures in place, but also the possession of political agency with respect to these institutions. Decentralized government in which women possess only a token presence provides a good illustration. Here the failure to engender politics and policy is rooted in the local as much as the macro. In this case we can see how state policy both reflects and structures policy in the household, the neighbourhood and the village. The status of women is not an issue, gender is not part of a discourse. Consequently women have at best the legal status of citizenship as constituted in that country.

Political agency cannot be engineered. In many instances unequal progress in the different arenas is due to a lack of synergy between economic development and political representation. Historically, pressure for specific rights has often followed on from particular experiences of economic development. Today, rights are often introduced from outside and are not necessarily sustainable in terms of support and mobilization from below. Again, women's rights might be a case in hand whereby it is we – Western donors, academics, liberal-minded people – who insist on them having a full set of rights immediately. While this might be justifiable in terms of oppression and discrimination, do women demand all these rights today? When arguing against intervention in another country's politics, J. S. Mill said that people must achieve freedom for themselves; only thus can they develop 'the virtues needful for maintaining freedom' (Mill 1867: 175). There is a strong contemporary argument – supported not only by liberals because of its anti-paternalism, which extends it to the relationship between a state and its peoples – that members of a political community must seek their own freedom (Walzer 1977: 87).

While agreeing with the need to avoid institutional engineering, we would argue that intervention to facilitate political space from both above and below is possible. In focusing upon the local, our research has sought to locate and explore the types of political agency on the part of the poor that can be facilitated. As some of the chapters illustrate, marginalized groups are often adept in operating in complex ways not only to cope with poverty, but also to challenge it. They sometimes go beyond the actions Scott (1989) describes as those of the first resort, such as foot-dragging, dissimulation, non-compliance, feigned ignorance, desertion, pilfering, etc., also organizing or utilizing social forms of organization in a strategic fashion in an attempt to change their condition of poverty. It is these actions by the poor and the extent to which they articulate political agency within the institutional structure that interventions should identify and that support should be based upon.

What Informs our Thinking on Political Space?

There is a range of literature and thinking that we have drawn upon in our thinking on political space. To begin with the contested nature of political space and the variations within and between countries that this gives rise to, this draws upon a number of theoretical sources, among which are the discussion of hegemony by Gramsci (1971) and Foucault's discussion (1976) of how power is reproduced through the acceptance of its organization and of its effects as the norm within society. These arguments are pertinent in relation to an understanding of the contested nature of the state, of poverty, and the importance of discourse in constituting them. The debate concerning the relationship between democracy and development has been a recurrent theme, from Huntington's discussion (Huntington 1968) of the need for strong government and democracy as chronologically following on from economic growth, to more recent studies, such as Moore's (1996), which suggest that the evidence is more positive in favour of democracy. The rich literature on civil society, social movements and state formation by, among others, Keane (1998), Lukham and White (1996) and Thompson (1993) have also been sources of inspiration. Dimensions they have introduced into the consideration of political space include concerns with the nature of the state, its hegemonic role, the relationship between state and citizen, and the constitution of both the state and the local through discourse and practice (policy). With respect to the contested nature of political space, the discussion ranges from the use of coercive force to contested meanings rooted in different discourses. In this way political space emerges as part of a constantly shifting landscape of contest that is primarily about social actors winning positions rather than achieving decisive victories (Anderson 1976).

This has importance with respect to poverty and poverty reduction, in that the contested nature of political space reflects the relational dimensions of poverty. In most of the countries in which research has been undertaken, the elites in power have demonstrated or expressed a constitutional commitment to democracy. At the same time they have revealed an opposition to any transfer of power to popular institutions and an unwillingness to accept reform of the economic and political system. Consequently there have not been any significant changes in public policy. The fact of the matter is that there have been few attempts to introduce innovative institutional arrangements, and poverty reduction has not had too much success. Political agency from below, in particular from the poor, is all too often absent, yet it increasingly appears to be a necessary factor to effect such change and to consolidate it.

A second important area of debate that has informed our thinking are arguments concerning the development potential in democracy and the politics of democratization. Three sets of arguments are relevant here: those that make a general case for democracy; those that advocate a dynamic civil society as a means of achieving and consolidating democracy; and thirdly a variant upon the latter, in which the importance of social capital is stressed.

The general case for democratizing the South immediately raises the question of how to define democracy. The need to present such a definition would appear to be self-evident if one is to study the ways and means for the transition to democracy or to know when it is consolidated. Unfortunately, for many writers this has not been the case. With remarkable repetition, mainstream political scientists have seen the nature of the electoral process as the defining feature of democracy, together with the freedoms of speech and association necessary to make this process effective (Beetham 1994). In this school of thought the focus is more upon formal procedures than on institutional practices. The problem with such a procedural approach is that it tends to reduce the procedures to ends in themselves, such as regular elections, party political pluralism, and so on. At the same time it tends to leave out many other dimensions, such as the accountability and transparency of the civil service, the accountability of government between elections, the position of socially and economically marginalized groups *vis-à-vis* government and development policy, and much more.

With respect to the consolidation of democracy, this has often been measured in somewhat simplistic terms – for example, according to the longevity of rule by democratic government, or on the basis of electoral performance, such as the holding of successive free elections or the ability of an elected government to accept defeat in a subsequent election (Beetham 1994). As to the conditions suitable for democratization, again there is a tendency to approach this in a somewhat deterministic manner. Lipset has famously argued that the more telephones there are, the more democracy there will be (Lipset 1959), while Huntington identifies economic development at between US$500 and US$1000 per capita GNP as the jumping-off point for democratization (Huntington 1991).

Even when a minimalist conception of procedural liberal democracy is applied, its relevance, given the complexity of developmental and political factors in the South, is questionable and rarely acceptable to the countries concerned. One dimension clearly missing from the above is human volition. A second is the attention given to local politics and their role and relationship to the political system as a whole. A third is the unequal distribution of power rooted in economic, social and political inequalities and constraints and how these can thwart democratization. Finally,

following on from the previous point, we still need to ask how democratization can help the poor specifically, given their politically marginalized
status.

In seeking to identify the factors facilitating or hindering democratization, and to move towards the local, the concept of civil society has become
significant. Civil society clearly brings human volition into the discussion
of democracy, but what constitutes civil society and its location with respect
to the state on the one hand and the individual on the other is subject to
considerable debate and disagreement. The most widely accepted view is
that civil society lies between the household and the state. It is composed
of voluntary associations, non-state corporate actors and possibly political
parties; it is defined in terms of its relationship to the state as well as being
partly constituted by the state in terms of rights and formal recognition;
and it reflects the separation of economic and political power that characterized the emergence of liberal democracy (Törnquist 1997; Lukham and
White 1996).

As Törnquist writes, the common thesis on civil society and democracy
is that the former is the condition for the latter. It is therefore necessary
for the transition to democracy and its subsequent consolidation. Clearly
this argument on the role of civil society reflects some aspects of political
space. The important difference is that political space is rooted not in
organizations, as is civil society, but in the possibilities for groups of the
poor to bring about change through local organizations. A civil society in
which the poor have political agency might be the outcome, but political
space from the perspective of the poor is about the possibility for change.
Civil society is not a guarantee for such change.

More recently this thesis has been extended to say that for civil society
to support democratization, it also requires social capital. Basing his
argument on a comparative study of north and south Italy, Putnam has
presented social capital as being located in sets of horizontal associations
between people in the form of social networks and associated norms that
have an effect on the productivity of the community. The key feature of
social capital is that it facilitates coordination and cooperation for the
mutual benefit of the members of the association (Putnam et al. 1993). The
argument originally focused upon associations with a positive effect on
development, but the negative role of some groups has also been recognized;
for example the Mafia in southern Italy (Gambetta 1988).

Coleman (1988, 1990) broadens social capital to include vertical as well
as horizontal associations and includes the behaviour of other actors, such
as firms. Vertical associations are characterized by hierarchical relationships
and the unequal distribution of power. Social capital consists of a variety
of different entities, but with two elements in common: they all consist of

some aspect of social structure, and they facilitate certain actions of actors – whether personal or corporate actors – within the structure. Here the norms governing interpersonal behaviour are linked to the social structure beyond the association.

The third concept of social capital takes the structural dimension further and explicitly includes the social and political environment that enables norms to develop and shape social structure – formal institutionalized relationships and structures such as government, the political regime, the rule of law, the court system, and civil and political liberties. Here the arguments of North (1990) and Olsen (1982) on the importance of institutions to the process and nature of development are relevant to the discussion.

All three views of social capital stress the role of social relationships in affecting development, the argument being that, with the right legal and political context, these social relationships and the institutions they are located in will have a positive impact on development. Furthermore, as social capital can be acquired only by a group of people and requires a form of cooperation among them, these writers suggest that it should be treated as having the character of a public good. The argument then follows that, left to their own devices, associations and organizations will tend to underproduce social capital relative to the social optimum unless the group can internalize the externality involved, that is, the benefits that come from the group's engagement in markets. Because of this behaviour on the part of the members, horizontal associations with equity between members are more likely to succeed. The conclusion that the advocates of social capital arrive at, given its assumed potential in enabling development and democracy, is that support should be given to strengthen social capital and measures be taken to create an enabling environment that will encourage people to participate in local organizations.

A basic problem with the discussion of social capital is its general foundation in methodological individualism. This gives it a distinct instrumental flavour in which social capital is seen as a good in which individuals can invest and that yields a clearly predictable return. Moreover, the good is separated from the individuals and the social context in the sense that anyone can obtain a particular amount of social capital through more or less the same 'investments'. This 'homo economicus' thinking, where sentiments and moral beliefs are detached from and subjugated to calculations of the most lucrative alternatives to the individual, is seriously flawed when it comes to understanding social relations in which mutual obligations and support loom large.

It is important to recognize the significance attached to the role of social capital in current development thinking, not least because, in focusing upon local organizations, our research is exploring similar social phenomena and processes that are increasingly occupying the attention of donor agencies and development policy planners. Indeed, social capital has recently emerged as a buzz-word among donor agencies and with the World Bank in particular. In its 1997 *World Development Report*, the Bank argued that there is a need to open up a 'democratic space' in countries in order that public institutions can be reinvigorated. There should be better administrators and administration, and more checks and balances to make for the effective and efficient use of public resources. Also said to be needed is a reinvigoration of the state through the enhancement of rules and restraints, competitive pressure, and voice and partnership. With respect to poverty reduction, the *Report* states that sustainable, shared, poverty-reducing development has five crucial ingredients: a foundation of law; a benign policy environment including macro-economic stability; investment in people and infrastructure; protection of the vulnerable; and the protection of the natural environment.

To this strategy has now been added social capital. Under the World Bank's Social Capital Initiative the argument is being developed, grounded in ongoing research, that there is a need to identify existing institutions, social relationships and networks that contribute to growth and poverty alleviation, as well as those that impede it. Projects can then be enhanced by utilizing these social relations and institutions, by investing in them to make them more inclusive of the intended beneficiaries (especially the poor), and by enhancing their social capital. Reforms that create an enabling environment for these institutions can be supported: towards good governance, the enforcement of property rights, an independent judicial system, a competent and transparent bureaucracy, and mechanisms to promote dialogue and resolve conflict between actors.

The move towards social capital and the requirement it places upon the World Bank – in this instance, to understand better the nature, role and organizational forms of social capital within a country prior to developing policies and designing projects – are to be welcomed. When this is combined with poverty and social assessments it may well be that matters of local ownership and sustainability will be better served. Yet the criticism of civil society and social capital remains, particularly when one addresses the interests of the poor and poverty reduction. While better local organizations might be selected and enabled, will the poor gain political agency in the face of entrenched opposition?

Much that has been written on democracy, civil society and social capital is relevant to our thinking on political space, and discussions of the different approaches within these have to some extent informed our approaches. Where we differ can be summarized in the following points.

First, while the importance of civil society and social capital is rooted in a historical analysis of democracy, it tends to abstract the institutional forms that have arisen and the social relations embodied within them and to turn them into ends in themselves. As in the more general discussion of democratization, this tends to neglect the role of political agency in both the process of institutional formation and in institutional politics. Institutions and their functions and roles become ahistorical. For example, Putnam has been criticized for failing to recognize that the degree of civicness fluctuated over time, and for his approach being more a case of applying a model to history than a study of history. When such an argument is generalized and applied to the needs of democratization and development in the countries of Asia, Africa and South America, its ahistorical roots and the danger of assuming causation from correlation render it extremely problematical.

Second, in the present context political space is based upon the local analysis of specific forms of poverty and the organizing practices of the poor on the one hand, and the political trajectories of the state, its policies, socio-economic natures and historical constitution on the other. Rather than applying a model of development our desire is to explore development in context and in terms of the social actors whose actions have shaped that context. The usefulness of the term 'political space' is accordingly assessed against its ability to provide a meaningful understanding of political processes and their implications for poverty reduction: it does not constitute first and foremost a normative proposal for the reorientation of policies and development assistance.

Third, power and the study of power relations are central to our research. Institutions need to be examined in terms not merely of their institutional capacity, but also of the political and socio-economic interests they represent. We need to ask who sits in the office, what discourse and system of categories they use to carry out designated duties, what are the powers of inclusion and exclusion asserted by individuals and the socio-cultural practices they carry, and similar questions. Political space encourages the exploration of such complexities at the local level.

Fourth, by focusing on political space it is possible to take up the comparative analysis of the different experiences in order not so much to generate a model, but to bring the local and the poor into development studies and development policy through a better understanding of the role of the local in the politics of democratization, development and poverty reduction.

One further conceptual input into the thinking of political space needs to be mentioned, not least because we have been asked previously why we should not speak of 'room for manoeuvre' when formulating a concept of political space. Clay and Schaffer (1984) introduced the concept of 'room for manoeuvre' in order to discuss the space that is assumed to exist in making policy choices – choice assumes alternatives – and the space in which individuals can find themselves with respect to the implementation of policy and programmes. For example, an administrative officer at district level is often able to determine the poverty-reducing effects of a particular programme because of the degree of decision-making authority he or she possesses. Just as there might be degrees of room for manoeuvre in the selection of policy for the individual based in the organization and management structures of an institution, so it can also be argued that the concept should be extended to all social actors, institutions or otherwise.

The utility of such a usage is that it enables the examination of political and developmental opportunities from the perspective of different social actors and the institutional systems they find themselves in. To this can be added a focus upon the poor and poverty reduction. Room for manoeuvre could be used in this way to support the analysis of the poor's ability to affect public policy or the implementation of a programme. It can also be used to explore how individuals negotiate their way to an objective within a given political and social context by using personal connections, kinship networks, and so on – playing the system as best one can. An analysis of the room for manoeuvre is primarily based on the actor's view, be it a group, an organization or an individual. The concept can lead us to understand the constraints and limitations as experienced by the individual actor, who, nevertheless, may influence and enlarge its room for manoeuvre through particular strategies. However, the limitation of room for manoeuvre lies in its lack of focus upon the social forces and structural relations that constitute institutions and their practices. While room for manoeuvre might provide an assessment of the possible and impossible at a particular point in time, it cannot capture the processes that give rise to a particular context, a particular political space. By using the notion of political space, we are therefore seeking to understand the broader conditions for political action rather than the particularities facing specific actors.

Approaching Diversity, Agency and Non-dichotomous Analyses

In addition to the endeavour to construct a political contextualization for poverty reduction by marginalized groups and local organizations, the chapters in this book contribute to the development of conceptual approaches emphasizing diversity, agency and non-dichotomous analytical understandings. Although these issues increasingly receive attention, their importance is by no means fully recognized. Diversity continues to be overshadowed by universalistic categories and approaches; the particularities of specific activities and processes are being sacrificed at the altar of reductionism; and subtle differences and continua of social practices are being exposed as dichotomies (Booth 1985; March and Olsen 1984).

The studies in the book all emphasize issues such as diversity, open-ended change, the actions and strategies of groups and individuals, and the interplay of micro and macro processes. The contributions are based on case studies of particular localities and seek to understand processes of political struggle and the changing nature of actors' strategies. While the influence of structures and embedded institutions to various degrees is underlined, focus is directed not only to the ways in which people respond to ever-changing conditions, but also to the strategies with which they try to create new possibilities and improve their living conditions.

People's actions and strategies are seen as especially important, since they provide a path into the understanding of social change, a path that seeks to avoid a teleological bias. By studying specific localities in their complexity and by focusing on the actions and strategies of particular groups within that locality, it is hoped to confront and question ideas that are too often taken for granted by both the development researcher and the development practitioner. The focus upon action and agency implies, moreover, an emphasis on the open-ended nature of social change. The struggles and confrontations in relation to poverty reduction and political spaces are ambiguous and indeterminate, and there is no sound foundation for arguing that specific power configurations within a particular political space will necessarily bring about poverty reduction.

The interplay of micro and macro processes is also at the heart of the book, but this is not to say that the micro is subordinated to the macro. Although the latter is typically beyond the control or direct influence of actors in a locality, it can be negotiated, disputed and transformed by them. From the point of view of local studies, it is also important to notice that the macro cannot be equated with national and international issues and the micro with the local. In a locality, migratory patterns, historically embedded social tensions and economic changes may all be significant factors that actors cannot control, but to which they are obliged to react. Likewise, national level questions are affected by micro processes of social interaction which are not confined to specific localities. This reinforces the need to examine the interplay of micro and macro issues in both local and supra-local studies.

The particularities of social situations are often overlooked because they do not fit the general picture or because they make the basis for action and policy-making too complicated. Of specific interest in the present context is the fact that the study of Third World politics has concentrated much on national politics in relation to international relations and particular socio-cultural traits, partly to the exclusion of local politics (Hydén 1983; Clapham 1985; Randall and Theobald 1985; Sandbrook and Baker 1985; Cammack, Pool and Tordoff 1988; Manor 1991; Bayart 1993). There are many studies of local politics in South Asia because of the longstanding experience with local government in this region, and elsewhere the study of local politics has been approached through questions of social movements, land conflicts, ethnic tensions, and so on. Thus, aspects of local politics have been addressed in different ways, but a widespread interest in local politics as something different from and supplementing national politics has begun to emerge only since the end of the Cold War and the re-emergence of a concern for democracy.

Our interest in local politics is characterized by, among other things, the following features. Local politics cannot be derived from national politics because the historical and contemporary particularities of a locality influence the nature of local political processes. These may, in turn, have repercussions for national politics, since the two are often linked in subtle interdependent ways. An understanding of local politics is accordingly necessary in getting to grips with national politics, which cannot be analysed solely in terms of national class struggles or state–society interactions.

Furthermore, local politics is much more than formal political processes. Despite the creation of local formal arenas for political competition and popular participation in more and more countries, local politics encompasses many spheres and touches upon questions of religion, ethnicity, market structures, and so on. The basis of influence and legitimacy, as well as of political struggle itself, are to be found both inside and outside formal political institutions. Also, the pervasiveness of local politics is important; social interactions cannot be excluded from the sphere of politics, and social and economic change is an intrinsically political process in terms of struggles for power and influence. The frequent claim that someone is 'not involved in politics' usually refers to a particular type of politics, a particular set of political activities, from which that person wishes to distance or disassociate herself or himself.

The state being an important institution linking local and national levels is central to the understanding of local politics. Here, we understand the state not as a monolithic unit with clear divisions of labour, coherent policies and uniform goals, but as different, heterogeneous, competing organizations responding to diverse conditions, some of these organizations possibly being more closely linked to non-state actors than to the state as such. Nevertheless, different state organizations do share a set of practices and an ideal of social organization, for which reason the state can be perceived as being monolithic in particular situations. This duality of the state is important in the context of local politics, since non-state actors in a locality have to confront the Janus-like nature of state organizations that can play the cards of dialogue and state authority interchangeably.

Many states are currently undergoing significant changes due to economic and political pressures. These changes have greater complexities than notions such as 'rolling back' or 'good governance' are able to capture. While service delivery may be declining, the state is not necessarily perceived to be less present or less powerful at the local level. At the same time, various kinds of organization, including NGOs, have entered some areas that previously were the state's exclusive domain. Local politics needs to be seen in this context of a changing state and changing social actors, and again the particularities of these processes of change differ from one locality to another and need to be understood when analysing local politics.

A couple of remarks on the notion of local politics are needed, since the term 'local' carries with it a number of inappropriate associations. Recently, two criticisms have been raised in relation to the notion of the local (Ferguson 1997). First, it has been argued that there is nothing local any longer, if there ever was, since ideas, organizations and economies are linked throughout the world. So-called local organizations are financed from abroad, ideas and needs are formed by the commercials of transnational corporations, and economies are, although to different degrees, being globalized. This cannot and should not be denied, of course, but it does not invalidate the notion of the local. Although permeated by many non-local processes, a social locality, whatever its contested boundaries, is understood by the relevant actors in relation to its surroundings, its negation or its 'other'. What characterizes a locality is a somewhat shared and at the same time often contested understanding of what belongs to it and what does not. This does not imply that local organizations are completely local in the sense that their resources, activities and ideas belong exclusively to a given locality, but simply means that in one way or another these organizations are associated with a particular locality in contradistinction to other localities or a broader social setting.

The second criticism is that, in the study of African politics, 'the local' as an analytical level is related either to a negative perception of static traditional practices and primordial attachments or to positive notions of civil society and its progressive nature. While this may be true for parts of the literature, it does not follow that studies of the local have to continue along these normative lines. Thus, in the present context there is nothing isolated, static, familiar or normative about local politics. It is thoroughly influenced by national and international processes; the number and nature of social actors taking part in it change, due to migration, economic opportunities, new social practices, and so on; and it is as much the object of strategic and rational considerations as any other human interaction.

Nor should local suggest that this kind of politics is any less important than national politics. The local is particularly used to delineate processes at a sub-national level, recognizing the fact that nation-states are still a crucial feature of social and political organization at all levels. By discussing processes at a local level the assumption is that these processes are somewhat autonomous from other, in particular national, processes and need to be studied not in isolation, but on their own terms.

Forms of social organization are often being dichotomized, thus neglecting both intermediate forms and the possibility that a specific social situation simultaneously manifests an ambiguous combination of different social organizations. In our endeavour to understand local politics, political space and the strategies of marginalized groups, we do not consider the public/private and the traditional/modern dichotomies to be particularly useful. Although different interests, practices and discourses can be related to the public and private spheres respectively, it is more important to recognize how actors straddle the spheres and exploit the officially established distinction between them (Berry 1993). Resources within one sphere are often used for purposes in the other, and in most social contexts actors do not consider them to be clearly separated. Thus the distinction is important to recognize as an element used in political struggles, but it is less useful in analytical terms.

The dichotomy between traditional and modern is also flawed and has always been so. Traditions are not very traditional, but usually invented for particular purposes, and so-called modern practices are always interpreted in a historically specific context. The dichotomy is all the more problematic since it is sometimes used, explicitly or implicitly, to identify progressive and conservative forces. Again, the dichotomy may be used by social actors in concrete struggles, but this does not make it valuable for analytical purposes. The analysis of social action and local politics easily becomes too rigid and stereotypical if it is uncritically based on dichotomies of this kind, which have their theoretical roots in modernization thinking and seldom correspond to the actors' perceptions.

One way of overcoming dichotomies and predefined distinctions with respect to patterns of authority is to examine the different ways in which power is legitimated. Powerful actors typically employ different ways to legitimize their position by drawing on different ideas and discourses that are all perceived to be appropriate. Thus, in a given locality, the point is to map a network of powerful actors and the resources and discourses they utilize. This network could be called a system of governance, as it is experienced by the various social groups in the locality. Using such an approach, it becomes possible to identify and understand manocuvring in and between different institutional spheres, and to depict the way in which authority is encountered from below. Hence it is useful to talk about local organizations in a general manner encompassing all organizational entities within a locality and avoiding predefined distinctions between public and private, external and indigenous, religious and secular, and so on. Depending on the particular context, certain distinctions will then appear to be crucial if they help to describe the system of governance.

The Contributions

One dimension of political space concerns the institutional channels for accessing political processes. In Bolivia, a Law of Popular Participation was promulgated in 1994 that officially aimed at creating the basis for political participation by local organizations and the rural population. Anne Marie Ejdesgaard Jeppesen in Chapter 2 analyses the mixed response to this seemingly far-reaching reform and puts it in the context of long-standing popular struggles with the state as an enemy. Furthermore, she carefully describes the changes that have taken place in a particular municipality in the department of Cochabamba after the first elections were held. Although it is one of the municipalities where peasant organizations (the *sindicatos*) have gained prominent influence, it is clear that, for example, the women have little access to decision-making, and that it is difficult for the municipal government to address the structural constraints faced by coca leaf producers. The chapter deals with the important question of whether the political inclusion of hitherto marginalized local organizations reduces their ability to challenge the conditions of marginalization.

In neighbouring Peru, the situation is substantially different. Neoliberalism is the name of the game, and there is no indication of substantial devolution of state prerogatives to locally elected councils. Furthermore, the rural population seems to regard the state not as the enemy, but rather as a saving angel that may help provide *progreso* after a decade of devastating violence and terrorism. Karsten Paerregaard in Chapter 3 goes through three decades of substantial national political and economic turmoil and relates it to the social changes in Alto Cunas in the central highlands of Peru. Although pervasive in nature, national events and changes are not directly reflected locally, but are being moulded by the history and social relations of Alto Cunas. The peasants have used their long-standing organizational practices to counter the attempts of the military regime of the 1970s to create cooperatives and the Shining Path's destruction of local organizations in the late 1980s. Nevertheless, the chapter clearly demonstrates the profound impact of national politics on local political space and the ability of the rural population to improve its conditions.

The study from Tomatlán in Western Mexico explores this relationship between changing policies and people's strategies in detail. Accessing credit and aid funds has become a significant feature of rural livelihood strategies, and the negotiation and contestation of state services and resources characterize people's everyday interaction with state officers. However, this is not a cost-free affair, since interaction may entail forms of dependency and clientelism. Magdalena Villarreal in Chapter 4 analyses a national programme designed to support diverse forms of production in rural areas and demonstrates how different discourses are being used to legitimize claims to resources. In this sense, actors are constantly seeking to explore and push the limits of political space in directions that suit their interests. Another conclusion arising from the study is the extent to which different producers benefiting from the programme struggle to repay their debts in order to build relations of trust and to provide the basis for future support. A great deal of manoeuvring is taking place, and networks and alliances are significant resources in that respect. Moreover, the history of Tomatlán, with its strong political movements, an independent peasant union and spontaneous resettlements, provides a particular background for the continuing negotiation of political space.

The social and political practices used by marginalized groups for influencing decision-making are crucial to understanding the conditions for poverty reduction. In many African countries, institutions related to the chieftainship and so-called traditional leaders have been moulded by such practices. This is also the case in Angónia in western Mozambique, where chiefs have become very important social actors, partly due to the post-war national political struggles, and partly because they are the only authority in many rural areas. Astrid Blom in Chapter 5 analyses the relationship between the chiefs and different social groups, examining a number of land conflicts and the way in which the poor seek to negotiate their interests in this respect. An important conclusion is that the poor have been able to secure land in a large proportion of the cases where chiefs have arbitrated in land conflicts. In view of the lack of other local authorities, the chiefs and their concern with people's needs are clearly better for the poor than the law of the jungle. Thus the chapter demonstrates that the institution of chief not only reflects attempts by local elites to control the rural communities, but also constitutes a political opportunity for marginalized groups to exercise their interests.

The question of land is also central to Chapter 6 by Amanda Hammar. She analyses the discourses, narratives and practices of naming linked to land in Zimbabwe and shows not only how land has different meanings to different constituencies, but also how discourses and practices of naming are used strategically to promote particular interests. The chapter vividly documents how 'traditional' and 'modern' discourses are interrelated and sometimes used almost interchangeably by the state. Thus different actors have no difficulty in picking a language to support the legitimacy of their claims. These issues are carefully discussed in relation to the notion of Communal Lands and with respect to a specific case of eviction of settlers in the district of Gokwe North in the north-western part of the country. Although marginalized groups such as settlers and squatters are significantly constrained by the spatial politics linked to Communal Lands and by various powerful local actors seeking to exploit remunerative opportunities in relation to land, they are not stripped of power. Discourses on justice, empowerment and human rights can be brought into play and provide a basis for contestation. Hence political space is very fluid, ambiguous and constantly disputed by many different actors.

In Burkina Faso, a contemporary process of democratization and de-centralization is about to reorganize and enlarge the institutional channels used in accessing policy-making and implementation. Given this process, marginalized groups might be expected to increase their influence on politics and resource distribution. This is not the case, however. Through a study of the strategies of NGOs in Yatenga province, Lars Engberg-Pedersen in Chapter 7 argues that politics is perceived to be a dangerous game by many and that the political space for poverty reduction in general is quite limited. The poor and poverty do not figure prominently in political discourses, and despite widespread practices in organizing, marginalized rural groups have very little experience in influencing policy-making at any level. A historical understanding of the Burkinabè state and of the socio-political specificities of Yatenga is emphasized in the attempt to explain the nature of political space. Furthermore, it is concluded that although the political space for poverty reduction is limited, politics is omnipresent, and NGO leaders develop different strategies to manoeuvre in this politicized environment.

Chapter 8 by D. Rajasekhar reveals the diversity of experience of local organizations and of the poor in India. Based upon a study of two villages in the Indian State of Tamil Nadu, it focuses on the one hand on the livelihoods of the small and marginal farmers and the landless in the village, and on the other on the role of NGOs operating in the locality. The latter have emerged as part of the more general growth of local NGOs in India, supported by the fact that both government and donor agency programmes have increasingly pursued poverty reduction through such local organizations. The chapter demonstrates that the presence of institutional channels in the form of local government and of NGOs in particular, with programmes and resources directed towards poverty reduc-tion, is not enough. Since the identification and design of such programmes remains far removed from the locality, and since the marginalized and the excluded fail to become involved, the potential for poverty reduction cannot be realized. Not least the local discourse on poverty and the lack of awareness of the social and political practices of the poor in challenging poverty appear to undermine the political agency of the poor in bringing about poverty reduction through such channels.

Bangladesh has one of the highest number of NGOs in the world, and since 1985 it has experienced different types of local government. Accordingly, one may expect a vibrant civil society and well-established institutional channels for accessing politics. On the basis of two case studies, Kirsten Westergaard and Abul Hossain discuss in Chapter 9 whether the poor have been able to profit from this situation in a national political context of strongly clientelistic practices. They explore the social and economic changes over a 20-year period in a village in northern Bangladesh and examine their consequences for local government elections. The second study deals with two NGOs and the ways in which they have also supported groups of poor in elections for local government. One overall conclusion is that the poor have generally experienced improving economic conditions either as a result of new economic opportunities or through NGO support. The picture is more mixed with respect to the elections of representatives of marginalized groups. Either the poor do not exploit an emerging political space, or their elected representatives are quickly absorbed by the clientelistic relations, or else they are confronted by strong and sometimes violent action by political elites whenever they succeed in obtaining a firmer hold on seats in local government.

The state of West Bengal has followed a different development path from that of Bangladesh following partition in 1947. Most notably, the coming to power in 1977 of a Left Front government in the state, led by a communist party, has seen a more radical programme of agrarian reform and decentralization of government than in Bangladesh. Chapter 10 by Neil Webster seeks to explore the way in which specific groups of the poor engage with the state and government policy to develop a pro-poor development trajectory. It suggests that the introduction of institutional innovations for greater popular participation is not in itself sufficient to secure a process of public policy formulation or implementation that serves the interests of the poor. It is argued that political agency on the part of the poor is required, and that the specific local dimensions of poverty present in the area of the case study have required a more direct political agency than can be provided through the state. The case study focuses upon Adivasi or 'tribal' women in south-west Bankura District who have organized silkworm cooperatives since the early 1980s and are now playing a leading role in the programme of community forest management being implemented in the area.

The final chapter seeks to draw some general lessons on the basis of the nine case studies. It discusses the relationships between marginalized groups, local organizations, the state and political space. Although no comparative methodology has been used to streamline the case studies – which, moreover, differ in their theoretical points of departure – important observations are made regarding a number of issues: the political agency of the poor, the strategic use of discourses, the limits of institutional reform, the contested nature of poverty reduction, and the significance of political space in challenging the conditions of marginalization.

Bibliography

Anderson, P. (1976) *Arguments in Western Marxism*, London: Verso.

Baulch, Bob (1996) 'Editorial. The new poverty agenda: a disputed consensus', *IDS Bulletin*, 27, 1: 1–10.

Bayart, J. P. (1993) *The State in Africa: The Politics of the Belly*, London: Longman.

Beck, Tony (1994) *The Experience of Poverty: Fighting for Respect and Resources in Village India*, London: Intermediate Technology Publications.

Beetham, D. (1994) 'Conditions for democratic consolidation', *Review of African Political Economy*, 60: 157–72.

Berry, Sara (1993) *No Condition is Permanent: The Social Dynamics of Agrarian Change in Sub-Saharan Africa*, Madison and London: University of Wisconsin Press.

Booth, David (1985) 'Marxism and development sociology: interpreting the impasse', *World Development*, 13, 7: 761–87.

Cammack, P., D. Pool and W. Tordoff (1988) *Third World Politics: A Comparative Introduction*, London: Macmillan.

Chambers, Robert (1989) 'Editorial introduction: vulnerability, coping and policy', *IDS Bulletin*, 20, 2: 1–7.

— (1995) *Poverty and Livelihoods: Whose Reality Counts?*, Brighton: Institute of Development Studies.

Clapham, Christopher (1985) *Third World Politics: An Introduction*, London: Croom Helm.

Clay, E. and B. Schaffer (1984) *Room for Manoeuvre*, London: Heinemann.

Coleman, James S. (1988) 'Social capital in the generation of human capital', *American Journal of Sociology*, 94: 95–120.

— (1990) *Foundations of Social Theory*, Cambridge, MA: Harvard University Press.

Escobar, Arturo (1995) *Encountering Development: The Making and Unmaking of the Third World*, Princeton, NJ: Princeton University Press.

Ferguson, James (1997) 'Transnational topographies of power: beyond "the state" and "civil society" in the study of African politics', paper read at conference Concepts and Metaphors: Ideologies, Narratives and Myths in Development Discourse, 1998, at Karrebæksminde, Denmark.

Foucault, M. (1976) 'Disciplinary power and subjection', reprinted in S. Lukes (ed.) (1986), *Power*, Oxford: Basil Blackwell.

Gambetta, Diego (1988) 'Mafia: the price of distrust', in D. Gambetta (ed.), *Trust: Making and Breaking Cooperative Relations*, New York: Basil Blackwell.

Gramsci, A. (1971) *Selections from Prison Notebooks*, London: Lawrence & Wishart.

Huntington, S. (1968) *Political Order in Changing Societies*, New Haven, CT: Yale University Press.

— (1991) 'Democracy's third wave', *Journal of Democracy*, 2, 2: 12–34.

Hydén, Göran (1983) *No Shortcuts to Progress*, London: Heinemann.

Keane, J. (1998) *Civil Society: Old Images, New Visions*, Oxford: Polity Press.

Lipset, S. (1959) *Political Man*, London: Heinemann.

Lukham, R. and G. White (eds) (1996) *Democratisation in the South: The Jagged Wave*, Manchester: Manchester University Press.

Manor, James (ed.) (1991) *Rethinking Third World Politics*, London: Longman.

March, James G. and Johan P. Olsen (1984) 'The new institutionalism: organizational factors in political life', *American Political Science Review*, 78, 3: 734–49.

Mill, J. S. (1867) 'A few words on non-intervention', in *Dissertations and Discussions: Political, Philosophical and Historical. Vol. 3*, London: Longman.

Moore, M. (1996) 'Is democracy rooted in material prosperity?', in Lukham and White 1996.

North, Douglass C. (1990) *Institutions, Institutional Change and Economic Performance*, Cambridge: Cambridge University Press.

Olivier de Sardan, Jean-Pierre (1995) *Anthropologie et développement. Essai en socio-anthropologie du changement social*, Paris: APAD-Karthala.

Olsen, M. (1982) *The Rise and Decline of Nations: Economic Growth, Stagflation and New Social Rigidities*, New Haven, CT: Yale University Press.

Procacci, Giovanna (1991) 'Social economy and the government of poverty', in G. Burchell et al. (eds), *The Foucault Effect: Studies in Governmentality*, Chicago: University of Chicago Press.

Putnam, Robert D. with Robert Leonardi and Raffaella Y. Nanetti (1993) *Making Democracy Work: Civil Traditions in Modern Italy*, Princeton, NJ: Princeton University Press.

Randall, V. and R. Theobald (1985) *Political Change and Underdevelopment: A Critical Introduction to Third World Politics*, London: Macmillan.

Sandbrook, R. and J. Baker (1985) *The Politics of Africa's Economic Stagnation*, Cambridge: Cambridge University Press.

Sano, Hans-Otto (1996) *Enabling Strategies and State Intervention. Policy Action and Major Problems of Livelihood in Dryland Villages in Iringa District, Tanzania*, Roskilde: International Development Studies, Roskilde University.

Scott, J. (1989) 'Everyday forms of resistance', in F. Colburn (ed.), *Everyday Forms of Resistance*, New York: Sharpe.

Swift, Jeremy (1989) 'Why are rural people vulnerable to famine?', *IDS Bulletin*, 20, 2: 8–15.

Thompson, E. P. (1993) *Customs in Common*, London: Penguin.

Törnquist, O. (1997) 'Making democracy work', in L. Rudebeck et al. (eds), *Democratisation in the Third World*, London: Macmillan.

UNDP (1997) *Human Development Report 1997*, New York: Oxford University Press.

UNDP (1998) *Human Development Report 1998*, New York: Oxford University Press.

Walzer, M. (1977) *Just and Unjust Wars*, New York: Basic Books.

2

Reading the Bolivian Landscape of Exclusion and Inclusion: The Law of Popular Participation

Anne Marie Ejdesgaard Jeppesen

Discussions about poverty alleviation and popular participation in development planning have become increasingly important in debates about development in Latin America and elsewhere. The social costs of structural adjustment programmes have been recognized by most international development institutions and banks (Lawton 1995), and institutions such as the World Bank, USAID and the UNDP stress the necessity and importance of poor people's participation in development planning and participation in civil life as one of the necessary means of overcoming situations of poverty (World Bank 1997; Atal and Øyen 1997: 17).

Many Latin American researchers are critical of the performance of these relatively new initiatives in incorporating different social groups into the decision-making processes. While there is no question about the positive sides of democracy, the doubts concern the possibilities of influencing and having a voice in fora where decisions of importance for national development planning are being made. Why talk about popular participation and poverty alleviation in a period when neo-liberal policies are still dominant throughout the region, policies that, according to some scholars, seem to exclude certain groups from participation? Jelin, for example, states that 'While democratic discourse becomes hegemonic, the reality of economic relations is in contradiction with it. Indeed, there is a double discourse: a discourse of participation and a non-discourse of economic exclusion' (1997: 28). Vilas, referring to the Latin American state, talks about a 'dislocation between representative institutions and political decisions, between the spheres in which people participate and the spheres in which decisions are made which determine the living conditions for those same people' (1997: 20). The consequence is what he sees as a 'reclusion of policy' from public control and participation, which does not apply equally to all: 'the declining involvement of unions and civic associations in public policy debates contrasts with the maintenance, and at times the strengthening, of participation by business associations or particular firms' (ibid.). Is this view too pessimistic?

This chapter discusses the Bolivian Law of Popular Participation (LPP) promulgated in April 1994 by the Sánchez de Lozada administration (1993–97). The explicit goals of the law are to create a more just distribution and better administration of public resources, to promote economic growth and development in the countryside, and to advance political participation in general and the participation of local organizations in decision-making processes in particular (LPP, Artículo 1).

Poverty is widespread in Bolivia. In the rural areas, where 42 per cent of the Bolivian population live, 90 per cent of all families are estimated to live in poverty (Informe Social 1995: 63). It seems very important to promote growth and development for these people. Furthermore, the law implies a legal recognition of forms of local organization, which formerly have largely been ignored, and an attempt to incorporate the peasants' systems of self-rule into local development planning.

It seems that this law totally contradicts the critical views of Jelin and Vilas. The overall ambitions of the law look very positive. Why, then, did the law meet with so many protests and so much opposition? Why were poor people in the countryside not pleased? Why did the peasants' unions and the labour movement launch a series of protests? And why did some of them later change their minds?

This chapter will examine the different types of problem involved in the implementation of the law and will explore some of the attitudes of the different actors involved at the different levels of Bolivian society – peasants, peasant leaders, local authorities, government employees and politicians. One aim is to discuss how different actors, at both local and government levels, influence the real outcome of the LPP and actual political spaces through different kinds of negotiation and alliance. This implies seeing political space for poverty reduction as defined much more by negotiation, contestation, confrontation, resistance and local power relations than by government politics or consent.

The chapter will also discuss how political participation and exclusion in the countryside in Bolivia have historically been linked to different politics of space and to the ordering of space, and how this may explain some of the critical voices raised against the LPP.

The Sánchez de Lozada Administration

According to Carlos Hugo Molina, the national secretary for popular participation, the work that later crystallized into the Law of Popular Participation was initiated in 1990, when a multidisciplinary group of people, politicians and academics started discussing a reform of the Bolivian Constitution. At this time the MNR, or National Revolutionary Movement, was in opposition to the Jaime Paz Zamora government (1989–93). One of the participants in these early discussions was the later president, Gonzalo Sánchez de Lozada, leader of the MNR.

The MNR is the political party that came to power after the popular uprisings in 1952, which were to be called the National Revolution. The first MNR government of Paz Estenssoro of 1952–56 carried through the nationalization of the mining industry and the agrarian reform, two major changes that in many respects transformed the Bolivian society and economy. The MNR still has many followers in rural areas because of this historical role.

Having won the elections in 1993, the Sánchez de Lozada administration implemented various reforms and changes to the Bolivian economy and the political and administrative system. Not all these reforms were well liked by the population. Because of their high social costs, structural adjustment policies have been met with resistance from many sectors of the population. Many of the political reforms have also been met with opposition, for instance the agrarian reform, called Ley INRA, the reform of the school system, the new system of pensions, and the Law of Popular Participation. Often these reforms were carried through without much in the way of previous public debates. For example, the LPP is probably one of the government's most radical and ambitious projects, but it was kept a secret until just before it was due to be discussed in parliament, which – because nothing is really a secret in Bolivian political life – naturally gave rise to all kinds of rumours and prejudices. The very way in which these processes were implemented caused confrontations between the government and its citizens (Calderón and Laserna 1995: 105).

Furthermore, the government of Sánchez de Lozada was a very self-contradictory type of administration. On the one hand it promoted popular participation, changing the official self-image of Bolivia into one of a 'multi-ethnic society' by granting territorial rights to the indigenous population, promoting teaching of the indigenous languages in school, and so on. At the same time, however, it repressed popular demonstrations, arrested union leaders, killed protesting peasants and miners and continued the paramilitary campaign in the coca-growing areas of Chapare.

In almost all cases where human rights were violated, the guilty persons were not prosecuted because of the 'culture of impunity' that has survived in the political parties (Última Hora, 5 May 1997). This nourished the widespread negative perceptions of politicians and political parties (La Seguridad Humana 1996).

The Law of Popular Participation

The LPP 'municipalizes' the country, as the Bolivians say, which means that, while before April 1994 there were only 13 municipalities, mostly provincial and departmental capitals, now there are 311. These municipalities have autonomous elective governments and, more importantly, the LPP provided these municipalities with a budget in the form of a 20 per cent share of national taxes proportional to the number of inhabitants. The LPP includes the rural area and its inhabitants within the jurisdiction and responsibility of the municipality. This implies a reorganization of the national territory, as we shall see below.

The LPP defines as the 'subjects of the Popular Participation the Territorial Base Organizations (OTBs), expressed in the communities of the *campesinos*, the indigenous peoples and the neighbourhood committee organized according to their own traditions and laws' (LPP, Article 3). These organizations can be given legal recognition if they represent the whole population, urban or rural, living in a specific area. To register as an OTB, the organization has to present its 'book of minutes', the statutes or the regulations according to the nature of the organization, to the administrative authority, which cannot refuse to allot legal status to the organization if these demands have been fulfilled. Only one organization can be recognized within each territorial unit.

The OTBs together form a Vigilance Committee (VC) with one representative from each *canton*.[1] The VC, a new representative body introduced by the LPP, is supposed to be the intermediary between civil society and the municipal government. It has the right to supervise and control the work of the municipal government, and the obligation to participate and cooperate in the planning and the carrying out of works for the common good, thereby expressing the interests of the 'subjects' of popular participation, the OTBs (LPP, Articles 7 and 8). It is interesting to note that the LPP does not define the space or the territorial limits of the OTB. The LPP is based on the presence of already existing organizations defining themselves as belonging to a specific place, or as representing the population in a specific area. The LPP, so to say, labels subjects who were already there but who had never been recognized! The following section will examine the history of these 'subjects' and the reasons for their existence, focusing on the peasants' organizations in the rural areas.

The Politics of Space and Participation: A Historical Perspective

One way of understanding why the Bolivian peasantry are opposed to a law that was meant to benefit them is to examine the historical processes that have led to their present situation of poverty and marginalization. This perspective will also demonstrate how radical the ambitions of the LPP are, and what profound changes in the rural areas it is seeking.

The integration of the rural area and its citizens into the jurisdiction of the municipal government means breaking centuries-old traditions of political and social exclusion of the rural population. In Bolivia the different states and governments have exercised their power to organize land and territory and to name and re-name places and groups of people according to shifting political needs and different political ideologies. This was never done without resistance from the indigenous population, yet mostly it succeeded. This political and social exclusion of the majority of the Bolivian population has been based on racial classifications and the ordering of space. As Lefebvre states, the ordering of space is not neutral. It is historically rooted, extremely political, and should not be imagined as something separate from social relations (Lefebvre 1998).

When the Spaniards arrived in 1535 in what was to be called Upper Peru, today's Bolivia, they did not encounter 'empty space', but found a well-established, sophisticated society, divided into administrative units based on territory or space. The basic form of organization within this society was the *ayllu*, a clan of extended families living together in a specific area, where they shared land, animals and crops. Everything belonged to the community, which distributed land to the different families according to their necessities. The *ayllus* had land or colonists in various ecological regions, which made it possible to exchange products from the valleys and the lowlands with products from the high plain within the circles of the extended family. Several *ayllus* together formed a district, and several districts constituted a territory.

The Spaniards partially broke this system during the period of the Toledo reforms (1572–76), when the indigenous population was concentrated in *reducciones*, permanent fixed villages or nucleated *comunidades indígenas*, rural Indian communities. Viceroy Francisco Toledo's purpose was to make tax collection more efficient and to secure the supply of labour to the silver mines, for which he needed control over population and space (Klein 1992: 39). Thus the indigenous population was gradually forced off its land, obliged to live in a specific place and to deliver labour to the Spanish Crown and its representative, and furthermore to pay taxes. To guarantee the smoothness of this system the cooperation of the indigenous leaders, the *kurakas*, was essential (Klein 1992; Larson and Harris 1995).

Toledo thus founded a form of organization for colonial territory that gradually resembled what Mamdani, talking about the colonial state in Africa, calls 'the bifurcated state' (1996: 16). Such a state was based on two different but interrelated systems of rule defined by location and space: in the cities, centralized, direct rule, based on civil society and civil rights (for the white, male, literate population); and in the countryside indirect, decentralized rule based on violence and coercion, the collaboration of rural tribal authorities (in Bolivia the *jilacatas* and the *kurakas*), community culture and customary law. Needless to say, the Spanish colonial system also was based on profound racism (Harris 1995: 353).

The Toledo reforms also initiated the gradual economic and social homogenization of the indigenous population, to such a degree that today being an Indian (or a peasant) almost automatically means being poor. As Harris states: 'Indians are a class to whom accumulation of resources has been progressively denied' (Harris 1995: 75).

After independence in 1825, the Bolivian territory was divided into nine administrative units called departments (*departamentos*) with their capitals, for example the department of La Paz, the department of Cochabamba, etc. In some areas the logic of this territorial division was constructed according to the limits of the *latifundia* or *hacienda*, sometimes imposing divisions on indigenous communities, making the land of one community belong to two different *cantones* or provinces. The municipality still constituted the local government of the cities or urban centres created exclusively for these units, from where control was exercised over the rural areas and its inhabitants, the indigenous population, through the *latifundia* or *hacienda*. Political participation such as voting was an affair exclusively for the literate and largely white population, the indigenous population not being considered citizens. In 1951, just one year before the National Revolution, the voting population consisted of 200,000 persons out of a population of 3 million. At the presidential elections that year only 54,000 votes were registered (Klein 1992: 232).

The National Revolution of 1952 and the Agrarian Reform of 1953 changed these relations. The new regime established universal suffrage and also freed the indigenous population from the constraints on their freedom of movement. The *hacienda* disappeared in many parts of the country, and with it the landed magnates.

The new small landowners, now officially named *campesinos* (not Indians any more), organized in base unions or *sindicatos*, which became the basic organization and system of self-rule for the indigenous rural population communities in most rural areas in Bolivia. In some areas where peasants still live in *ayllus*, the *sindicato* exists as an organization parallel to them.[2] Agreements are made and conflicts solved at meetings where everybody living in the community is present. Molina Saucedo characterizes this as 'the democracy of consensus' and defines it as consisting of 'discussions until a consensus is reached and the obligation of the leaders to subjugate themselves to it' (Molina Saucedo 1996: 73).

These community organizations formed their own networks through an organizational structure uniting *sindicatos* into *sub-centrales, centrales* and *federaciones,* since 1979 organized in the nationwide *Confederación Sindical Unica de Trabajadores Campesinos de Bolivia* or CSUTCB, affiliated to the National Trade Union Congress or COB. The *sindicatos* became the 'development agents' of their territory, where normally no school, health clinic, road or irrigation system was constructed without their initiative and work. Only on rare occasions could the rural communities count on help or assistance from the state or the municipal government (Ramírez Velarde 1996: 112).

Nevertheless, these community organizations remained marginal to the institutional organization of the municipalities. The rural areas continued to have two types of organization, on the one hand the official institutions of the state, and on the other the community organizations for the rural population. One of the creators of the Popular Participation Act stresses the fact that in Bolivia one must distinguish between the real local government, which is the community organization of the peasants, and the local authorities of the municipality created by the constitution with the purpose of managing public resources. Before April 1994 there was total separation between the two (Molina Saucedo 1996: 73). Only urban dwellers voted in the municipal elections, or in some cases maybe communities close to the urban centre also participated, but in fact half of the country was in 'no man's land', excluded from the system of municipalities. Formal limits or boundaries did not have great significance or importance. Mostly the local mayor defined the limits of his jurisdiction according to his own personal wishes (Ramírez Velarde 1996: 113). Also the attitude among the local mayors was very often that the rural communities were not their responsibility, since they were attended to by the *sindicato* (ibid.).

Bolivia thus continued being what Vilas calls a 'weakly integrated territory' where, at the regional or local levels, social or political institutions and practices could persist that did not exist from the point of view of the central authorities (Vilas 1997: 13). Rockefeller, for example, describes how until 1984 the indigenous leaders of the *ayllu* were expected to go down to San Lucas, the regional capital, on a weekly basis to sweep the mayor's patio, bring eggs to the municipal authorities, and gather and cut firewood for them as a part of their (unpaid) obligations to the white community (1998: 187). Officially these practices had been abolished in the 1952 National Revolution.

The Image of the State as Enemy

Peasants reflect on these historical processes in the political document from the VII Congress of the CSUTCB. In the section on 'Our history and identity', it says:

> The Quechuas, Aymaras, Guaranís, Urus-Chapayas, Mojeños, Ayoreos, Chiquitanos, Yukis, Mosetenes, Chimanes, Sirionós, Yuras, Trinitarios and others have for thousands of years constituted the original nations ... Our knowledge corresponds to a communitarian society of equality and equity where human life is of permanent solidarity. (VII Congreso, p. 55, author's translation)

According to the document the harmony of the ancient societies was broken 'by the foreigners who came to usurp our territory and take away our riches by coercion and violence' (ibid.: 55). They contrast this ancient society with the present capitalist society, which they see as based on 'the principles of individualism, egoism, personalism, cannibalism, and which leaves aside the feelings of solidarity, cooperation and collaboration, which characterized our peoples.' (ibid.: 62).

The document sees the LPP as one of three instruments being used by the Sanchez de Lozada administration to defend its class objectives and guarantee the interests of imperialism.[3] It stresses the fact that in many places the community organizations of the peasants and the organizations of the indigenous groups of the Oriente exist as alternative and parallel organizations to the Bolivian state, and expresses concerns about how the 'oligarchy' now intends to make the political control of the communities more efficient through the official recognition of the traditional authorities of the communities. The peasants see themselves as oppressed, dominated and exploited, and in opposition not only to capitalist society, as is evident from these short extracts from the document, but also to the government, the state and most political parties.

Nevertheless, more recently peasants' organizations have changed their attitude towards the LPP. The attitude of the peasants is still hostile, but the hostility has new elements in it. The Political Document criticizes the LPP because it 'municipalitizes' conflicts and 'takes away the responsibility from the state to solve the hundreds of problems which exhaust workers in the countryside and in the cities' (ibid.: 63). However, the peasants have decided not to stay outside the process, but to 'radicalize the popular participation to the extreme' in order to become the 'zealous controllers of the money that belongs to the people and not to allow corruption either among politicians from the government party or among peasant or indigenous leaders' (ibid.: 75).[4]

In spite of the undisguised opposition to state and government, this attitude in fact corresponds quite well to the intentions of the LPP and may be one of the reasons for its relative success in some rural municipalities, although there are many problems of various kinds, as we shall see below.

Boundaries and Names

Boundaries and limits Before 1994 there was no national registration of the territorial boundaries of the municipality jurisdiction or the different *cantones*. The Ministries of Health and Education defined their districts without any reference to either the political division or the social organization of the population, a fact which could cause some confusion at the local level when people tried to approach the different state representatives.

During the first year after the LPP was introduced, an Inter-Ministerial Commission of Boundaries was appointed with the purpose of coordinating the different maps and lists of five different ministries to define the boundaries of the new municipalities and their *cantones*. In this process all sorts of problems arose. According to the records, two municipalities existed in an area where no one lived. In another area three municipalities existed but had never been officially registered, although elections were held there on a regular basis. Lots of communities protested because they had been placed in the wrong place or because their boundaries had been drawn wrongly (Ramírez Velarde 1996: 118). But as Ramírez Velarde, one of the intellectuals who designed the LPP, concludes: 'At the end we will have a clear and precise political division of the country, an important basis for the planning and administration of the territory' (ibid.: 122).

The subjects of popular participation The LPP defines three different kinds of organization as the 'subjects of popular participation' – the peasants' communities, the indigenous peoples and the neighbourhood committees – thus embracing people in the rural area (i.e. the highland sand valleys of the western part), the jungle areas (in the eastern lowlands) and the cities. In fact, most of these people (apart from the indigenous peoples in the jungle areas) are already organized in a nationwide organization, the Central Obrera Boliviana (COB) or National Confederation of Workers, which has played a very important political role since the 1952 National Revolution. Why not name the base unions of the COB the 'subjects of popular participation'? It is evident that the state does not want 'subjects' who are organized according to their profession or their work (or class) to participate in local politics. On the contrary, the 'subjects' should be organized according to where they live, which is to forget the fact that people may live in several places, according to season and the patterns of migration.

In areas such as mining centres, where the base union of the miners did not include all the individuals living within the area, the LPP means a serious reduction in the union's political and maybe even social role. In the past the miners' trade unions were the most representative social organizations in the mining centres, and together with the parallel organization of women, the Amas de Casa, they could speak on behalf of almost the whole community (Nash 1979). They have been very active in the struggles for democracy and against the military dictatorships, but because of the way the 'subjects of the popular participation' are being defined, they are being ruled out. The miners still regard the LPP as one of the 'damned laws' of the former government.

Other problems arise when the community does not live in a fixed, limited space, but consists of semi-nomads, of which there are several groups living in the jungle areas of Chimán, Parque Isiboro Sécure and Ibiato. Some of these groups have been asked to present a sketch of the area their communities occupy to be accepted as an OTB. This raises fear of having the territory 'mapped' by the authorities, and consequently of having it sold off in the future to others and thereby losing it.

Some municipalities have forced indigenous communities in the eastern lowlands to register as peasant communities, claiming: 'We cannot give them legal recognition as indigenous people because they speak Spanish just like we do. Maybe they were Indians in the past, but today they are not any more.' If these groups register as indigenous people, they can claim territorial rights. This would be against the interests of the big timber companies and the cattle breeders, who use land belonging to indigenous territories (Arias Durán 1996: 151).

Not all communities have a book of minutes. A group of Mosetenes, indigenous people in the jungle area, wanted to register as an OTB. Their book of minutes was an enormous tree where the history of the people was inscribed in the bark. But as the LPP says that the registration should respect the practices and customs of the people, the community received their legal recognition (Arias Durán 1996: 146).

In the rural areas of the western part of the country, the high plain and the valleys, the situation is different, and it seems that the LPP was really designed for these areas. As mentioned above, the LPP combines the two systems that existed previously: the official organizations, i.e. the municipality, based on representation and the election of political parties; and the peasant community organizations, based on traditions of participation and consensus and defined by space. But even here the registration of the OTBs has not been without conflict. In the first place the name caused resistance, because the LPP not only gives names to already existing organizations, it renames them. In so doing, some organizations suddenly find themselves with a name (Territorial Base Organization) that enables them to be a part of Popular Participation; other organizations, which are not renamed, are excluded.

Peasant leaders protested: 'If they change our name (*sindicato*, *ayllu*, *tenta*, etc.), what they really want to do is to change our organization, and transform it so that it can be managed by the government' (Urioste and Baldomar 1996: 34). The problems and dissatisfaction reached such levels that the government was forced to agree to accept the names of the specific organizations (*sindicatos campesinos*, *ayllus*, *pueblos indígenas*, etc.) instead of the OTB at a meeting in April 1995 with the peasants' organization, the CSUTCB, the organization of the indigenous peoples of the Eastern Lowlands, the CIDOB and the COB.

Second, local authorities and political parties have tried to manipulate the process. In some areas departmental government representatives organized 'their own' OTBs, appointed new leaders and had the organization registered. It has been a long fight for the community organizations, the *sindicatos*, in these areas to fight for the annulment of these 'false' OTBs and have their own organization registered as an OTB.

It is clear that the LPP involved negotiation, manipulation and contestation at both state and local levels from the very moment of its creation. The following section will examine how the LPP was implemented at the local level.

Processes of Popular Participation

The first elections after the introduction of the LPP were held in December 1995. It was only after these elections that the LPP could be implemented in many areas and show its potential at the local level. I have chosen to analyse the changes the LPP provoked at the local level and the problems concerning its practical implementation in three different, but interrelated, areas: 1) representation; 2) participation; 3) the use of economic resources.

It is around these three areas that local power relations are concentrated, negotiated, contested and changed, and ultimately the political spaces for poverty reduction and popular participation defined. The discussion of the three areas will be based primarily on the processes taking place in one municipality, Villa Tunari, in the province of Chapare, Department of Cochabamba, which will then be compared with the more general patterns.

Villa Tunari The small village of Villa Tunari[5] is one of three municipalities in Chapare Province. The urban centre, which bears the name of the whole municipality, has only 1,987 inhabitants, but the whole jurisdiction consists of 81,136 persons according to the self-diagnosis of the municipality. Fifty-eight per cent of the population live in the rural areas. About half the population are migrants from other provinces of Cochabamba Department or from the Andean Departments of Oruro and Potosí (Censo de 1992: 29). For the most part people have come to colonize the jungle areas in Chapare because of poverty.

The typical crops grown by these farmers are rice and yucca, mainly grown for subsistence, as well as lemons, oranges, mandarins, bananas and other tropical fruits. The main cash crop is the coca leaf, which on the one hand provides the families with an income, but on the other hand also causes repression and violence. It is common practice for the army and special police units (often lead by North American soldiers) to get into the villages, physically assault the peasants and their families, destroy their property and arrest them. Women and children are not excluded from this harassment.

Living conditions in general are very difficult. Basic services are generally poor and inadequate. Most villages have no electricity, clean drinking water or roads, and many places are cut off during the rainy season. Eighty-seven per cent of the population is considered to be poor (Calderón and Laserna 1995: 109). There is a high degree of infant malnutrition and illnesses like malaria, yellow fever, tuberculosis, leishmaniasis and all kinds of infections. The infant mortality rate is 180 per 1,000 live births (national figures are 96 per 1,000). Thirty-three per cent of the female population and 16 per cent of the male population are considered to be illiterate.

The peasants are organized in *sindicatos*, with their *sub-centrales*, *centrales* and federation. The Tropics region also has a group called the Five Federations, which is connected to the CSUTCB and the nationwide Confederation of Colonizers.

When the LPP was introduced in 1994, the *cocaleros* or coca leaf growers were opposed to it, just like many other groups in Bolivian society. But reality, and their own political cleverness, opened their eyes to the new political possibilities in the law. The coca-leaf producers were among the best-organized peasants in Bolivia, and at the municipal elections in December 1995 they won the elections in three municipalities in the tropical Chapare and Carrasco Provinces of Cochabamba. One of the three municipalities is Villa Tunari.

Representation The mayor in Villa Tunari, Felipe Cáseres, is a peasant and a coca leaf grower, as are four of the seven members of the municipal council. Also an experienced peasant union leader, Felipe Cáseres lived in the countryside until he was elected mayor but he has now moved to the urban centres. In a way this act symbolizes what has become one of the big changes after the LPP was introduced, namely that political power has shifted, so that the rural has imposed itself on to the urban. There is no doubt that the municipal government now represents the rural population.

This is not the case in all municipalities in Bolivia. Things have stayed more or less the way they were, with the mayor and the majority of the councillors coming from the urban centre. The December 1995 municipal elections increased the number of mayors and councillors of indigenous or peasant origin (the two being almost synonymous in Bolivia) to 25 per cent of the total, so although some changes have occurred there is still a serious level of exclusion of indigenous groups from local (and national) politics.[6]

Another important representative body in the municipal government is now the Vigilance Committee (VC). This does not function in Villa Tunar. Unfortunately this is a general problem. As mentioned previously, the VC is supposed to articulate the interests of the OTBs – the peasant communities, and so on. The election of the members, one per *canton* in most areas, is one of the *cargos* or duties of the male community members. There are no resources attached to the functioning of the VC. The municipal government is obliged to provide the VC with the necessary facilities (such as an office and furniture), but as some municipalities are so poor that they can hardly furnish the office of the mayor, they are not likely to give an office to the VC. In one village I visited in the Department of Chuquisaca, the VC had an office they paid for themselves but they had only two chairs for the ten members. Some representatives from remote *cantones* have to walk for one or two days to reach the road where they can take a lorry. They have to pay for their transportation, and if they have to stay in the urban centre overnight, they have to pay for the accommodation as well. This is almost impossible for peasants living at subsistence level. Therefore it is often the VC member living in the urban centre who has most control over the plans and work of the municipality. It also means that in many cases little information will reach the people living in the rural areas.

These simple, practical problems impede the functioning of the VC. Very often those participating in the VC lack the technical skills that would enable them to carry out their control, and there are no training facilities or technical advisers. In addition, VC members often have to confront traditional racism and paternalism, to the extent that just gaining access to the mayor can be a considerable problem.

In many places the political parties try to influence the elections to the VC. This is not quite in accordance with the ideas of the law since the VC should represent community organizations, but the reality is very different from this apolitical image of the peasant communities. Party politics and political patronage are often present.

In Villa Tunari, however, the problems are of a different nature. In some municipalities the mayor can feel somewhat isolated from the rural areas (interview with the mayor in Camargo, Chuquisaca) but in Villa Tunari the mayor has no chance to isolate himself, since there are thousands of eyes watching him. At the meetings of the Five Federations group of peasants, municipal politics are discussed and decisions are made that later have to be carried out by the municipal government. The mayor is seen as the representative of the peasants, and they have elected him for this job, just as they could have chosen him for one of the other leadership posts in the community. What is in other areas the responsibility of the VC is in Villa Tunari part of the politics of the peasants' union. Social control is very strict, but it is not carried out by the VC. This may cause problems in the future if discontent and internal divisions arise within the union structure.

Participation According to the LPP the OTBs have the right to 'propose, request, control and supervise the implementation of works and the rendering of public services according to community needs' (Article 7). The municipal government is required to draw up a five-year development plan, the PDM or Plan de Desarrollo Municipal, and an annual operative plan, the PAO or Plan Anual Operativo, on the basis of projects proposed by the communities, the OTBs. This is interpreted in various ways in the different municipalities. In Villa Tunari it led to a process of participatory planning that reached even the smallest and remotest communities.

This process took a whole year and was initiated by a meeting where 'social actors' were identified, that is, a 'mapping' was made of the different institutions and organizations working in the administrative area. The outlines of participatory planning in the municipality were presented to the different social actors during workshops held in three different places in the area, which is the largest in the Department. The next step was a three-day training seminar with community leaders, who afterwards carried out 'self-diagnoses' in their communities. To do this they were provided with the necessary material, such as pencils and paper, and forms based on the principles they had all agreed upon during the training seminar. The 'self-diagnosis' focused on two themes: 1) problems; 2) potentialities. The idea behind this was to urge people to think also of solutions to their situation of poverty. On the basis of the 200 lists handed in by the communities, the consultancy firm contracted by the municipality produced a municipality self-diagnosis. This was discussed at a meeting with community leaders, and on the basis of this a five-year development plan was elaborated. The last step was to draw up a PAO for 1997 containing the planned projects and priorities of the municipality, which was presented to and discussed with representatives from communities at a workshop held in Villa Tunari.

This planning process has been more thorough and participatory in Villa Tunari than in most municipalities including the neighbouring municipality of Puerto Villarroel, where the peasants are also in charge of the local government (see Booth et al. 1997). This is because of on the one hand a municipality favourable to participation, and on the other hand a very well-organized, well-informed, highly aware population. A third factor is that the municipal government contracted a very good consultancy firm to do the training and the data analysis. Many municipalities use consultancies to carry out different kinds of job, from the elaboration of the PAO and the Development Plan to the implementation and supervision of the actual development project. The services of the consultancy firms vary considerably.

In many municipalities participation in local development planning is limited to the submission of project proposals. The communities apply directly to the mayor, and there is no overall coordination or discussion of the prioritization of the use of resources in which the OTBs participate. This results in a lack of general information about the municipality's development plans, and a lack of awareness about general problems and development priorities.

By now people in the rural areas know that the municipality has resources at its disposal and that they are supposed to submit projects, but not necessarily that they might also participate in decision-making. As Nicod states, 'the municipality governments do not know the real meaning of the word participation' (1996: 76), and apparently many peasants continue to think of the mayor as good, when he acts like a godfather who gives the community what it needs. The idea of a mayor who wants participation is impossible (cf. Arias Durán 1996: 163). These problems and attitudes are, of course, not only due to a lack of consciousness in the rural population in general but also to the weaknesses of peasants' organizations in many areas.

Women are virtually absent from all decision-making fora. The structures of power in Bolivia, in both politics and civil society are characterized by a 'masculine monopoly' (Alanes Bravo 1997: 5) at decision-making levels. There are very few women, if any, who are mayors, very few women in the municipal councils, hardly any women in the VCs and no women representatives of OTBs. In fact women's participation in local government in Bolivia declined after the introduction of the LPP. It might be suspected that this is due to the old saying that where money and power enter, women are squeezed out, but in fact the very system of representation constructed under the LPP effectively excludes women.

The OTBs as the LPP defines them are men's organizations. The community organizations are constituted by landowners, and very few women own land (Informe sobre el avance de las mujeres en Bolivia 1994: 39). In the ancient *ayllu* structure, the system of reciprocity of male and female still exist, but the person representing the community to the outside world is usually male. This is, of course, also reflected in elections to the VCs. In addition, the traditional political parties are almost exclusively male organizations.

In Chapare there is a strong women's organization affiliated to the National Federation of Female Peasants in Bolivia, Bartolina Sisa (FNMCB.B.S.).[7] The women of Chapare and Carrasco organized a march to La Paz in January 1996 to talk to the government and the wife of the president 'woman to woman' (Agreda et al. 1996: 145). It is a 600-kilometre walk from Cochabamba, and the women had to walk on small paths in the mountains to escape the police and to cross mountains about 5,000 metres above sea level. It took them a month, but in doing so they gained the respect not only of their home communities but also of Bolivian society in general. The march also strengthened the women's organization itself.

Women also have to confront the police and the army in the coca-growing areas, often being harassed sexually as well; as a consequence, men now know that they need the active participation of women. This is, however, not reflected very much in the political life of the unions, and even less in the municipal government. In Villa Tunari there is one female councillor, but she is from one of the traditional political parties, not from the peasants' organization. In this respect Villa Tunari is no different from most other municipalities in Bolivia.

Use of resources The LPP 'transfers [to the municipality governments] the physical infrastructure of education, health, sports, secondary roads, and micro-irrigation, with the obligation to administer, maintain, and renovate it' (LPP, Article 2b). As we saw earlier, the municipal government receives from the state 20 per cent of national taxes in proportion to the number of inhabitants in the jurisdiction. In 1994 the average per capita public investment by the municipal governments was US$1.2. In 1995 this had gone up to US$20.6 (Ministerio de Desarrollo Humano 1997: 82).

The first municipal government in Villa Tunari (after the introduction of the LPP), a traditional, urban local government, renovated the public square, paved the main road in the urban centre and had electricity brought to the central square and the main road of the village. This was very much in line with the priorities of most municipal governments when they received the first money from the state: to renovate the town hall, the square, the churchyard, the 200 metres of road passing by the town hall, etc. More than 50 per cent of all the resources budgeted in 1995 at a national level were planned for such activities (Ministerio de Desarrollo Humano 1997: 81). The symbolic values of such places and buildings should not be underestimated, but these priorities do reflect old ways of thinking about the responsibilities of the municipality, or in other words, of urban domination over the rural. But some things have changed – for instance, in many places in the Bolivian countryside one can see new school buildings as a visible sign of money that has now come to the rural areas.

In Villa Tunari the development plan reflects both the needs of the communities as expressed in the self-diagnosis and the needs of the local authority in controlling its area. The plan is based on four pillars: better living conditions, better health conditions, better access to markets, and the promotion of a productive transformation of the region. The plans are to construct roads, schools, hospitals and health clinics; to provide electricity, clean drinking water and better houses with lavatories; to build centres for the study of agriculture and technical skills and provide tree nurseries and marketplaces and meeting centres for the communities; to promote traditional 'fiestas' and celebrations to support a sense of belonging and community; to register who lives where, who owns what land; to limit the illegal expansion of the villages and the frontier into the jungle; to limit the amount of garbage and pollution from human excrement; and to make regulations concerning construction of houses (see Jeppesen 1997).

Compared to these ambitious plans, the PAO seems very poor. In an interview with Felipe Cáseres, the mayor, in February 1997 he explained to me that their needs were many, but that unfortunately the municipality had the resources only to improve health conditions and education, and there was no money for the promotion of a productive transformation. In his opinion and in that of many other people I talked to, the main hope for the future was to improve the health and education of the children. The municipality will therefore concentrate its resources on providing breakfasts for schoolchildren, some new classrooms and the improvement of existing classrooms, some new houses for schoolteachers, the improvement of existing health clinics, and also the construction of some marketplaces, roads and warehouses for agricultural products and tree nurseries.

These plans do not differ very much from plans anywhere else in Bolivia, although they may transfer more resources to rural areas, and they do not include prestige projects like a new town hall, football stadium or something similar.

On the one hand the priorities of most municipalities reflect the negligence of the Bolivian state, the fundamental lack of attention to the population in the countryside and its basic need for health and education. On the other hand these priorities focus more on services than on production. This is understandable but unfortunate, especially in a municipality like Villa Tunari, where dependency on coca leaf production is causing serious problems for everyone living in the area.

This is in fact a general problem in the countryside: the municipalities tend to invest their money in improving basic services such as schools, roads and health clinics (if not the public square), all very necessary investments, but still areas that will not improve the income level of the municipality or its inhabitants.

Many local governments lack the technical skills to plan, implement and supervise projects. Consequently they are dependent on the knowledge of consultancy firms or outside planners and donors. In some cases unhealthy relationships evolve between the private and the public, causing project budgets to swell unreasonably. Some small communities suddenly find themselves with a very elegant school, while they are still living in clay houses without water, electricity or sanitation – except that the school soon starts to fall apart because only half the cement estimated was put into the construction!

Political Spaces for Poverty Alleviation?

In the hands of the Sánchez de Losada administration, the Bolivian state did in fact set up a new set of rules with the LPP, so to speak opening up a space for popular participation at the local level, a popular participation that could lead to an alleviation of poverty for the Bolivian peasantry. But as Carlos Vilas emphasizes, we should not focus so much on rules and procedures that we forget 'the configuration of power relations and ... the modes in which actors interpret rules, negotiate around them, and apply them as a function of power resources which are distributed unequally' (Vilas 1997: 11).

There is no doubt that the LPP has produced a change in the allocation of public resources and of power, and that this represents a fundamental change in Bolivian society. The LPP also gives local organizations a role in decision-making and the right to control local government planning and spending. But the configuration of power relations that has existed throughout Bolivian history has resulted in the gradual marginalization, political exclusion and impoverishment of the indigenous population. When, or if, Bolivian peasants enter the new political space opened up by the law, they enter on unequal terms.

On the other hand, the same processes that have led to exclusion from the municipalities and from local political life have probably also been one of the causes of the existence and relative autonomy of local peasant organizations and their system of self-rule.[8] It is one of the aims of the LPP to incorporate these organizations at the lowest level of the state, the municipality, through a redefinition of the municipality and its responsibilities and a reorganization of its territory. While the political and social organization of the Bolivian landscape used to mean the exclusion of the peasants, the new organization is intended to lead to their inclusion.

But inclusion and participation have a price. According to Lefebvre the way in which space is organized by the modern state means an 'imposition of homogeneity and transparency everywhere within the purview of power and its established order' (Lefebvre 1998: 383). In Bolivia this process is very clear. From the perspective of the peasants this 'imposition of homogeneity and transparency' may not be to their advantage. The state they have known and recollect in their documents is not a benevolent state: on the contrary, it is the enemy. This also applies to local power elites. When the peasants express fears of corruption and of their leaders being co-opted by either the political parties or other influential groups, this fear is based on everyday experiences of the misuse of public resources and power. This means that 'subjects' who are highly opposed to the state, for example the coca leaf growers, have now decided to become a part of this state at the local level, to become 'the zealous controllers of the money that belongs to the people'.

The outcome of these struggles at the local level depends on the strength of the peasants' organizations and on their capacity to negotiate and create alliances to obtain access to information and to influence decisions – that is, their capacity to transform the well-defined political space of the law into channels of influence and power. This means contesting local power relations.

The case of the coca leaf growers in Villa Tunari is very special. They are now in charge of the municipality, not because of a process of inclusion, but because they themselves have taken over power. There is no easy answer to the question of how their organizations could become so strong (see Jeppesen 1997), but one element may be that they are also in charge of the organization of space, and have been so from the start of the colonization of the area. The migrant can obtain new land in the area only by paying a fee to the local *sindicato*, which will then allocate the plot (Blanes and Flores 1982; Arrueta Rodriguez 1994: 50). Also, peasants in Chapare who have left their place of origin to become colonists of a new territory may also have left behind old traditions of subordination and become more independent and self-confident. In fact the overall impression one gets when talking to people in Villa Tunari about popular participation is one of enthusiasm and hope, in spite of their bitterness over the repression and control of the police and the army. The mayor, Felipe Cáseres, summed this up in one interview by saying: 'The Law of Popular Participation is like an instrument for the people who have never before been taken care of. Now we are not clients any more.'

In the Bolivian case of the Law of Popular Participation, a potential framework for poor people to influence the allocation of economic resources at the local level, was planned at state level. While the way the law was designed reflects different political and personal interests, at the local level it can be said that it enabled a political space for poverty reduction that had not been defined as planned for in advance. This political space is in fact defined by the different types of alliances between individuals, political parties, groups of persons and institutions. In the fights between the different actors at the local level to create these alliances, the historic exclusion of specific social groups plays a crucial role. The starting point for Bolivian peasants is one of marginalization, not one of being a 'subject of popular participation'. Where they have had success, it has been through their ability to draw upon their own capacities to organize and to contest the institutional opportunities that the LPP has brought. Here they have demonstrated a capacity to be agents in their own development.

Notes

1. The municipal jurisdicion corresponds to the administrative *sección de provincia*, which is divided into several *cantones*. One may find several OTBs in one *canton*, but they can send only one representative to the VC.

2. Conflicts between the two types of organization, the *ayllu* and the *sindicato*, exist in some areas, such as Northern Potosí, where peasants refused to organize in *sindicatos*. The *ayllu* structure is still very strong in these areas. See Rivera Cucicanqui 1990.

3. The other two instruments are educational reform and the privatization of state-owned enterprises.

4. The following is based on my own fieldwork in Villa Tunari in Chapare Province, Department of Cochabamba, on visits to other areas and municipalities and on the little research done so far.

5. See also Jeppesen 1997.

6. Indigenous people number from 71 per cent to 85 per cent of the population, depending on the definition used. See Ströbele-Gregor 1994: 106.

7. The organization was founded in 1980 and bears the name of an important indigenous woman, Bartolina Sisa, who fought the Spaniards in the most important Indian uprising together with her husband Tupac Catari in the 1780s. They were, of course, both brutally killed.

8. Peasants' organizations were co-opted by the military governments of the 1960s and 1970s in what was called the military–peasant pact (*el pacto campesino–militar*). At the local level, however, they did not play any political role.

Bibliography

Agreda, R., Norma Rodríguez O. Evelin and B. Alex Contreras (1996) *Mujeres cocaleras marchando por una vida sin violencia*, Cochabamba: Comite Coordinadora de las cinco Federaciones del Trópico de Cochabamba.

Alanes Bravo, Zulema (1997) *La mujer en los sindicatos: Bajo el signo de la discriminación*, La Paz: Cedoin.

Arias Durán, Iván (1996) 'Cotidianidad e interacción: el proceso social de Participación Popular', in Ministerio de Desarrollo Humano 1996.

Arrueta Rodriguez, José Antonio (1994) *Campesinado, Coca y Estado. Sindicalismo y movilización de productores de coca en torno al Plan Trienal de Lucha contra el Narcotráfico. Cochabamba, 1987–1989*, Cusco, Peru: Centro de Estudios Regionales Andinos 'Bartolomé de Las Casas'.

Atal, Yogesh and Else Øyen (eds) (1997) *Poverty and Participation in Civil Society*, New Delhi: Abhinav Publications/UNESCO Publications.

Blanes, José and Gonzalo Flores (1982) *Campesino, Migrante y Colonizador. Reproducción de la economía familiar en el Chapare tropical*, La Paz: CERES.

Booth, D., S. Gilsby and C. Widmark (1997) *Popular Participation: Democratizing the State in Rural Bolivia*, Stockholm: SIDA.

Calderón, Fernando G. and Roberto Laserna (1995) *Paradojas de la modernidad. Sociedad y cambios en Bolivia*, La Paz: Fundación Milenio, CERES.

Censo de 1992, Provincia: Chapare, Volumen 11, Cochabamba, Bolivia: Ministerio de Desarrollo Sostenible y Medio ambiente, Instituto Nacional de Estatistica.

Chalmers, Douglas A. et al. (eds) (1997) *The New Politics of Inequality in Latin America*, Oxford: Oxford University Press.

Harris, Olivia (1995) 'Ethnic identity and market relations: Indians and Mestizos in the Andes', in Larson and Harris 1995.

Informe sobre el avance de las mujeres en Bolivia. Comité Nacional Preparatorio de la Cuarta Conferencia Mundial de la Mujer (1994) Subsecretaría de Asuntos de Genero, La Paz: EDEBOL.

Informe Social Bolívia 2 (1995) La Paz: ILDIS–CEDLA.

Jelin, Elisabeth (1997) 'Towards a culture of participation and citizenship: challenges for a more equitable world', in Yogesh Atal and Else Øyen 1997.

Jeppesen, Anne Marie Ejdesgaard (1997) 'Peasant organizations and development in a rural municipality in tropical Bolivia', paper for the third LORPA seminar at Institute for Social and Economic Change, Bangalore, November 1997.

Klein, Herbert S. (1992) *Bolivia, the Revolution of a Multi-ethnic Society*, Oxford: Oxford University Press.

Larson, Brooke and Olivia Harris (eds) (1995) *Migration in the Andes. At the Crossroads of History and Anthropology*, Durham, NC and London: Duke University Press.

Lawton, Jorge A. (ed.) (1995) *Privatization amidst Poverty! Contemporary Challenges in Latin American Political Economy*, Boulder, CO: Lynne Rienner Publishers.

Lefebvre, Henri (1998) *The Production of Space*, Oxford: Blackwell.

Ley de descentralizacion administrativa. Ley No. 1654 (1997) República de Bolivia.

Ley de participación popular (LPP) Ley no. 1551 de 20 de Abril (1994) República de Bolivia.

Mamdani, Mahmood (1996) *Citizen and Subject: Contemporary Africa and the Legacy of Late Colonialism*, Kampala: Fountain.

Ministerio de Desarrollo Humano (1996) *Apre(he)ndiendo la Participación Popular. Análisis y reflexiones sobre el modelo boliviano de descentralización*, La Paz: Secretaría Nacional de Participación Popular, Ministerio de Desarrollo Humano.

Ministerio de Desarrollo Humano (1997) *Bolivia: Participación Popular en Cifras. Resultados y proyecciones para analizar un proceso de cambio*, La Paz: Secretaría Nacional de Participación Popular, Ministerio de Desarrollo Humano. Direccion de Asuntos Económico–Financieros, Vol. II.

Molina Saucedo, Carlos Hugo (1996) 'Decisiones para el futoro', in Ministerio de Desarrollo Humano 1996.

Nash, June (1979) *We Eat the Mines and the Mines Eat Us: Dependency and Exploitation in Bolivian Tin Mines*, New York: Columbia University Press.

Nicod, Chantal (1996) 'Seguimiento al proceso de participación popular en los municipios de Chuquisaca', in Rojas Ortuste 1996.

Plan de Desarrollo Municipal Sostenible, 1997–2201, Gobierno Municipal de Villa Tunari. Presentación Preliminar, Villa Tunari, Diciembre 19 de 1996, Elaborado por CIDES.

Ramírez Velarde, Luis F. (1996) 'Recuperación de la consciencia territorial', in Ministerio de Desarrollo Humano 1996.

Rivera Cucicanqui, Silvia (1990) 'Liberal democracy and ayllu democracy in Bolivia: the case of northern Potosí', *Journal of Development Studies*, 26, 4: 77–121.

Rockefeller, Stuart A. (1998) 'Political institutions and the evanescence of power: making history in highland Bolivia', *Ethnology*, 37, 2: 187–207.

Rojas Ortuste, Gonzalo (ed.) (1996) *La Participación Popular: avances y obstáculos*, La Paz: Unidad de Investigación y Análisis Secretaria Nacional de Participación Popular Grupo-DRU.

La Seguridad Humana en Bolivia: Sociales y Economicas de los Bolivianos de Hoy (1996) La Paz: PRONAGOB; PNUD; ILDIS.

Ströbele-Gregor, Juliana (1994) 'From Indio to Mestizo ... to Indio. New Indianist movements in Bolivia', *Latin American Perspectives*, 21, 2: 106–23.

Última Hora (1997).

Urioste, Miguel and Luis Baldomar (1996) 'Ley de participación. Seguimiento crítico', in Rojas Ortuste 1996.

Vilas, Carlos M. (1997) 'Participation, inequality, and the whereabouts of democracy', in Chalmers et al. 1997.

World Bank (1997) *World Development Report 1997: The State in a Changing World*, Oxford: Oxford University Press.

3

The Vicissitudes of Politics and the Resilience of the Peasantry: The Contestation and Reconfiguration of Political Space in the Peruvian Andes

Karsten Paerregaard

Since the late 1960s Peru has experienced significant changes. Politically, the country has lurched between shifting and often opposing ideologies depending on the political credos prevailing in the global arena: state protectionism and nationalism in the 1970s, democracy and socialism in the 1980s, and neo-liberalism and developmentism in the 1990s (cf. Alvarez Rodrich 1995; Wise 1997). Economically, Peru has gone from material prosperity and the expansion of the public sector via very high inflation and recession to economic liberalization accompanied by extreme poverty and inequality. Simultaneously, rural–urban migration and growing globalization have transformed the power hierarchy and undermined the ethnic divisions on which post-colonial Peruvian society is based. Over the past 30 years, this transformation in Peruvian society has incited the spread of modern lifestyles and the creation of new identities among Peru's indigenous and peasant populations and triggered social conflicts and political instability in the country's rural areas.

The aim of this chapter is to explore how shifting economic and political conditions at the national level are articulated in Peru's peasant society. It is argued that the peasant community constitutes a principal link between Peru's rural population and the state, and that peasants use the community not only as an arena to play out internal struggles and conflicts, but also as an organizational tool to negotiate dominating power structures and generate rural development. The chapter suggests that, rather than regarding regional or local processes of change as mere reflections of shifting economic and political conditions on the national level, peasants make power relations forged at an extra-regional level the object of contestation and reconfiguration at the regional and local levels. In order to study this process, the chapter explores changes at regional and local levels over a period of three decades, with particular attention to how state intervention and political conflicts are represented and enacted as power relations and strategic resources in the everyday life of the peasant population.

From Revolution to Neo-liberalism

When the military staged a coup in 1968 and overturned the elected government of Fernando Belaúnde only three years after democracy had been restored in the country, Peru was about to write a new chapter in the political history of Latin America. Rather than defending the privileges of the wealthy and dominant sections of the population, as military regimes usually do on this troubled continent, the new military rulers of Peru, led by General Juan Velasco, were induced by a reformist and, in the eyes of some, revolutionary ideology aimed at transforming Peruvian society in order to alleviate poverty and diminish social inequality. As evidence of such a policy, an agrarian reform was introduced in 1969 that radically changed the land tenure pattern in the country's rural areas to the benefit of the Peruvian peasantry, particularly the most impoverished and exploited (Matos Mar and Mejía 1980).

The 1969 land reform broke the economic and political power of Peru's agrarian ruling class and made the landless tenants on the *haciendas* the owners of the land they tilled, primarily as members of the newly established cooperatives (Hunefeldt 1997; Skar 1988: 43–72). Different types of cooperative were established by the new regime on the coast and in the highlands, where the former *haciendas* varied in terms of organizational structure and production pattern (Seligmann 1995: 56–76). The two dominant types of cooperative were the SAIS (Agrarian Societies of Social Interest) and the CAP (Cooperatives for Agrarian Production), the first recruiting its members from among the former workers of the *haciendas* as well as the surrounding peasant communities in the highlands (thus combining two distinct production systems), the second including former workers of the sugar and cotton *haciendas* on the coast (Caycho 1977; Matos Mar and Mejfa 1980: 161–252).

During its first years in power the military regime had considerable success in changing the country's economic and political power structure in favour of the marginal sections of the population. After General Francisco Morales Bermúdez replaced Velasco in 1975, however, the political reform process was brought to a halt and the economy started to show signs of recession, which triggered popular discontent (Gorman 1997). In 1980 the military withdrew to its barracks and called for democratic elections, which ironically brought former President Belaúnde back into power twelve years after General Velasco had forced him into exile. Not surprisingly, expectations that the new administration would introduce democratic reforms and prompt economic progress were high (Mauceri 1997).

Yet worse times were ahead for the Peruvians. Not only did the second Belaúnde administration fail to control growing inflation or to spark economic growth, but from 1980 to the mid-1990s Peru experienced one of the most violent conflicts in its post-colonial history, due to the insurrection of two Marxist-oriented guerrilla movements. As Sendero Luminoso (Shining Path) and the MRTA (Túpac Amaru Revolutionary Movement) gained popular support and political influence, Andean peasants found themselves caught in a fierce civil war between the Peruvian military and the rebels, with high casualties, particularly among the civilian population. Paradoxically, the conflict, which originated in the extreme poverty and social inequality that historically has reigned in Peru, only made worse the economic and political situation of the poor and marginal sections of the Peruvian population, whom the rebels (or terrorists, as they soon became) were claiming to defend. At the end of the 1980s, the political panorama and future prospect of *progresar* (making progress) looked more gloomy than ever, not only for Peru's poor, but also for large groups of middle-class Peruvians as well.

If Peruvians consider the performance of the Belaúnde administration poor, they remember that of the APRA government, which followed under the leadership of Alan García, as disastrous (Glewwe and Hall 1994). In 1987, after two years in power, the government had completely lost control of Peru's political and economic crisis. The deprivation and distress caused by this development further contributed to the discontent of the poor about the country's ruling parties and their uncertainty about its political future. To them, the 1980s represent a lost decade in Peru's contemporary history, a time of crisis in which they turned their eyes towards other parts of the world, particularly the USA, Europe and Japan, in search for *progreso*. At the end of the APRA government's five-year term, this craving for improved living conditions had taken the form of a mass exodus, which further gathered strength in the 1990s.

The surprising election of president Alberto Fujimori in 1990 stands as a turning point in Peru's modern history. Although Fujimori, the son of poor Japanese immigrants, ran his election campaign without economic funds or a political programme, he beat Mario Vargas Llosa – Peru's world-famous novelist, who represented the country's ruling class – in a spectacular run-off with the overwhelming support of the less-privileged population (Durand 1997; Cotler 1998). The victory became a watershed in Peruvian political history because Fujimori was identified not only as representing the interests of the poor but also as having the same origin as the poor as the son of migrants who had suffered racial prejudice and economic poverty. Once he was in power, however, circumstances looked daunting. The war between Sendero Luminoso, the MRTA and the Peruvian military was generating fear, social chaos and destruction in almost every part of the country, paralysing the efforts that the state and foreign development agencies had made during the 1970s and the early 1980s to develop Peru's impoverished rural areas. Further, inflation of more than 6,000 per cent annually was crippling the national economy, which was now declining at an alarming speed.

In 1992 new hope arose among Peru's poor when Fujimori staged his famous *auto-golpe*[1] and neutralized most of the country's rebel and terrorist activities (Degregori 1997; Mauceri 1995). This highly unconventional and undemocratic move, which concentrated the power of the state in the hands of the president and his ruling party, produced much criticism from the country's traditional political leaders and international opinion, yet to the majority of poor Peruvians of Andean origin living either in impoverished communities in the highlands or in shanty-towns next to the big cities the *auto-golpe* represented a blow against the economic and political establishment by a man who meant business when promising to beat inflation and terrorism. In effect, many Peruvians felt that they had passed the worst and that progress was within reach. Yet today, it is far from sure that the country's impressive record of foreign investments and economic growth will eradicate poverty in Peru (Gonzales de Olarte 1995; Moncada and Webb 1996). On the contrary, there are many signs that the number of rural as well as urban poor is on the rise (Figueroa et al. 1996: 35–48). Although inflation has been brought under control and terrorism beaten, Fujimori's economic policy has not generated many new jobs and wages are still very low. Likewise, agricultural production is stagnating due to a lack of capital and government support.

During the 1990s, under the Fujimori administration, the country experienced a fundamental change in the class structure and the ethnic division of the Peruvian population, with old forms of social inequality being effaced and new patterns of differentiation emerging (cf. Golte 1995). In effect, many middle-class families of mestizo origin who have experienced a traumatic setback in economic and social status over the past ten years today belong to the growing section of urban poor in Peru. Conversely, a growing number of Andean peasants and migrants are exploiting new sources of income and ascending the social hierarchy (cf. Adams and Valdivia 1991).

The breaking up of Peru's ethnic divisions has to a large extent been caused by the rural–urban migration process, which brings poor and marginal people into direct contact with the national and global society. In the 1990s, this development was accompanied by a modernization process that has improved the country's infrastructure, particularly the transport and communication system, and provided Peru's marginal areas with roads, telephones, parabola antennae and other modern facilities. Similarly, the state has strengthened its presence and improved public service systems in rural areas, often in competition with the increasing number of local NGOs and international development agencies that have been mushrooming in Peru since the violence was brought to an end. Finally, Peru's rapidly growing tourist industry is breaking ground as a new source of income in the city as well as in the countryside.

Peru's economic and political development over the past 30 years can be divided into three stages: 1) the reform period of the military government in the 1970s, which changed the economic and political basis of Peru's rural power hierarchy; 2) the restoration of democracy in the 1980s, which also heralded the outbreak of political violence and the deterioration of the country's economic crisis; and 3) the introduction of neo-liberal politics by a democratic but also authoritarian government in the 1990s, leading to the defeat of Peru's terrorist movements, the increased modernization of Peruvian society and economic recovery.

The aim of this chapter is to explore the Peruvian peasantry's response to changes in national politics and economic development during these three periods of Peru's contemporary history. In order to do this I examine, historically and ethnographically, how the shifting political and economic environments on the national level in the 1970s, 1980s and 1990s are articulated in the peasant communities of the Alto Cunas, an area situated in the Junín department of Peru's central highlands on the eastern side of the Mantaro Valley. Moreover, I explore to what extent the political and economic environment in each of the three decades has either instigated or thwarted the creation of a political space in favour of the poor – whether institutional mechanisms, poverty discourses and social practices for influencing politics have been available to reduce poverty among the peasant population.

Peasant Communities and the Struggle for Land in the Alto Cunas Area

There exist approximately 5,000 peasant communities in the highlands of Peru, of which 3,312 are recognized by the Peruvian state (Hunefeldt 1997: 122). The inhabitants of these communities make up the backbone of the country's rural population and share many linguistic and cultural traits of colonial or pre-Columbian origin. Not only are native languages such as Quechua and Aymara still spoken in large parts of Peru's peasant communities, but their inhabitants wear clothing, perform rituals and practise agrarian rituals identified as indigenous. In effect, the creole and mestizo populations, who primarily are urban dwellers and historically have played a dominant role in Peru's economic and political development, regard the peasants living in these communities as the descendants of the country's pre-Columbian peoples. In contemporary Peru, however, the ethnic label of 'Indians' thrust upon the Andean peasantry by the outside world has become highly controversial; indeed, most of Peru's rural population do not identify themselves as indigenous. Rather than employing ethnic or cultural categories, they refer to economic position or regional origin when accounting for their identity (Paerregaard 1997: 250).

While the notion of Indianness originates from the Spanish conquest, the blurring of Peruvian ethnic categories and identities goes further back to the time when different Andean population groups were integrated into the Inca state through a resettlement policy called *mitmaq*. The aim of this policy was to unite the region culturally and linguistically by resettling local populations and creating ethnic colonies in different parts of the empire. Some Andean populations, however, resisted the Inca expansion and the *mitmaq* policy. Among these were the Huancas, who inhabit the Mantaro Valley and other parts of the central highlands of Peru. When the Inca empire was conquered in 1532, they became the Spaniards' most loyal allies, an alliance that turned out to be crucial for the region's political and social history during the colonial and post-colonial periods.

In 1572, Viceroy Toledo introduced the policy of *reducciones* in Peru and other Andean countries. Once again the native Andean population became the object of a resettlement policy, this time with the aim of consolidating the peasant population in villages designed along Spanish lines, with a plaza and a church in the centre (Wightman 1990: 9-44). Consequently, local kin groups (*ayllus*) were brought together from different areas in a single village to form the roots of Peru's modern peasant communities. In the Mantaro Valley the policy of *reducciones* led to the formation of peasant communities with a strong internal organization. The appearance of a well-organized peasantry in the central highlands was due not only to the region's thriving economy but also to the Huanca's alliance with the Spaniards after the latter had conquered the Inca empire. The new colonial administration allowed the Huanca native leaders (*kurakas*) to maintain their role as local authorities in the region's rural society for several centuries after the conquest. Unlike other parts of the Andes, where a Spanish-controlled *hacienda* system hampered the formation of peasant institutions and representations, it was only in the high *punas* above the agricultural peasant communities of the Mantaro Valley, where the frigid, dry climate made sheep-raising a profitable activity, that the large estate flourished (Mallon 1983: 39). These estates were initially controlled by a group of *kuraka* families who used their position within the native communities to gain access to labour and to expand their landed possessions in the highlands in the period after the conquest. Later these lands came into the hands of Spanish and mestizo settlers, who formed the basis of what was to become a *hacienda* system based on sheep-ranching and mining in the highlands (ibid.; Smith 1989: 49).

One of the communities that emerged in the Mantaro Valley in the aftermath of the *reducciones* policy was Mito. During the colonial period it became a prosperous village in the region, controlling not only vast areas of farm land in the Mantaro Valley, but also pastures in the Alto Cunas area located in the high *punas* (Alberti and Sánchez 1974: 51–60; Castillo 1964a). As the region experienced a massive influx of outsiders in the late seventeenth century, the percentage of lands owned by mestizos increased dramatically, thus triggering class and racial tensions in many peasant communities (Mallon 1983: 38, 45). The immigration of non-Indians led to a process of *mestizaje* (mestization) in Mito and other villages, which deepened social differentiation within the peasant population and caused a shift in the communities' local power hierarchy. In effect, the last *kuraka* families lost the land they had retained in the Alto Cunas area (Samaniego 1980: 51), while the emerging mestizo families gained control, economically as well as politically, over the *puna* herders. Among these mestizos was the Lozano family of Mito, who became the owners of the Alto Cunas area, including what are today the villages of Chaquicocha and Usibamba.[2] In order to make the herders work for them, the Lozanos organized the local population as *huacchilleros* (Martínez Alier 1973: 9–13; Samaniego 1980: 45, 49; Smith 1989: 35–7). In return for tending the animals of the Lozano family, the herders received agricultural products and some of the offspring as payment.

Over the years the *huacchillero* arrangement became a profitable business for the Lozano family and other mestizo groups in Mito. Not only did they re-sell the products they received from the Alto Cunas herders in the Mantaro Valley, but many of the public works in Mito, such as street-cleaning and bridge construction, were carried out by the villagers of Usibamba and Chaquicocha, who were commanded to do corvée labour *(faena)* by the municipality of Mito (Alberti and Sánchez 1974: 52). The church in Mito also benefited from the compulsory labour recruitment of Alto Cunas herders who were obliged to work for Mito's religious brotherhoods *(cofradías)*.

Periodically, tensions arose between villagers in Usibamba and Mito, and when new mines opened in the central highlands at the turn of the century, offering the herders an alternative to the unequal division of labour and exchange imposed by the powerful mestizo families of Mito, the tension between the two groups escalated into open conflict. The herders could now opt to sell their products directly on the new markets that emerged in the wake of the mining economy instead of bartering them with Mito. As a result, in 1907 the Lozano family of Mito sold the pastures of the Alto Cunas to the local herders, an event that initiated Usibamba's and other communities' struggle for their economic and political independence.

The peasant institutions that emerged in the Alto Cunas area in the twentieth century were not only the product of long struggles for land rights and political autonomy with surrounding communities and *haciendas*, but also the result of internal conflicts over land and communal organization. The village of Usibamba provides one of the most interesting cases of community reorganization in Alto Cunas's contemporary history. Like other Alto Cunas villagers, the Usibambinos continued to live from sheep- and cattle-herding up to the middle of the twentieth century. As the population was scarce, access to land remained free. However, demographic growth and the introduction of agricultural production induced the villagers to alter the land-tenure pattern and restructure the communal organization (López 1981).[3] This development was also promoted by the land claims made by landless peasants from the Mantaro Valley, who migrated into the area during the first half of the twentieth century. As a result of this development, in 1937 the local population formed a so-called *comunidad campesina* (peasant community). Although this institution was established in order to control individual villagers' access to land, it soon turned into the central arena for internal conflicts. The first serious incident occurred between 1958 and 1959, when the majority of villagers decided to *igualizar* (equalize) access to land (Usibamba n.d.) at a community meeting. This decision entailed the village's land being parcelled out among those villagers classified as *cotantes* or descendants of *cotantes*, i.e. the original or native village population who fought against Mito and bought the pastures from the Lozano family in 1907. In effect, land was made private property and reserved as the special privilege of one group of villagers (the 'native' population, labelled *cotantes*) while the rest of the population (those who migrated after the village gained its autonomy) was made landless.

The 1970s: Agrarian Reform in Alto Cunas

The land reform process implemented by the military government of General Velasco altered this development dramatically. In the early 1970s government agents from SINAMOS[4] visited peasant communities all over the Peruvian highlands to promote the land reform and encourage peasants to abolish private property in land, redistribute it among the villagers, and establish rural cooperatives to encourage the communally organized production and commercialization of agricultural products. While the agents were quite successful in mobilizing peasant support in favour of the government's expropriation of *hacienda* land, their attempt to make them change the existing land tenure pattern within the communities and enforce a communal redistribution in favour of the landless and less privileged groups of villagers bore less fruit. One of the communities in Peru that actually did comply with the reform act was Usibamba. SINAMOS agents visited the village on several occasions encouraging the villagers to carry out a *restructuración de la tierras* (land restructuring), the official term used in the act for abolishing private property in community land and redistributing it in equal shares among the villagers. And as the villagers of Usibamba reacted promptly and thus became among the first in Peru to carry out the decision to redistribute land on a communal level, they were presented as national pioneers in the reform process by government officials. These even pictured Usibamba as a model of how other peasant communities in Peru could transform social relations and foster economic development in the country's rural society.

The decision to comply with the land reform act, which was taken at a community meeting in 1972, provoked an internal conflict among Usibamba's population. While the majority of the villagers (including those who had been denied land rights when the community decided to introduce private property in land between 1958 and 1959) enhanced their land rights in connection with the SINAMOS proposal to carry out a *restructuración de la tierras* and hence welcomed it, Usibamba's minority of large landowners, who had gained exclusive rights to community land 14 years earlier, repulsed the government's interference in the village's internal affairs. As the abolition of private property in land represented a threat to their economic position, this group of villagers bitterly resisted the SINAMOS proposal. However, in the light of the political discourses in favour of Peru's poor and landless population that swept through the country in the 1970s, the rhetorics of Usibamba's founding *cotantes*, who hold a particular historic right to village land because of their heroic fight against the mestizo families of Mito, were no longer applauded by the majority. In effect, the villagers decided to abolish private property in land and the right to inherit it, and to redistribute it in equal shares among those households granted status as members of the newly established peasant community (see Tables 3.1 and 3.2).

To become a member of the community, villagers have to meet a number of requirements and pay an inscription fee.[5] This gives them the right of usufruct to a specific number of land lots which they cannot sell or rent.

TABLE 3.1 Social stratification and land distribution in Usibamba before the land reform of 1972

Category of community membership	Number of villages as percentage of total population	Average size of land for each villager (hectares)
Upper strata: more than 5 ha	22	10.2
Middle strata: between 0.1 and 5 ha	59	2.1
Lower strata: landless	19	0
Total (percentage or average)	100	3.85

Each household is granted the usufruct of approximately five hectares, of which two are irrigated and three non-irrigated. However, retired villagers, widows and single mothers receive only a total of 2.5 hectares. In return for rights over land, household members are required to participate in the weekly or monthly labour corvée organized by the community and to take on different political and administrative posts in the village's communal organizations. Single males and villagers who are either physically absent because of migration or simply cannot afford to pay the inscription fee are precluded from rights over land.

In 1972, the villagers established a community cooperative (*empresa comunal*) responsible for the marketing of the community's herd of more than 2,000 sheep and a number of cows and bulls, and the management

TABLE 3.2 Land distribution of community members in Usibamba after land reform (in 1981)

Category of community membership	Percentage of total community members	Average size of land for each member (ha)	Average number of lots of each member (ha)	Average size of lots for each member
Active members: only married males	62.2	5.18	8.37	0.62
Retired members, widows and single mothers	38.8	2.30	4.26	0.54
Total (percentage or average)	100	3.73	6.32	0.58

of a communal shop, a truck and several agricultural machines (including two tractors). The purpose of the cooperative was to generate an income to be distributed among its members. Those households that were already members of the community automatically became members of the co-operative too, with the right to benefit from the different kinds of services it offered (the renting of agricultural machines, the use of the community's truck, purchasing in the shop, and so on). In addition, they were granted the right to receive water from an irrigation canal built with the assistance of a German aid agency in the early 1970s.

In 1972 Usibamba also became associated with the SAIS Túpac Amaru, the first agricultural and pastoral cooperative established by the military government in the Peruvian highlands and one of the largest. The SAIS model was designed to transform the landless tenants and rural workers of the former *haciendas* into members of rural cooperatives, which would pay them a monthly salary and assure them rights to health care, schooling, housing and other kinds of social services.

By associating neighbouring peasant communities with the newly estab-lished agrarian cooperatives, the military government hoped to promote economic development in Peru's rural society. Hence the land reform act granted the inhabitants of the country's peasant communities the right to receive part of the future profits of the cooperatives, which also provided the associated villagers with social services similar to those offered to SAIS workers. Furthermore, by stimulating growth and development among the associated peasantry, the government hoped that the SAIS would reduce former land conflicts with neighbouring peasant communities (cf. Hune-feldt 1997: 120). Yet the SAIS model failed to solve the urgent problems of increasing poverty and land conflicts among the peasantry. Economically, most of the cooperatives established by the military government in the highlands were too inefficient to promote development in the neighbouring communities (Torres Rodriguez 1979: 823–4), and as peasants in the Peruvian highlands are generally reluctant to waive the historical claims they hold to land encroached upon by the ex-*haciendas*, the SAIS had little success in solving existing land conflicts (Hunefeldt 1997: 112–15).

The social and political predicaments inherent in the SAIS model seriously affected the relationship between the SAIS Túpac Amaru and Usibamba. Of the 16 peasant communities associated with the SAIS, the village was appointed as the principal recipient of economic support. Yet Usibambinos continue to claim large areas of pastures lost to the Cerro de Pasco Corporation before the company's properties were expropriated by the Peruvian state in 1970. Bitterness and agony against the SAIS is particularly prevalent among elder villagers, who argue that the land currently held by the SAIS should be divided between the associated communities. Moreover, as the majority of the cooperative leaders were recruited among the former employees of the Cerro de Pasco Corporation, they made little effort to alter the paternalistic bonds traditionally informing peasant–*hacienda* relations (cf. ibid.: 116).

Despite its limits the SAIS model has played an important role in promoting the reorganization and redistribution of land rights within the associated communities and improving public services among peasant families. In the Alto Cunas area, the economic support and technical assistance that Usibamba has so far received from the SAIS Túpac Amaru has helped thwart the growth of internal differentiation among the villagers. Likewise, when the neighbouring Chaquicocha carried out a land reform process in 1980 similar to the one Usibamba implemented eight years earlier, thus reinvigorating the reform spirit that dominated the region in the 1970s, it received support from Heroínas Toledo, one of the smallest SAIS in the area.[6]

Today, only a handful of the 53 SAIS established by the military government in the Peruvian highlands exist. Some lasted only a few years, disintegrating because of internal conflicts. Others were dissolved because of economic problems and inefficient management. Yet others, such as the SAIS Heroínas Toledo, with which Chaquicocha was associated in 1973, were destroyed by the Shining Path during the years of political violence in the 1980s and early 1990s.[7]

The 1980s: Political Violence in Alto Cunas

The Shining Path initiated its violent struggle against the Peruvian state in April 1980, on the very same day the first democratic elections were held after twelve years of military dictatorship. During the early 1980s the insurgents limited their activities to three of Peru's highlands Departments (Ayacucho, Apurímac and Huancavelica). From 1985 the violence spread to other parts of Peru, and before the decade was out only a handful of the country's 24 Departments had been spared the terror that followed the fierce showdown between the rebels and Peru's armed forces. The Mantaro Valley was one of the regions most effected by the political violence, and in 1995 the rebels declared the Alto Cunas area liberated territory. The police and armed forces responded by classifying it a *zona roja* (red zone). The outcome was a so-called *guerra sucia* (dirty war), in which the civilian population played a role as the pawns of the insurgents as well as the military. The villagers in the area remember the following five years as a time of fear, deprivation and even starvation.

One of the ways the conflict affected the lives of the local population was that transport in the area became a perilous undertaking. Buses and trucks were frequently forced to stop or were attacked by the rebels, who would charge so-called *cubos* (war taxes) from the drivers, inspect the passengers' identity and, in some cases, execute individuals found to be 'enemies of the people'. As the Alto Cunas peasants are very dependent on the regional and national economy and sell most of their produce at the weekly markets in Chaquicocha, Chupaca and Huancayo, transportation is conventionally extensive in the area. Sendero's attempt to sever the peasants' links with the regional and national markets therefore stirred up much anger and frustration. One male peasant in Chaquicocha told me that when the insurgents blew up a small bridge that connects the area with the highway to Huancayo, the largest city in the region, travellers were forced to walk the rest of way up to the Alto Cunas villages, thus dangerously exposing themselves to watching rebel patrols. This same informant recalled that on one trip from Huancayo to Chaquicocha a squad of *cumpas* (an abbreviation of *compañeros*, i.e. comrades, and a popular term for the rebels) stopped the van he was travelling in and ordered everybody to get out. After a close inspection the passengers were allowed to reenter the van and continue the journey except for two individuals who were forced to stay behind with the rebels. 'None of us ever knew what happened to them,' he exclaimed.

A particularly terrifying experience for the Alto Cunas inhabitants were the nightly visits by squads of *cumpas* who called for meetings in the central square in the village to indoctrinate the villagers and carry out *judicio popular* (popular justice) – that is, to interrogate individuals accused of moral crimes such as adultery and rape. After a brief 'trial', the victim would be punished in public. As the Shining Path condemned all forms of political activity apart from those authorized by the organization itself as a threat against *la guerra popular* (the popular war), political collaboration with the state and the formation of independent peasant organizations were also punished. In response, villagers holding administrative and political offices resigned from their posts.[8] Moreover, in Usibamba and Chaquicocha the Shining Path forced the villagers to dissolve the cooperatives established in the 1970s and to partition the communally owned sheep and cattle herds among the villagers. Another crime that was punished was the exploitation of fellow villagers. One middle-aged man who owns a small shop in the village of San Juan de Jarpa told me that he spent several years sleeping outside in the surrounding mountains out of fear of revenge by a local squad of *cumpas*, who accused him of being a 'capitalist'. Similarly, a shop situated near Chaquicocha, on the highway from Huancayo to Alto Cunas, which was owned by a businesswoman from a village in the Mantaro Valley, was blown up. According to the villagers of Chaquicocha, the owner was killed by a patrol of *cumpas*.

Villagers relate that armed groups of insurgents toured the villages at night paying personal visits to the homes of the villagers in order to coax or simply coerce them into sending sons, daughters or husbands as Sendero recruits. In effect, many were afraid to work in the fields during the day and hid in caves outside the villages at night. A woman who defied the ruling order of the Shining Path and formed an independent *club de madres* (mothers' club) in Usibamba to solve the growing health and food problems of the village's infant population told me that for almost three years she lived in fear of a local group of the Shining Path, who repeatedly visited her to 'discuss' her conduct in village affairs. The woman explained that when someone came looking for her she would know whether they were *cumpa*s by the way they knocked on the door. She also said that she agreed with her neighbours to warn each other by making a noise with their kitchen pots when the insurgents made nightly visits. Whenever she received such a warning, she would hurry her husband and son to escape through the back door. Miraculously, the woman was not killed by the *cumpas*. When asked why, the woman replied, 'I dared to face *los terrucos* [the terrorists] and ask them what good all the violence did to a humble peasant woman and ask them whether they didn't have a mother themselves'.[9]

In 1990, shortly after Fujimori was elected president of Peru, the army established military camps in Chaquicocha and several other Alto Cunas villages and within two years had gained control of the area. In effect, all subversive activities were suppressed and new village authorities elected. However, to many Alto Cunas villagers, the defeat of the Shining Path was achieved not through the intervention of the military but because of the *rondas campesinas*; that is, autonomous armed peasant self-defence groups. Originally the *ronda* organization was created by *hacienda*-owners and Indian peasants in the northern highlands to fight cattle-rustling. In the late 1980s, it was introduced in the central and southern highlands to mobilize Andean peasants in the fight against the Shining Path, now constituted as village-based peasant paramilitary units trained and equipped by the Peruvian army. While the Peruvian army initially encouraged and trained the Alto Cunas population to form *rondas*, their success was the result of a desire among the local peasantry to organize themselves to resist local *cumpa* squads' frequent abuses against villagers. In fact, the army did little to support the *rondas*. The villagers recount that when the military established camps in the villages of Bella Vista and Chaquicocha, they treated the locals as though they were all *terrucos*. Moreover, the officers required the peasantry to provide food and firewood free and allowed the soldiers to abuse civilians. One villager in Bella Vista told me of a sergeant whom he described as particularly mean accusing the local *ronda campesina* of supporting the *cumpas*. In the words of this villager,

'The soldiers were so scared of the *terrucos* that they never dared to leave their camp at night and suspected everybody of being their enemy,' adding that 'We in the *ronda* were the ones who actually faced *los terrucos* and we were even accused by *los milicos* [the military] of being *terrucos*.'

As in other parts of the Peruvian highlands the spread of subversion in the Alto Cunas area was a response to the continuous withdrawal of the state, which the rural population had experienced since the land reform period because of the country's growing economic crisis (Hunefeldt 1997: 115). Initially, one group of villagers openly supported the Shining Path by helping it gain control over peasant institutions and establishing a power base in the area. Before physically entering the Alto Cunas villages the Shining Path established a clandestine network of agents in the area, often through local schools. The first *cumpa* reported to be active in the area was a schoolteacher from Ayacucho working in the village of Shicuy, which he used as a stronghold to establish local networks in Sulcán and other neighbouring villages.[10] In Usibamba, a number of villagers also cooperated with the Shining Path. One villager told me that he was appointed local squad leader when the Shining Path took control of the village. The man refrained from revealing the details of his performance as squad leader, but other villagers affirmed to me that he showed few signs of repentance while carrying out his mandate. However, when I met the man in 1997, he was acting as the leader of the local *ronda campesina* in Usibamba, an office he had occupied since the *ronda* was established there in 1990. Even more surprisingly, no villager expressed discontent with the apparent inconsistency of this villager's performance as community leader.[11] Clearly, his continuous drifting in and out of offices according to the shifting political environment reflects a highly pragmatic notion of politics among Alto Cunas peasants, who tend to identify with rather than contest the existing power hierarchy. This notion of politics seems to suggest that it is by representing and reconfigurating extra-regional power relations and the replication of dominant discourses on poverty, political conflict and development within their own community institutions and rural life-world that peasants develop social practices for influencing politics.

Yet to most villagers, the years of political violence in the late 1980s were a time of fear when those who had relatives in Huancayo or Lima left the area, while the rest survived by avoiding all contact with the authorities or armed forces. Villagers say that it was also a time of starvation and deprivation, when many gave up agricultural production and slept in caves or primitive shelters in the surrounding hills and mountains. Those who lived from commercial activities or public transport were particularly exposed. They either refrained from doing business at all or kept their shops open or transported passengers for limited intervals during daylight.

Arguably, this was a period with little or no space at all for political change in favour of the poor, and without the possibilities of drawing on national discourses on poverty and land rights that dominated on the national arena in the 1970s. Nor did peasant institutions enhance their representation or room for manoeuvre at the local and regional levels, as happened during the land reform period. On the contrary, many of the economic and political achievements of the 1970s were actually lost. Similarly, it was often those who had benefited most from the land reform process – the poor and the landless – who found themselves exposed to persecution by either the terrorists or the military and who suffered most from deprivation in the 1980s.

The 1990s: Neo-liberalism in Alto Cunas

At the entrance to Chaquicocha the visitor is saluted by a decaying board that says *Pacificación. Camino a la Victoria* (Pacification. The Road to Victory). Although few seem to pay attention to this sign any more, it stands as a reminder of the Peruvian Army's defeat of the Shining Path and thus marks a watershed in the contemporary history of the Alto Cunas population. It was placed there in 1991, the same year President Fujimori[12] visited Chaquicocha to honour the army's presence in the area and encourage the local peasantry to join the newly established *rondas campesinas*. The president, who arrived and left by helicopter, donated a small van to all the villages in the area and promised to build a new school in Chaquicocha.[13] During his visit a military parade was arranged with the participation not only of the army regiment stationed in the area but also of the local *rondas campesinas*, *clubes de madres*, school students from Chaquicocha and Usibamba, and so-called *licenciados* (former conscripts in the Peruvian army).

Fujimori's visit to the Alto Cunas area was a carefully planned attempt not merely to mobilize the peasantry in the Peruvian army's fight against the Shining Path, but also to construct an image of himself as a strong man who meant business when talking about fighting terrorism and generating development in the countryside. As the newly elected president needed political support for the neo-liberal programme introduced after his 1990 victory, he began to tour the Andean highlands and visit remote rural peasant communities to persuade the Peruvian peasantry that he was their man. In Chaquicocha, his attempt bore fruit. Whatever support the Shining Path received from the local Alto Cunas population in the late 1980s shrank rapidly in the early 1990s (Taylor 1998: 49–53). During the three years of Shining Path dominance in the area, their excessive use of terror and violence convinced the villagers that the *cumpas* had little to contribute in terms of economic and social development. Meanwhile, the formation and growth of *rondas campesinas* in the Alto Cunas villages took the form of a social movement. The *rondas* symbolized what the local population identified as social order and progress and rapidly replaced the political function of the peasant communities, whose leaders were systematically persecuted by the terrorists as well as the military. A year after Fujimori's visit to Chaquicocha, all the villages in the Alto Cunas area had formed a local *ronda campesina*.

Yet what contributed even more significantly to the peasants' increasing resistance to the Shining Path was the new role the Peruvian army and the state came to play in rural society under the Fujimori administration. This new balance of power was conveyed by two concepts, *pacificación* and *reactivación*, which influenced not only Alto Cunas peasants' configuration of the post-Shining Path political space, but also the moulding of political life in Alto Cunas in the Fujimori era. In essence, the new political space rested on an implicit understanding between the state and the local peasantry: if you help us fighting the *terrucos*, we shall help you revive development in your villages. Symbolically, Fujimori's 1991 visit to Chaquicocha orchestrated the local peasants' re-encounter with the Peruvian state in the aftermath of the defeat of terrorism and provided the ingredients to render visible the power hierarchy, as well as the room for manoeuvre available within this arrangement. It would be a mistake to take the participation of the villagers in the parade organized in honour of Fujimori solely as evidence of their approval of the state's new role in area. However, the enthusiasm the villagers demonstrate when showing photographs of themselves marching in front of the president, recalling the visit and expressing the expectations they have regarding Fujimori's promise to deliver peace and generate development in the villages suggests that he was successful in linking anti-terrorist policies with dominant discourses of nation-building and economic progress. Moreover, these discourses provided Fujimori with the rhetorical gunpowder to create a political alliance with the peasantry that was to be of crucial importance to Peru's development in the 1990s.

The term *pacificación* refers to the united effort of the *rondas campesinas* and the Peruvian army not only in defeating the *terrucos* on the battlefield but also in reinforcing and legitimizing peasant ties to the Peruvian state and the Fujimori government. Although peasant loyalty to the state has strong historical roots in the Peruvian Andes (Mallon 1995), it was weakened during the post-land reform period in the late 1970s and throughout the 1980s because of Peru's economic and political crisis, a situation the Shining Path cunningly took advantage of (Hunefeldt 1997: 115). The *pacificación* process of the early 1990s aimed to restore this loyalty by making the peasantry a partner in Fujimori's anti-terrorist policy. This linked the struggle against Peru's two rebel groups (the Shining Path and MRTA) to the nation-building process and equated waging the fight against the *terrucos* with being loyal citizens and thus good Peruvians. In other words, as partners in Fujimori's anti-terrorist policy, the Alto Cunas peasants would be treated as faithful subjects of the Peruvian state and therefore be entitled to the economic opportunities and social and legal rights conventionally denied Andean peasants.

One important tool in Fujimori's anti-terrorist policy was *la ley de arrepentimiento* (the Act of Repentance), which pardoned individuals accused of terrorism who confessed and repented their subversive acts in public and revealed the identity of their fellow rebels. Although the act was administered in an extremely arbitrary manner, it had an important impact on the local and regional discourse of political activities and state loyalty and thus on peasants' notion of social order. It gave people who had joined the *terrucos* 'mistakenly' the opportunity to change sides and praised those who had rejected the Shining Path's rhetoric of violent rebellion. While a small group of villagers either refused to repent or were simply made to 'disappear' by the military in the aftermath of the defeat of terrorism and thus denied any right to a pardon, the majority saw the acts of public repentance as an opportunity to be reconciled with the state and to get back to normal life. Numerous villagers even turned themselves in to the *rondas campesinas* that were in charge of administrating the new act. Later the *rondas* arranged public meetings on the central squares of the villages, where the 'sinners' made *juramentos* (oath-taking), signed an *acto de compromiso* (document of pledge) and turned in other companions. As a result, subversive activities decreased significantly in the villages from 1990 to 1993, when the army finally withdrew from the area. That year also marked the end of the era of *pacificación* and the beginning of the *reactivación*.

In 1993 Fujimori was riding on a wave of popularity in Peru. One year after his *auto-golpe*, the echo of the 1992 capture of Shining Path leader Gúzman and the first indications of economic recovery after the *Fuji-shock*[14] were being felt throughout Peru. Many Peruvians came to believe that there was light at the end of the tunnel. Of course, as the wake from these changes in the country's political climate reached the Alto Cunas area, expectations among the population regarding the state's participation in local development began to rise. Terrorism had been suppressed, and now people wanted to taste the fruit of *la Victoria* so exultantly heralded on the sign at the entrance to Chaquicocha. The first step in restoring the social order was the election of new village authorities that had been repressed by the rebels in the late 1980s. In many villages the new leaders simply took up the work of those who had been ousted from their offices by the Shining Path in the 1980s.[15] Economically, the weekly markets in Chaquicocha and Chupaca once again became the centre of commercial transactions in the area, which encouraged the peasants to take up agricultural activities again. Likewise, the villagers who had escaped the Shining Path terror and the military began to return to their homes. Finally, in Usibamba, Chaquicocha and Jarpa the villagers re-established the community cooperatives destroyed by the insurgents in the 1980s.

The destruction of the SAIS cooperatives, which had a dominant economic and political role in the area during the 1970s and early 1980s, created a new political space at the local and regional levels that the peasants were quick to fill. As the *rondas'* military and political role began to decline during the *reactivación*, peasant communities once again emerged as the principal political institution in the area.

Another important institutional change in the post-violent period was the reappearance of private NGOs in the Alto Cunas area. In San Juan de Jarpa the villagers decided to reactivate a former community cooperative established in cooperation with a religious NGO before the violence broke out. Today, CAUSA 'Alto Cunas', a multi-community cooperative that promotes commercial activities (handcrafts, meat, wool, etc.), offers social services to individual households and runs a credit institution for members of the cooperative. Similarly, numerous NGOs are currently working in Usibamba and Chaquicocha, including several national NGOs (PANFAR and PRISMA) and two foreign NGOs (MISERIOS of Germany and CEVEMO of Holland). As part of the Fujimori administration's anti-poverty programme implemented in 1990 to alleviate the social effects of its neo-liberal policies, several government-controlled organizations (PAR, PRONAA, Vaso de Leche, etc.) have worked in the area offering food and health services to peasant families. Likewise, state agencies such as FONCODES and FONAFOG (see Wise 1997: 91) have provided either direct finance or loans to improve livestock and construct new irrigation canals in Chaquicocha and Usibamba.

The state's growing presence in the area and direct participation in the local development process in the 1990s is the outcome of a policy that uses government funds as a means not only of winning the support of the peasantry in the fight against terrorism, but also of configuring the political space that emerged in the wake of Fujimori's neo-liberal programme (ibid.: 92). Thus many of the social services and public works that were conventionally administered by the Ministries of Health, Work and Education are today managed directly by the Ministerio de la Presidencia (the Presidential Ministry). Needless to say, the numerous announcement boards placed in the Alto Cunas villages, informing the local population that the Presidential Ministry was responsible for building schools, improving roads, providing health care, and so on help to remind the villagers that their implicit understanding with President Fujimori in 1991 is still in force.

Conclusion

The Alto Cunas peasants have demonstrated a remarkable capacity to adapt to Peru's changing political environment. Crucial in this process of contestation of, as well as identification with, the shifting power hierarchies that link the peasantry to the regional and national domains are the peasants' own organizations. In the 1930s the peasant community became the main institution for villagers to resist neighbouring *haciendas*' attempts to encroach on their land. Later, as agriculture was extended and the pastures were parcelled out in the 1950s and the 1960s, the community became a central arena for villagers' internal struggles over land rights.

Yet the community is not just the product of the peasantry's own organizational practice: it is a legal institution promoted and recognized by the Peruvian state in the twentieth century to integrate the Andean population in the nation-building process and to foster development in the country's rural society. In the early 1970s, the community became an important vehicle for promoting the land reform act implemented by the military government among the peasantry. It was also the main institution integrating the peasantry into the newly established SAIS and the village-based cooperatives. While some Alto Cunas villages such as Usibamba and Chaquicocha came under the strong influence of neighbouring SAIS and government agencies, others, such as Jarpa, were supported by local NGOs. However, although the external agents that triggered the land reform process and the formation of cooperatives in the 1970s and early 1980s varied, it was the peasant community that constituted the central arena for organizational change and the articulation of state–peasant relationships throughout the Alto Cunas area in this period. This leads us to conclude that peasants not only reproduced the dominating power hierarchies within the community, but also used them to reconfigure and even contest the political space outlined by the state.

As already demonstrated, the Peruvian state was virtually absent as a development agent in the Alto Cunas prior to the period of violence in the late 1980s because of the economic crisis. To the peasantry, the entry of the Shining Path was therefore seen as a natural response to the weakening of the Peruvian state and their increasing frustration at not making *progreso*, particularly when comparing the Bermúdez and the Belaúnde governments' apparent lack of interest in generating change in rural society with that of the Velasco regime in the first half of the 1970s. Not surprisingly, the insurgents met little resistance from the local population when entering the Alto Cunas villages between 1985 and 1987. To the villagers, the political space of the 1970s – when the national power hierarchy was articulated directly with their own peasant institutions and when a national discourse designed by the military government on poverty and land rights swept through the country – had been replaced by a gap in peasant–state relations in the 1980s that at best left the villages to their fate and at worst made them the object of abuses by the government bureaucracy and the local police. Yet Alto Cunas peasants soon realized that the Shining Path's severance of their ties with the regional and national power structures only restricted their options in making *progreso* and made them the victims of local squad leaders' arbitrary use of violence. Certainly, the *terrucos* allowed little if any political space for social practices at local or regional levels to influence politics or negotiate with the dominating power hierarchy. Likewise, the only public discourse allowed in this period consisted of revolutionary slogans and Maoist rhetoric.

The rise of the *rondas campesinas* represented a vivid example of Alto Cunas peasants' organizational skills and institutional capacity. Although the idea of forming *rondas* in the Alto Cunas area was originally introduced by the Peruvian army to gain the support of the peasants in the fight against the Shining Path, they soon took the form of a genuine peasant movement that expanded from northern Peru to almost every part of the Peruvian Andes. Indeed, during the early 1990s the *rondas* replaced the community as the peasants' main institutional vehicle in contesting existing power hierarchies and resolving internal conflicts and struggles among the villagers. One of the reasons for the rapid spread of *rondas* was that this institution reinserted the peasants into the Peruvian society and reaffirmed their traditional loyalty to the national state. This allowed them to make legitimate claims to the regional and national power hierarchies. In return for their help in fighting terrorism, they earned acknowledgement as loyal subjects and good Peruvians, and with it the government's support in fostering development in their villages. Once the Shining Path had been beaten, President Fujimori sensed the political potential of this alliance and stretched out his hand by keeping his promise to help relaunch development in the Alto Cunas area.

Throughout the 1990s the Peruvian state became increasingly present in the Alto Cunas area. Together with several national and international NGOs, the Presidential Ministry has become a central agent for development in the area, taking over the position formerly occupied by the SAIS and the cooperatives created in the 1970s. Although the Fujimori administration tried to control and to a certain extent limit the political space available to the Alto Cunas population through its anti-terrorism policy, there are a number of signs that the growing presence of the state, improvements in the infrastructure and the reactivation of the national and regional economies have provided peasants with new opportunities to organize and make *progreso*. As more peasants today exploit trade and alternative sources of income, and as rural–urban as well as transnational migration pave the way for new livelihoods, the Alto Cunas population is increasingly looking beyond local and regional power hierarchies when negotiating and contesting their position in Peruvian society. Such a development not only implies that traditional peasant institutions have become less important in rural people's struggle to make *progreso*, it also questions the existing power hierarchy, which rests on a close alliance between the state and its rural subjects.

My argument is that peasants' organizations in Peru's highlands can be seen as a vehicle for reconfiguring and contesting the changing nature of national and regional power hierarchies. I also suggest that peasants to a large extent identify with and thus reproduce the political hierarchies dominating the extra-regional level, and that they employ a highly pragmatic attitude when trying to exploit the political space available at any given moment. While Alto Cunas peasants adopted the national discourse on land reform of the 1970s and carried out a redistribution of communal land in favour of the landless, they adapted to the Shining Path's violent presence in the area in the 1980s by either tacitly approving of the ruling order or simply disappearing until the power hierarchy changed rhetorics and practice. And when the military and the state reappeared in the area in the 1990s, they soon changed sides again, now joining the newly established *rondas* and adopting the dominant discourse on terrorism, developmentalism and nationalism. Unlike the political space available in the 1970s, when the peasants were encouraged to take on an economic class identity and make claims to land and political rights, or in the 1980s, when the ability to influence not only extra-regional but also local politics changed dramatically and peasants experienced a serious setback in terms of their own social practice for political change, the political space for creating changes from below has re-emerged in the 1990s, although in a less democratic and autonomous form than in the 1970s. Thus the Fujimori government's authoritarian management of public resources, which promotes development and *progreso* in rural areas on the condition of loyalty to the state, seriously limits peasants' room for manoeuvre at the local and regional levels. Yet as the dominant role of the *rondas campesinas* declines and the peasant community recaptures its previous function as the peasants' principal vehicle for articulating relations with the state and other extra-regional power hierarchies – and as the political promises of generating development in Peru's impoverished rural areas fail to deliver because of an ailing neo-liberal policy and stagnating agricultural production –

Fujimori is likely to lose some of the tight control he has enjoyed over the Peruvian peasantry so far. Whether such a shift in the relationship between the local, regional and national power hierarchies will produce more space for influencing the politics of poverty reduction from below remains to been seen.

Notes

1. Literally, *auto-golpe* means a coup against oneself, but in the Peruvian context the term refers to Fujimori's closure of the democratically elected parliament and re-appointment of himself as president. For more information, see Cameron 1997.

2. Unlike Usibamba, Chaquicocha was originally under the jurisdiction of Orcotuna, a community situated in the Mantaro Valley. However, after a bloody conflict between Orcotuna and Mito over the control of the Alto Cunas population, Chaquicocha passed into the jurisdiction of the latter (Castillo 1964b: 8). In 1938 Chaquicocha achieved official recognition as a *comunidad indígena* and thus achieved political autonomy (ibid.: 9).

3. Another implication of demographic growth is the place of migration in villagers' livelihood strategies, whether as seasonal and temporary migration to the regional mines, permanent out-migration to Huancayo and Lima, or transnational labour migration to the USA.

4. SINAMOS means Sistema Nacional de Mobilización Social (National System for Social Mobilization). This agency was established in 1971 by the military government to mobilize popular support for its reform policy (Matos Mar and Mejía 1980: 129). It was dissolved in 1978 (ibid.: 176).

5. The requirements are that the villagers are either born in Usibamba or are the offspring of locally born villagers, that they are either married males or female widows, and that they have permanent residence in the village (that is, they must be non-migrants).

6. While Usibamba was encouraged by the Peruvian state and the SINAMOS agency to abolish private property in community land in 1972, a local Catholic NGO (PROCAD) played a crucial role in proposing and outlining a plan to carry out land reform in Chaquicocha eight years later. For a comparison of the two cases, see Paerregaard 1987).

7. Many of the cooperatives established during the military government of the early 1970s were destroyed by the Shining Path. In the central highlands, where the largest and most productive of the cooperatives were situated (see Hunefeldt 1997: 129), only the SAIS Túpac Amaru resisted and succeeded in repulsing the attacks of the Shining Path.

8. In peasant communities in Peru, local administrative and political offices such as mayor, justice of the peace, and the police representative are occupied by local peasants elected from among the adult male population.

9. This woman explains that after the Shining Path was thrown out of the Alto Cunas area in 1990, she happened to meet the leader of the terrorist squad that had tried to terrify her and her family in the late 1980s on the streets of Huancayo. She claims that the man used to work as a schoolteacher in the area and that he, unlike many other *terrucos*, was an educated person. Her anger with the squad leader was so great that she cursed the man and accused him of being a *cobarde* (coward) in front of all the passers-

by. She told me that although he never replied, at least she felt content, because 'I told him the truth'.

10. Villagers recount that the teacher became a *cumpa* leader in the area and that he was feared for his cruel and merciless execution of individuals not willing to cooperate with the Shining Path. Eventually, he was himself killed by the villagers.

11. I first got to know this man in 1983–84 during my original field research in Usibamba. Sons of one of the largest landowners in Usibamba before the land reform, he and his brother openly opposed the community's decision to abolish private property in land in 1972. They often explained to me that they would exploit whatever opportunity they had to overturn the decision and return the land that had been confiscated in 1972 to the previous owners. Notwithstanding this attitude to the land reform process, the man was one of the community's two *delegados* (representatives) at the *asamblea general* (general assembly) of the SAIS Túpac Amaru in the early 1980s. His brother also held political office in the village. Today, the brother lives in the USA, where he is working as a sheep-herder in California.

12. This chapter was written before Fujimori was ousted from presidential office in November 2000.

13. A villager in Usibamba who recounted the details of Fujimori's visit to me made little effort to conceal his enthusiasm about the president. He exclaimed 'And can you imagine? He arrived straight from heaven! The first Peruvian president to visit our humble village.'

14. The *Fuji-shock* is a popular term for Fujimori's unexpected introduction of a neo-liberal polilcy in August 1990 by freeing the prices and thus paralysing the country's economy (see Wise 1997: 84). For many Peruvians, the brutal shift to a free market economy was associated with much uncertainty and confusion, as prices initially skyrocketed, and large sections of the national workforce were laid off.

15. Chaquicocha and Usibamba are both administrative sub-units (*anexos*) of the district of neighbouring San José de Quero. Hence political mobilization and the appointment of village leaders are subject to local interests and personal networks and do not follow regional or national party political lines.

Bibliography

Adams, Norma and Néstor Valdivia (1991) *Los otros empresarios. Etica de migrantes y formación de empresas en Lima*, Lima: Instituto de Estudios Peruanos.

Alberti, Giorgi and Rodrigo Sánchez (1974) *Poder y conflicto en el valle del Mantaro (1900–1974)*, Lima: Instituto de Estudios Peruanos.

Alvarez Rodrich, Augusto (1995) 'Del estado empresario al Estado regulador', in J. Cotler (ed.), *Perú 1964–1994. Economía, sociedad y política*, Lima: Instituto de Estudios Peruanos.

Burt, Jo-Marie (1997) 'Political violence and the grassroots in Lima, Peru', in D. Chalmers, C. Vilas, K. Hite, S. Martin, K. Piester and M. Segarra (eds), *The New Politics of Inequality in Latin America: Rethinking Participation and Representation*, Oxford: Oxford University Press.

Cameron, Maxwell (1997) 'Political and economic origins of regime change in Peru: the eighteenth brumaire of Alberto Fujimori', in M. Cameron and P. Mauceri (eds) 1997.

Cameron, M. and P. Mauceri (eds) (1997) *The Peruvian Labyrinth: Polity, Society, Economy*, Pennsylvania: Pennsylvania State University Press.

Castillo, Hernán (1964a) *Mito: The Orphans of its Illustrious Children*, Ithaca, NY: Cornell University.

— (1964b) *Chaquicocha: Community in Progress*, Ithaca, NY: Cornell University.

Caycho, Hernán (1977) *Las SAIS de la Sierra central*, Lima: ESAN.

Cotler, Julio (1998) '"Popular deluge", the informal sector, political independents, and the state in Peru', in M. Vellinga (ed.), *The Changing Role of the State in Latin America*, Boulder, CO: Westview Press.

Degregori, Iván (1997) 'After the fall of Abimael Guzmán: The limits of Sendero Luminoso', in M. Cameron and P. Mauceri (eds) 1997.

Durand, Francisco (1997) 'The growth and limitations of the Peruvian right', in M. Cameron and P. Mauceri (eds) 1997.

Figueroa, Adolfo, Teófilo Altamirano and Denis Sulmont (1996) *Social Exclusion and Inequality in Peru*, Geneva: International Labour Organization.

Glewwe, Paul and Gillette Hall (1994) 'Poverty, inequality, and living standards during unorthodox adjustment: the case of Peru, 1985-1990', *Economic Development and Cultural Change*, 42, 4: 689–717.

Golte, Jürgen (1995) 'Nuevos actores y culturas antiguas', in J. Cotler (ed.), *Perú 1964–1994. Economía, sociedad y política*, Lima: Instituto de Estudios Peruanos.

Gonzales de Olarte, Efraín (1995) 'Transformación sin desarrollo: Perú 1964–1994', in J. Cotler (ed.), *Perú 1964–1994. Economía, sociedad y política*, Lima: Instituto de Estudios Peruanos.

Gorman, Stephen (1997) 'Antipolitics in Peru', in B. Loveman and T. Davies (eds), *The Politics of Antipolitics: The Military in Latin America*, Wilmington, DE: SR Books.

Hunefeldt, Christine (1997) 'The rural landscape and changing political awareness: enterprises, agrarian producers, and peasant communities, 1969–1994', in M. Cameron and P. Mauceri (eds) 1997.

Isbell, Billie Jean (1978) *To Defend Ourselves: Ecology and Ritual in an Andean Village*, Prospect Heights, IL: Waweland Press.

López, Gloria Rivas (1981) 'Un análisis prelinimar de algunos efectos de la crisis económica sobre la economía campesina: el caso del Alto Cunas', paper presented at II seminario sobre Campesinado y Proceso Regional, Huancayo, Peru.

Mallon, Florencia (1983) *The Defense of Community in Peru's Central Highlands: Peasant Struggle and Capitalist Transition 1860–1940*, Princeton, NJ: Princeton University Press.

— (1995) *Peasant and Nation: The Making of Postcolonial Mexico and Peru*, Berkeley: University of California Press.

Martínez Alier, Juan (1973) *Los huacchilleros del Perú*, Lima: Instituto de Estudios Peruanos.

Matos Mar, José and José Manuel Mejía (1980) *La reforma agraria en el Perú*, Lima: Instituto de Estudios Peruanos.

Mauceri, Philip (1995) 'State reform, coalitions, and the neoliberal autogolpe in Peru', *Latin American Research Review*, 30, 1: 7–38.

— (1997) 'The transition to "democracy" and the failures of institution building', in M. Cameron and P. Mauceri (eds) 1997.

Moncada, Gilberto and R. Webb (eds) (1996) *Cómo estamos? Análisis de la Encuesta de Niveles de Vida*, Lima: Instituto Cuánto.

Paerregaard, Karsten (1997) *Linking Separate Worlds: Urban Migrants and Rural Lives in Peru*, Oxford: Berg Publishers.

Palmer, David Scott (ed.) (1992) *The Shining Path of Peru*, New York: St. Martin's Press.

Samaniego, Carlos (1980) 'Campesinado en el valle del Mantaro, Perú', *Estudios Andinos*, 9, 16: 31–72.

Seligmann, Linda (1995) *Between Reform and Revolution: Political Struggles in the Peruvian Andes, 1969–1991*, Stanford, CA: Stanford University Press.

Skar, Harald (1988) *The Warm Valley People: Duality and Land Reform among the Quechua Indians of Highlands Peru*, Göteborg: Göteborgs Etnografiska Museum.

Smith, Gavin (1989) *Livelihood and Resistance: Peasants and the Politics of Land in Peru*, Berkeley: University of California Press.

Taylor, Lewis (1998) 'Counter-insurgency strategy, the PCP–Sendero Luminoso and the civil war in Peru, 1980–1996', *Bulletin of Latin American Research*, 17, 1: 35–58.

Torres Rodriguez, Oswaldo (1979) 'Reforma agraria y cooperativización en la Sierra Central peruana', *América Indígena*, 34, 4: 813–29.

Usibamba (n.d.) *Historical archives of the village of Usibamba*.

Wightman, Ann (1990) *Indigenous Migration and Social Change: The 'Forasteros' of Cuzco, 1520–1720*, Durham, NC: Duke University Press.

Wise, Carol (1997) 'State policy and social conflict in Peru', in M. Cameron and P. Mauceri (eds) 1997.

4

The Voice and Representation of the 'Poor': Striving for Government Aid in Western Mexico

Magdalena Villarreal

Political space is about voice and representation. In this book, we are seeking to focus upon spaces in which the voices of those considered 'impoverished' can be heard and their interests represented in poverty alleviation policies. I take the view that political breakthroughs in the participation of those from the lower echelons of society are not only attained within formalized and 'legitimate' spaces, but also sought and achieved within a range of everyday contests, negotiations and accommodations that take place between different actors or groups of actors, organizations and institutions where discontinuities in terms of interests and power are present. Most frequently achievement is only partial, and even where the ideal of a social order based on equal participation becomes a dominant discourse, this must constitute an arena of contestation as well, within which the interpretation of what 'equality' amounts to and how the identity of the participants is defined is subject to constant clarification and negotiation. This calls for a reconsideration of the kinds of arena in which political space is established and for a clarification of the multi-faceted nature of political agency.

In this chapter, I explore the ways in which political spaces are negotiated and constructed and the kinds of constraint faced by rural dwellers when struggling for a share in the distribution of government resources in western Mexico. Government programmes oriented towards curtailing the drastic escalation in rural poverty levels, unemployment and migration have ranged from subsidies for maize and other staple grain production, as well as for household consumption of milk and maize products, to credit for micro–agro–industrial enterprises, and breakfasts, food provision and scholarships for students at basic levels of education. Mexican rural livelihoods have come to depend on aid policies and government social programmes in a large way. But the country is now experiencing severe cuts in government expenditure geared to social compensation programmes

– largely due to restructuring measures imposed by the IMF – and negotiations over who is entitled to access and how to use scarce resources are becoming increasingly problematic.

I take the case of FONAES (Fondo Nacional de Apoyo a Empresas Sociales: National Funds in Support of Social Enterprises) as implemented in Tomatlán, Jalisco, located on the west coast of Mexico, to discuss the arenas in which political space is negotiated and the ways in which institutional channels for participation are utilized and transformed to represent a diversity of interests. The case of Tomatlán is appealing because here some low-income producers have reached a stage at which they are able to use political space to their advantage in their relations with the state. This has been made possible after long years of struggle for land and democratization. Another interesting feature is that some of the people who are now acting as state officers were previously anti-state activists who strongly encouraged democratization processes in the country. The skirmishes that are now taking place between producers and state officers provide a very good example of how forms of exclusion are reproduced despite 'democratic predispositions' and institutional apertures for participation.

The case sheds light on the ways in which interests are redefined in order to adapt to changing policies, the 'routes of access' that are created in striving for government funds and the socially negotiated character of emerging and pre-existing power relations. Viewed from a local perspective, the state is not a monolithic actor with a single, clear-cut agenda. The knowledge of this apparently straightforward fact provides the producers with room for manoeuvre. The opportunity to acquire credit entails access to information circles, as well as the ability to mobilize social and organizational resources by networking, cooperating and building relations of trust, but it also entails competition, exclusion and social differentiation. Access itself acquires a price leading to forms of dependency, control and clientelism wherein power and control are not necessarily wielded by state officers, who at times become the clients of local leaders and organizations.

The Nature of Political Space for Poverty Alleviation

All too often the notion of political space is narrowly framed within processes of class struggle and collective endeavour within public arenas. But the issue of poverty is imbricated with a range of processes entailing social discrimination and exclusion that also involve gender, race, kinship and other forms of social difference. Coalitions formed in struggles for access and control often include the association between 'dissimilar' actors (which can be classified as pertaining to different social classes), and frictions also take place between people considered to belong to the same social category who might become antagonists – for example, over political affiliation, loyalties and particular interests. Moreover, collective endeavours frequently conflate a diversity of, at times, discordant individual interests. Hence 'the voice of the poor' is often fragmented and erratic in its articulation.

On the other hand, the definition of 'the poor' is itself subject to negotiation within political spaces. It is often the crucial issue to be defined in order to establish priorities, allocate money, define programmes and link all sorts of specific interests, be they national, local or individual, public or private. Within political spaces, many kinds of negotiations are taking place, including the legitimacy of representation itself. The issue of who is to define the interests of the poor and act on their behalf is frequently an object of contestation. One cannot assume that those acting to represent the poor are actually promoting their interests. And because we cannot define *a priori* who the 'legitimate' representatives of the poor are, we can speak only of the ways in which struggles over poverty alleviation encounter other interests and struggles within political spaces.

Here the notion of political agency comes to the fore. Political agency entails specific conceptions of citizenship, rights and obligations, and presupposes a degree of knowledgeability concerning the workings of institutions and the ability to negotiate identities and representations. Political agency is often constrained by the lack of adequate democratic institutional channels, by the enforcement of discourses of exclusion, and by the naturalization of authoritarian and repressive practices. However, government endeavours to alleviate poverty may or may not include the participation of the 'beneficiaries' as one of the aims of the programme. This leads to differentiated forms of involvement by rural dwellers, but even 'top-down' programmes conceived of as charity can spark off lively contestations that can lead to changes in policies.

Political space entails a crystallization of strategies, organizational schemes and discursive practices whereby an actor or a group of actors are included in a particular contest for political gains. Such gains may or may not lead to a dramatic change in political systems. The spatial dimension may include territorial, symbolic or social arenas, and the political does not necessarily involve direct confrontation with the state. This, of course, leaves us with a vague notion of political space. But my argument is that the possibility of using political space to advantage lies precisely in such ambiguity, which is exacerbated by the ways in which public and private domains intersect to generate different identities. Confining spaces and issues to the sphere of the 'private' is often also a mystification that serves as a form of exclusion.

Underpinning the present discussion is the consideration that relations between state and society cannot be collapsed into a single form of explanation. As Pringle and Watson (1992: 67) argue, 'far from being a unified structure, [the state] is a by-product of political struggles'. They further explain that interests 'are constructed in the process of interaction with specific institutions and sites. The policies that ensue depend not just on the constraints of structures, but on the discursive struggles which define and constitute particular interests and the state at any one time' (ibid.: 70). This is evident in the processes by which poverty alleviation programmes are established in Mexico.

Poverty Alleviation Programmes in Mexico

A comparative study carried out by the World Bank and CEPAL (Comisión Económica para América Latina y el Caribe: Economic Commission for Latin America and the Caribbean) in the early 1990s[1] found that the per centage of poor in Mexico – calculated according to income – covered approximately 50 million of its inhabitants (around 60 per cent of the population), of whom 20 million were living under conditions of extreme poverty. In another study, Alarcón (1994) claims that in 1989, 69.4 per cent of the poor in Mexico were located in rural areas. But taking the view that poverty is not only about income, but about the quality of life – including housing, education, sanitary infrastructure and other basic needs (cf. Gendreau 1998: 16) – Bolvinik (1994) came to the conclusion that in the same period 83.1 per cent of the total Mexican population and 97.3 per cent of its rural inhabitants were poor. The intensity of poverty, calculated in terms of quality of life, is more acute in rural areas, where four-fifths of the population, classified as extremely poor, manage to survive on one-quarter of what has been calculated as the minimum level required to cover their basic needs (see Bolvinik 1994: 82–3). Such figures increased after the 1994 economic crisis, and this has favoured a further concentration of economic resources in the hands of a few.

The escalation of poverty in Mexico is generally linked to the collapse in the price of petroleum in the international markets, the rise in international interest rates, the low level of competitiveness of Mexican products in a globalizing world, badly managed financial policies leading to inflation and the crisis in national debt repayments, increased rates of unemployment and a decrease in investment in the country. The government was obliged to negotiate further loans with the International Monetary Fund, and signed agreements stipulating that structural adjustment measures were to be implemented. The policies that ensued were oriented at protecting and stimulating private investment in order to guarantee economic growth, encourage employment, reduce inflation and modernize production. Cuts in social welfare and public services were decreed. The highest costs of policies of structural adjustment were imposed on low-income households, most of which were located in rural areas (Gendreau 1998: 114).

In 1988 the new president, Carlos Salinas de Gortari, headed an ambitious policy of social restructuring oriented towards the liberalization and modernization of the economy. However, he started his presidential period in the midst of social discontent and accusations of fraud in his election. Poverty alleviation policies, the form of social compensation for those most affected by the harsh structural adjustment measures, became central to his policies as a means of legitimizing his government and warding off political unrest. But in order to secure political control, existing poverty alleviation programmes, which were generally linked to political groups previously in power, were abolished or minimized. Thus Coplamar (Coordinación General del Plan nacional de Zonas Deprimidas y Grupos Marginados: General Coordination of the National Plan for Deprived Regions and Marginalized Groups) – a programme to encourage production and bolster social welfare, both in the construction of infrastructure and by subsidizing basic goods for consumption – was cut down to specific regional programmes and almost disappeared. PIDER (Programa de Inversiones Públicas para el Desarrollo Rural: Programme for Public Investment in Rural Development), which primarily promoted cooperatives but also aimed to encourage better health and education services, was abolished, as was SAM (Sistema Alimentario Mexicano: Mexican food system), which provided credit and subsidies to encourage the agricultural production of basic grains.

Salinas created PRONASOL (Programa Nacional de Solidaridad: National Solidarity Programme) as the spearhead of his social policy, which included social welfare programmes oriented to health, education, housing, food supplies and urban services; regional development programmes involving the construction of roads and other infrastructure; and funds to be managed by the different municipalities and production programmes including agro-pecuarian and agro-industrial projects. Despite the fact that the president had decreed severe cuts in expenditures for social programmes, PRONASOL itself had an extremely high budget. In 1992 PRONASOL disbursements represented 4 per cent of national public expenditure and 7.7 per cent of social expenditure. While in 1989 it represented 6.6 per cent of total public investment, in 1992 it had reached 17.3 per cent (Valencia Lomeli and Aguirre 1998: 69).

From the outset, the programme was formulated within a framework of overlapping and at times conflicting arenas, which included negotiations with established political organizations – especially left-wing parties, which, it was feared, could capitalize on the general social discontent – but also concessions towards the president's own political allies involving government officials, particular entrepreneurs and ex-politicians, thus conflating individual and collective interests. Different political cliques within the government had to be considered, and the president's international image projected favourably in international arenas. PRONASOL is thus a clear example of the impact of social forces on policy processes. It was born out of the need to recognize poverty and do something about it. It should compensate for the painful structural adjustment measures and the changes in the Mexican Constitution, particularly those whereby land distribution and the privatization of *ejido* land was decreed to be at an end, but it should also provide political dividends and reduce anger and resentment.

It is therefore clear that we are referring to policy that is not directly oriented towards making a change in the political system as such, but towards making changes in order to guarantee a degree of stability and control. The political system in Mexico is based on the articulation of interests in a range of arenas in which processes of enrolment and co-optation are established. Hence it has become quite difficult to speak of clear-cut changes in the political system. Rather, one must focus on processes of change and on the implications that a particular configuration of spaces may have on such processes. The notion of political space cannot be limited to spaces opened up with the explicit aim of democratization or poverty alleviation, since social welfare policies are created in direct response not always to poverty, but to a larger arena of contestation where other issues are at stake and both national and international actors have a large say. Social forces in this case include the organized and unorganized poor, as well as those speaking in their name who are pursuing a wide range of interests.

Institutional channels and government discourse Participation of the 'poor' was a central issue in PRONASOL. President Salinas postulated that increased participation would encourage greater support for the political system, arguing that 'social welfare in the modern State does not sympathize with paternalism, which supplants efforts and inhibits character ... an elevation of the level of life can only be a product of responsible and mutually shared actions of the State with society' (Valencia Lomeli and Aguirre 1998: 65). Hence projects should be co-financed by government and the beneficiaries themselves, and implementation and decision-making should result from the combined efforts of government and programme participants. To this end, 'solidarity committees' were formed within the different municipalities that were elected in each community to be benefited, with the pretence of entrusting the allocation of resources to the organized beneficiaries themselves and encouraging their participation in policy decisions. In rhetoric, the aims of the programme were to build on representative local organizations in both urban and rural areas instead of establishing top-down bureaucratic structures. As Dresser argues (1991: 9), this emphasis on co-responsibility and community participation can be explained in part by the government's drive to enhance PRONASOL's accountability and effectiveness. However, popular participation in solving community problems also functioned to generate political support for government-sponsored development programmes, and consequently for the political system itself.

Hence the purposes of the programme were threefold. First, its aims were basically of a political nature: to provide social legitimacy for the Salinas government and avoid social upheaval. Second, the need was stressed to respect the general orientation of the current economic policy, namely congruence with a free market orientation supported by strong financial interests. Last but not least, it was important to encourage participation with the aim of generating the proper incentives and to help the poorest break the vicious circle of poverty. The difficulties of matching and merging such often contradictory intentions were evident, and different officials interpreted the programme's mission according to the priorities they deemed most relevant. Moreover, PRONASOL was selective in its distribution of resources. Politically critical regions, such as the state of Chiapas after the Zapatista uprising and the state of Michoacán, where votes had favoured an opposition party, were allotted large quantities of resources at critical periods.

FONAES (Fondo Nacional de Empresas en Solidaridad: National Funds for Solidarity Enterprises) was created as a sub-programme of PRONASOL to encourage the development of competitive enterprises as a longer-term goal, with the consideration that it was not only economic but social development that was to be pursued. This gave the programme a special challenge: to favour the creation of *social* enterprises, that is, enterprises that involved low-income producers and at the same time had an impact on community development. The aims of the programme as stated in its documents give priority to growth in terms of technical, economic, administrative, social and organizational aspects. Increases in production and better products were to be induced through the use of technical assistance, cost–benefit ratios were expected to improve, as were adequate administrative registers, and market penetration and control were to be attained. But projects should also generate local employment, retain a labour force in the region, improve the level of life of participants, and encourage the association of low-income producers with productive potential, thus seeking an impact on community welfare.

FONAES is a highly innovative programme compared to most government programmes in rural Mexico. The most relevant feature is the creation of a new form of association between the state and producers: that of partnership. Financial aid is not to be a gift, nor should it be credit: the producers should design viable projects, be they small industries, agricultural endeavours, cattle enterprises or other kinds of enterprise. A specialized government committee revises the projects and selects the best, after which state and producer become partners. The state provides the money and the producers provide land, labour and whatever other capital they can contribute to the enterprise. The state should not grant more than 30 per cent of the total cost of the project. Payments on capital will be made over a period of ten years (with no interest rate), after which profits will be divided up between the state and the producers.

Partnerships between state and producers were expected to generate a healthier relationship between them, first and foremost to break the much criticized vicious circle of paternalism, the patterns of subsidized production and unpaid credits. If they were partners, both state and producers would be interested in making the most of the capital provided. On the other hand, the state was willing to risk losses: as a partner associated with marginalized producers, the capital invested was considered high-risk. The programme was established all over the country and personnel allotted to each state to implement it. FONAES' greatest challenge was to get a number of successful enterprises off the ground, which, it was expected, would grow into strong social enterprises with democratic aims. If they were successful, the enterprises would have multiplier effects.

Thus, in line with the general orientation of PRONASOL, FONAES created formal channels within which beneficiaries could access resources and wield a degree of control over decision-making. However, although the initiative was squarely inscribed within a shared discourse of participation of the 'poor' in their own poverty alleviation, the agendas that underpinned the different actors' agreement were diverse.

Participation and Power

The establishment of solidarity committees generated interesting processes in terms of participation at local and regional levels. Although in many cases committees were formally instituted by a brief meeting organized by field officers and local participation was minimal, in others – especially where the beneficiaries were already organized within pre-existing associations – they were able to bypass local authorities who had traditionally wielded power and controlled government resources. But creating a space for 'the poor' opened access to a multiplicity of groups and individuals who, in one way or another, could legitimately claim to be spokesmen of the marginalized, and whose agendas differed from those of the programme. Many independent and left-wing organizations who had strongly opposed the Salinas administration decided to participate actively in local solidarity committees and increased their lobbying activities with the aim of influencing policy, but also to insure a share in the distribution of resources for the members of their organizations. Competition between diverse organizations, enhanced by political affiliations and long-held quarrels, hampered the chances of presenting a unified front that could influence the distribution of resources and more general policy formulations.

Projects had to be accepted by regional and federal offices in order to ensure their technical viability. Numerous badly designed projects were received and political pressure exerted to get them accepted. Central offices were often occupied by protesting unions who considered it their right to receive benefits. Officers complained that such organizations did not consider the main aim of the programme: to promote efficient enterprises. Rather, many leaders used the distribution of programme resources as a banner to promote affiliation to their organizations.

The first clients to receive the benefits of the FONAES programme were the rural organizations supported by the PRI (Partido Revolucionario Institucional: Institutional Revolutionary Party), the ruling party. Having agreed to sign the pact under which political reforms to the constitution had been made, the leaders were 'owed' special benefits by the state. Hence programme directors were obliged to attend to commitments acquired in higher political spheres and accept many projects that were doomed to failure. Failing to honour political alliances could jeopardize the stability of the programme and the permanence of the appointed officers, especially in view of the frictions and rivalry between different political cliques within the ruling party. Here there were not only conflicts over the allocation of resources to particular government programmes, but struggles over positions to determine the relevance of a particular policy within the larger framework of government plans. Adequate images must be projected at the precise time, and, of course, the programme must work. Thus the pressure to present outstanding results in tune with the free market orientation of the general development policy, and the need to secure loyalties from crucial political organizations, were unwritten elements that coloured and shaped the nature of negotiations within the 'participatory' spaces that had been introduced. The FONAES team had to manoeuvre within its own institutional spheres in Mexico City to sustain the programme and keep the budget flowing.[2]

In this way, participation in decision-making was demarcated by the actions of interlocking and often conflicting networks, where issues of legitimacy and representation were contested. To a large degree, links to key actors determined the identity of those involved, be they group leaders or government staff. And the issue of identity became crucial in the negotiations over access to financial support, drawing upon discourses of poverty alleviation to anchor positions of power. Although such contests took place within a specific arena – that of the FONAES programme – the stakes were often related to the attainment of power in other arenas (for example, the legitimacy of the Salinas administration, endorsement of loyalties towards certain factions of the ruling party, or the authentification of proper representation of 'the poor' by a political organization).

Here the notion of power as inherent in certain hierarchical positions, as controlling the wills and activities of those under its subjugation, is, of course, too static and all-encompassing, and makes too many assumptions concerning an ever-present powerful actor. Rather, one needs to make reference to arenas, to physical and symbolic spaces that are objects of control. It is obvious that control is never total and that it cannot be guaranteed indefinitely, but is constantly negotiated and restrained. Political space is necessarily inscribed within such socially restrained and repeatedly negotiated processes.

The Multi-faceted Nature of Political Agency in Tomatlán

Peasant groups from Tomatlán, in the state of Jalisco, were among those aspiring to receive the benefits of the FONAES programme. The director and his team placed their bets on associations such as these. The expectation was that, because of the level of political agency that had been attained in the region, and the ways in which they had encouraged demo-cratic organization and had challenged government corruption in the 1970s and 1980s, they would be able to adopt the programme as theirs, establish self-reliant enterprises and make the most of the resources provided. The team did not expect a smooth, democratic process; most of them had enough experience of peasant organization to know that interests change, conflicts take place and leaders are co-opted. However, they did face many 'surprises' in the implementation of the programme, many of which can be explained by the particular history of political organization in the region.

The struggle for access to resources and democratization had been a painful one in Tomatlán. In the 1950s, seven families controlled the municipality. Their dominion dated back to the previous century, when descendants of Spanish colonizers had deprived the local indigenous popu-lation of their land. The seven families owned most of the land, which they used basically for cattle-grazing. They were also traders, money-lenders and shopkeepers. Locals speak of that period as one of great scarcity and indebtedness towards the large landowners. Groups began to organize in order to recover the land, based on the agrarian laws established after the revolution. A number of landless agricultural workers from neighbouring states were invited to join such groups in order to strengthen the organization.

In the 1960s the government built a road linking the region to larger cities such as Puerto Vallarta and Melaque. In the 1970s a large irrigation project was initiated financed by the World Bank, the Inter-American Development Bank and the Mexican government. Such large public works brought with them a change in the social and political situation of Tomatlán. Because the construction companies needed cheap labour, many unemployed urban dwellers from other states, bricklayers, transporters and heavy machinery operators were brought in to work on the construction of the dam. Other immigrants included engineers, traders, government and bank officers, policemen, drug dealers and a few outlaws who were escaping justice in their home states and viewed the isolated region as a good place to pass unnoticed. However, the land that was to be irrigated was expropriated by the government, to be distributed later according to the guidelines of the new Law of Agrarian Reform. This attracted a horde of new immigrants, many of whom arrived with the hope of acquiring a piece of land. Possessing land was, in their eyes, the only way out of poverty. They could establish their own agricultural enterprises and not have to depend on occasional and badly remunerated jobs. Land could provide a steady source of income, and it also represented capital in their own names. Although *ejido*[3] land could not be legally sold, it gave them status and provided collateral in emergencies when they needed to borrow money.

Many eyes were set on the process of land distribution, and, from the 1970s to the beginning of the 1990s, Tomatlán was the site of a strong political movement. In the 1980s 16 groups organized themselves into an independent peasant union, La Unión de Ejidos de la Costa de Jalisco (The *Ejido* Union of the Coast of Jalisco). Although other producer organizations were also present including, for example, the Cattle Producer Association, the Association of Small Landowners (Asociación de Pequeños Propietarios, who in fact were mostly large landowners) and the local branch of the National Peasant Confederation (Confederación Nacional Campesina, linked to government), the *Ejido* Union was the only independent organization that represented the interests of the landless. Members scrutinized the agrarian law and consulted other leaders and organizations from other regions to learn what they were entitled to and what their rights consisted of. They lobbied in government offices, orchestrated road blocks, used press campaigns to protest against the illegal procedures and organized land invasions as a means of pressure. They also joined a left-wing national organization, the CNPA (Coordinadora Nacional Plan de

Ayala), in which a number of groups from different Mexican regions presented a common front in government lobbying. They shared experiences and tactics, and supported each other. Although the role of leaders in the Union was crucial, most decisions were taken in assemblies and tasks were often distributed in a balanced way.

By the end of the decade, the Union had won most of its demands for land. A consolidated group of leaders still continued to stimulate organization, mainly to favour the production and commercialization of their products. Nowadays, there is almost total consensus in terms of what the peasant movement meant for them: when asked, almost everyone responded that they learned that it is through organization and bottom-up pressure that peasants can make their voices heard and have their rights respected. One can speak of an almost generalized degree of political agency that was being exercised in terms of knowledge concerning the workings of the state, consciousness of their rights as citizens and skills in pushing through their legitimate demands.

But perhaps the producers came to understand the workings of the state only too well. The strategies used did not always have to do with straightforward pressure and self-reliance. The peasants discovered from experience that it was always better to reach high-level officers. On several occasions they spoke directly to the president (Echeverría at the time) and managed to push their demands and solve their problems. Friends who were well placed in government were also resorted to when a contact was needed. The groups also recognized how laws could be 'stretched' to include a diversity of interpretations that constrained them in exercising their rights. They learned to 'work' lower-level state officers, and they discovered that their soft sides could be detected and acted upon when the officers were invited for a drink, which they often were. Engineers in charge of the public works became quite wealthy, and state officers who allowed this were said to have received bribes. Although the Union denounced the illegal procedures, few changes took place.

In the years that followed, large government-managed agricultural projects came and went, most of them failures. Sometimes this was because of the mismanagement of water, sometimes because the necessary equipment was not bought, despite the fact that money had been allotted to it. The government rural bank dealt only with specific suppliers (which led the producers to suspect bribery), credit for producers was always late, and intermediaries took a large share of the produce. Dealings with the government bank had reached high levels of corruption. Local functionaries had encouraged non-payment by helping producers negotiate the payment of non-existent losses with insurance companies as long as they could receive part of the profits. The lesson was not lost on the local population.

Government was not monolithic, there were cleavages to be taken advantage of, diverse interpretations of laws and policies. In the scramble for resources, producers were being left out: input costs were soaring, the prices of their products were declining, and credits were increasingly unavailable Local producers saw the pilferage of funds and corrupt procedures being implemented in the various productive projects in the region. They learned to identify the differences between 'formalities' and 'realities' in the elaboration of government productive projects. And they did not fail to observe the inter-institutional rivalries, the lack of coordination and the power struggles between officials at different levels. Some organizations learned to use rivalries between officers to their advantage, subtly offering loyalty but expecting political favours in exchange.

In the meantime, frictions within the Union had led to divisions and dispersal. Diverse organized groups achieved a presence in the region: some affiliated to political cliques within the ruling party, others linked themselves with left-wing national organizations, while yet others remained independent. Most claimed to represent the poorest, although they often included the not-so-poor, that is, producers who had been able to increase their herds of cattle and establish themselves as intermediaries, and at times large landowners and cattle-owners. The composition of such groups was frequently transformed during election periods, associating in support of a particular candidate for mayor or regional deputy, with the hope that these would represent their interests better within the wider spheres of policy decision-making.

In the mid-1990s a significant group of producers joined El Barzón, a national movement of debtors which rallied against government neo-liberal economic policy. El Barzón acquired massive dimensions all over the country. In Tomatlán, most of those who joined were large, medium and small cattle-owners who had received credit from the official rural bank and were having problems in meeting their payments. Their previous experiences with the government credit had been a bonanza – they could acquire, for example, ten cows on a flexible and low-interest credit scheme and then pay off the debt with the sale of one or two head of cattle. But the 1994 devaluation of the peso had hit hard: many enterprises went out of business, and input costs and interest rates soared. The NAFTA treaty opened up the frontiers to American meat, and local cattle prices plummeted. The general complaint was that, under these conditions, producers could not pay their debts even if they sold their whole herds. Some did sell their cattle, houses, tractors and vehicles when they could no longer fend off government pressure, but others argued that government money belonged to the people who had paid taxes, and if it was going to be stolen by bureaucrats anyway, it was best not to pay. The Barzón movement encouraged non-payment. They demanded waiving the debts, arguing that national banking systems were protected with subsidies and yet still charged exorbitant interest rates, leaving producers to pay the price of the economic crisis. Later, they accepted forms of postponement and renegotiation. But for the cattle-producers in Tomatlán, the conditions for renegotiation entailed ten years of commitment to the bank, and, considering the risky nature of agricultural enterprises – due to climatological as well as economic and political adversities – many decided not to renegotiate and did not pay. This meant that they were blacklisted, which jeopardized their ability to access government credit programmes.

Hence more than a few rejoiced when they learned that a friend who had previously supported a peasant organization in the region was to direct a sector of FONAES. As one of the independent (meaning not affiliated to political parties or government organizations) leaders explained, of course their friend would be part of the state, but he would understand their economic predicaments and act with solidarity. He expected independent organizations to be supported again, and poor producers to be able to access government aid without the mediation of local and regional politicians.

However, the meanings of 'independent organization' and 'poor producers' soon became objects of contestation. In the 1990s political agency could not be confined to one dimension or type of struggle. It was wielded by several of the parties involved, at times entailing moments of contestation and conflict involving the negotiation and reinterpretation of rights in the pursuit of both individual and collective interests. Ascertaining their rights, acting in defence of their interests and recognizing the vulnerabilities of the state actually took groups in different directions.

A few leaders used political agency to collect pay-offs and negotiate privileges earned by committing their groups to loyal support of particular political groupings within the state. But the difference between success and failure related not so much to the kind of relation or the hierarchy of the person with whom they were linked, but to how such networks and linkages were used to acquire status, gain access to particular spaces and win battles.

Political agency did not necessarily entail the pursuit of what 'external observers' understand as 'the collective good' or 'the interests of the poor'. While the identification of extreme cases of virtue or corruption might be quite straightforward, the boundaries between 'legitimate' and 'illegitimate' interests were fixed circumstantially. Political agency was required to defend or contest the validity and legitimacy of particular interests or issues.

Equitable Development and the Identity of 'the Poor'

Tomatlán is not considered one of the most impoverished regions of the country, being one of the largest cattle producers in the state of Jalisco, and containing significant areas of papaya, mango, banana and coconut plantation. Drug trafficking is also an important source of income. However, although the flow of capital within the region has obviously increased, it is very unevenly distributed. Investors, company owners, traders and intermediaries are increasingly present, but indicators of progress are few. There are more satellite TVs, bars, trailers and hotels, but the number of schools has hardly increased and health services are quite inadequate. Many young people are discouraged from studying beyond secondary schooling because of the costs involved in travelling to larger towns, and for professional studies they must move out of the region altogether. One of the main household expenditures is health, since only simple illnesses can be treated in the region, and people have to travel to Puerto Vallarta – a city located 97 kilometres away – and pay for the services of private doctors and hospitals. Access roads to many of the villages in the municipality are inaccessible in the rainy seasons and remain in a very bad condition all year round, which limits their ability to transport their products to the market. Although for short periods sources of employment thrive and salaries are not low compared to other regions, wages are quite dissimilar. Income varies from US$1,400 to US$40 a month, the average being US$120, which is still below the poverty line. And, because of the relative isolation of the region, the cost of basic consumer goods is quite high.

On the other hand, although the production of papaya, banana, rice and sesame have brought significant profits, the risks are high, and only those with enough capital have been able to survive weather and market calamities. At least 20 per cent of the inhabitants of the region migrate to larger cities or the USA. While the region produces large amounts of cattle and milk, cattle is frequently sold lean before it has reached the weight that can render it cost-effective. As Lucía, a widow from Tequesquite, one of the villages in the municipality, expressed it:

> When my cow gives birth to a calf, my 'battle' is to keep it at least for a year, so I can obtain a bit more cash from its sale. If I can survive until the rainy season, the calf will have fed on fresh grass and can weigh more. But often sickness or other emergencies come along, and I have to resort to my calf. By the time I sell it, I am up to my neck in debts.

Lucía, like many other men and women in the region, carries out a diversity of income-generating activities to make ends meet and sustain her three daughters and one son. She picks tomatoes, a variety of plums and *nances* (a local berry), makes cheese, and raises chickens and pigs. Although it varies greatly, her average income is about US$70 a month, almost 50 per cent below what is considered the poverty line. On the other hand, Petra, from Nuevo Santiago, another of the villages in the municipality, is also a widow, but she manages to earn a monthly average of US$100. She sells milk, makes cheese and also grows papaya, although she has not been able to capitalize any of these activities. Milk and cheese are sold very cheaply at the time she can produce them, which is when the market is full. She sold two cows to invest in her papaya field and the produce was excellent, but the particular variety she had sown had such a low market price that she ended up giving most of the fruit to the cattle. Here lack of information concerning the workings of the market contributed to her failure. Furthermore, her mother, who lives with her and her family, has been sick for several years, and she has had to shoulder the costs of her treatment. Lucía and Petra were two of the few women who had joined groups aspiring to be included in the FONAES programme. But so were many other men, some of whom owned land, cattle, vehicles and farm implements.

The programme stipulated that projects should be group endeavours, and leaders of different political groups and several ex-Union leaders contacted FONAES officers to present projects. One of the leaders who had participated actively in the Union claimed that the programme really would benefit the poor, but, as later events showed, the 'poor producers' he had in mind were mostly those who had participated actively in the Union and who still respected and followed him as a leader, as well as his kin and friendship networks. These did in fact include very low-income producers, but also some who, although they were quite well off, were facing economic problems and could certainly use government help.

In some groups the inclusion of more wealthy producers – who in theory were not to be included in the programme – was in fact a mechanism of solidarity to incorporate the poorest. Lack of resources was an obstacle for the lowest-income rural dwellers. In order to enter a partnership relationship with FONAES, they had to possess land, a building, agricultural machinery, cattle, vehicles, fences or fodder, depending on the nature of the enterprise proposed, since FONAES would finance only 30 per cent of the cost of the project and producers had to provide the rest. By including more affluent members the enterprise as a whole was able to provide enough capital to cover its percentage.

A few groups were organized by the Central Campesina Cardenista (CCC), a branch of a national organization self-identified as left-wing, linked to a political party (PST or Partido Socialista de los Trabajadores, Socialist Workers' Party[4]), which claimed to have important contacts high in the government. The organization as such had not participated in the struggles for land in the region, but several ex-Union leaders had affiliated to it, thus granting it a degree of 'historical legitimacy'. The definition of 'poor' in this case was related to membership to their organization, which again included producers who could be described as destitute, but also some who were considered quite wealthy.

A local politician who had lost the election for mayor of the municipality headed a few other groups, as did a member of the ruling party who was linked to large cattle-owners in the region. The leaders organized meetings with their groups to discuss the proposals they would put forward, formulating their needs according to what they interpreted as the framework of the programme. Most of the groups decided to propose keeping cattle both for breeding and milking. Cattle had traditionally been a source of status in the region and were considered the only secure way to capitalize. They served as collateral for loans and a kind of 'insurance' that could be drawn upon in emergencies.

The FONAES team had hoped that the producers would be more resourceful and suggest more innovative enterprises. Cattle created ecological problems if they were not properly dealt with, and the revenues were generally not as high as those from other kinds of enterprise. Furthermore, cattle-owners had been the 'enemy' in the struggles for land, forever requiring extensive use of land and representing the 'rich' in the region. However, it was their policy and that of the programme to build upon the know-how and aims of the producers and to gamble on it, so the projects were sent to the FONAES committee for evaluation. Many projects were presented, a small percentage of which were accepted. I will focus here on the projects involving cattle, which in 1998 constituted 26 enterprises located in 16 different communities within the municipality, were being funded, entailing a total investment of 13 million pesos (approximately US$130,000).

In the initial stages, many members of the FONAES cattle-producer groups were debtors who could no longer resort to the government bank because of their unpaid debts. FONAES officers were conscious of this, but they were also aware of the complicated economic situation of the debtors and the impact on it of corruption within the government bank. Later, however, only producers who had cleared or renegotiated their debts with the bank were allowed access to the programme. Nevertheless, the fear of failure was present: would the producers work honestly with the programme or would they simply view it as government aid which did not need to be repaid? Had they learned the paths of corruption?

Their concern was not unjustified. Previous experiences with government programmes and undemocratic procedures had shaped particular

views of the nature of the state and the resources it was expected to
distribute. The notion of partnership was hardly ever fully understood by
the producers. Instead, they seemed to take the view that partnership with
an ambivalent entity such as the state – where, on the one hand, the
officials involved were not as interested in the financial dividends (which
would constitute the government's share of each enterprise) as they were
in political and social profits, and, on the other, they were likely to change
according to political circumstances and norms could be stretched and
resignified – was not the same as the kinds of partnership they normally
encountered in their economic endeavours. The general conviction was
that the producers – self-identified as poor – were entitled to state resources. It was their right to receive the benefits of the programme, the
result of years and years of struggle against the accumulation of capital in
the hands of a few. The government was obliged to 'redistribute' taxpayers'
money in favour of poor peasants as a measure of social justice.

Routes of Access and Mediation

Lucía and Petra were both included in groups that became FONAES
partners. But Juan, who had applied as part of the local politician's group,
was left out. His village is located in the mountain area surrounding the
irrigation district and is quite inaccessible because of the deplorable condition of the road that leads to it, which crosses two rivers that have no
bridges. He owns a few head of cattle together with his brother, but explains
that they can hardly make their ends meet because, although they have the
capacity to produce milk, it is impossible to get it to the market: by the
time they reach the main road it is spoilt. Juan believes his group did not
benefit because they were not affiliated to the 'proper' organization. In
fact, two other groups from his village were accepted, and it disconcerted
him to see that they had received their share of cattle, while he considered
that he was more entitled to help because he was 'poorer'.

Cristina, who is a member of a women's group in La Gloria, a village
located in the irrigation district, was also distressed because they had not
yet received any benefits under the programme. She explained that their
leader had betrayed them, and it was because of him that they had been left
out. Her group had been affiliated to the CCC, and she described how it
had been made to participate actively in political meetings and mobilizations,
for which they had to travel to Mexico City. They participated in the hope
of acquiring benefits such as government aid, but the leader received
resources from the programme for himself and his group, and then misused
the funds and even double-crossed his own group members. The women
consequently left the CCC, although they still hoped to receive the benefits

of the programme. As Cristina expresses it, 'We are holding on, we keep going, even if this means clinging on to the cows' tails!'

Organizations that were able to guarantee access to government aid managed to strengthen their influence *vis-à-vis* the locals, particularly after the drastic cuts in government welfare programmes. But access to the programme became a matter of conflict between local organizations and rekindled differences that had become problematic in earlier years. The resentment of from those who did not receive the benefits of the programme led to character assassinations – for example, linking those who had been accepted to drugs trafficking, and identifying them with outlaw immigrants who were only creating problems.

The matter became even more problematic when representatives of FONAES assigned to the region began to establish their own links and alliances with the aim of securing their space and position. As is the case with most federal programmes, regional officers resent the lack of autonomy. An officer from the state of Jalisco explained that 90 per cent of federal allocations of funds to the provincial states are already labelled for particular programmes and often for specific groups. Regional directors find themselves in a difficult situation, since their staff often have to follow direct orders from Mexico City and their authority is undermined. Jalisco officers resented the fact that some of the selected groups in Tomatlán had been 'imposed' from above. They took sides and at times participated in character assassination. Frictions within the groups thus permeated the institution and vice versa.

Conflicts between leaders acquired greater relevance because diverse forms of mediation were an indispensable element in the routes of access to the programme. As already mentioned, the process of project selection had not been as adequate as the FONAES team had hoped. But even in the case of those 'recommended' from above, the selection committee took pains to make the applicants reformulate their projects, in terms of both economic efficiency and social impact and community development. However, this constituted a double-edged sword, since skills were required to formulate projects according to the institutional criteria of sustainability and cost efficiency, which increased the need for experts and intermediaries.

Resources became available to people like Lucía, Petra and Juan only through the mediation of leaders and organizations who were able to work through information circuits and technicalities, as well as dealing with conflicts at diverse levels. However, producers' prerogatives in terms of choosing leaders or joining particular organizations were not simple. In their everyday life, each formed part of kin groupings, being linked to church, political or producer associations. They participated in several domains of village life, each of which involved particular loyalties, social expectations and commitments, the recognition of specific authorities, normative frames and established patterns of behaviour. Adherence to particular groups had social implications. Definitions, identities and values that were accepted, reproduced or contested within specific and often overlapping domains of interaction shaped the available possibilities for group representation and intermediation. On the other hand, interests were defined and fashioned within domains. Specific needs were legitimized, while others were trivialized or excluded.

The FONAES programme became a specific domain of interaction with which other local domains overlapped, but also conflicted. It was forged through a number of arenas of struggle, the first of which entailed the issue of access. As we have seen, in negotiating access both geographical and symbolic distance had to be spanned. Geographically speaking, diverse levels came into play: local antagonisms involving leadership and organizational influence, the regional government's struggle for political space, and negotiations at the level of federal politics constituted a series of diverse but interlocking and at times conflicting projects. The discursive practices within which interests were articulated all made reference to the poor and to poverty alleviation, but the rules of the game were contested, identities redefined and needs 'reinvented'.

Arenas of Struggle and Mechanisms of Control

Although local organizations (including, as we have mentioned, low- and not so low-income producers) participated in different fora in which decision-making concerning poverty alleviation policies were contested (the Barzón movement, political parties, municipal committees, etc.), it was at the level of implementation of specific programmes that political space was most often sought and negotiated.

Experience has led producers to understand that plans conceived at the top are reinterpreted and transformed during implementation. At times, producers complain that the president's aims are to benefit rural dwellers and that poverty alleviation policies are well designed, but that middle- and lower-ranking officers misinterpret and manipulate the programmes. When possible, they try to reach high-ranking officers to denounce the situation. But producers often trust their own skills in negotiating at the local level, which have been sharpened by their historical ability to adapt and manoeuvre in order to survive. This was particularly evident in the case of FONAES, where the overall aims and structure of the programme were accepted and respectfully referred to, although the interpretation of such aims and their implications were strongly contested.

Gaining access to the programme gave leaders a degree of legitimation *vis-à-vis* their groups, who believed in their power to transact at high levels of government. In turn, local groups' backing made the leaders strong in the eyes of programme implementers, who must negotiate the everyday operation of the enterprises. Producers managed to resist and negotiate aspects of control and wield a degree of power in crucial aspects concerning the implementation of the programme. In theory this is what participation is all about. However, this did not always mean that 'the poorest' would benefit, nor that 'productive' social enterprises as conceived by the programme were to be developed.

The first 'battle' to be fought concerned the composition of the groups. The programme clearly stipulated that the specific projects should entail collective endeavours in order to guarantee the social orientation of the enterprises. But government officials had learned from experience that producers tend to object to collective enterprises. Cooperatives and other forms of collective groups had been promoted and imposed since the beginning of the 1970s, and conflicts and malfunctioning had led to fiascos. However, they were willing to accept kin groupings and other forms of more flexible collectivities, in which individual producers take charge of their share of cattle, although they assemble as an enterprise that is officially the FONAES partner. The group as a whole is responsible for the operation of 'the enterprise', controlling and facilitating marketing and making sure payments are made. The producers translated such disposition as a right to a degree of autonomy. FONAES should not interfere with group membership and internal organization. Furthermore, the precise meaning of 'kin groups' was ambiguous. While government officials assumed that this meant that brothers, fathers, sons and, it was hoped, daughters and wives would work together as an enterprise, more than a few producers enlisted brothers who were not living in the village, and wives and daughters appeared as members but did not work in the enterprise, nor did they receive a share of the cattle. Hence in some cases identity as a kin group masked the accumulation of cattle in the hands of a few. The common association of family and kin with the 'private sphere' was a tacit but strongly enforced mechanism for excluding government from what producers considered should be respected as their autonomy and 'privacy'. Although this constituted a gain for the producers in terms of their space *vis-à-vis* the state, it reinforced the exclusion of women and reproduced patriarchal relations within the households.

Another issue involved the complicated calculations that had to be made to translate the producers' resources into numbers in order to account for their contribution to the project. At the beginning the programme itself provided staff to aid the producers in formulating their projects, but later the organizations brought in more skilled persons to write projects, and a few groups paid experts to do it. Such 'experts' encouraged the producers to include as many resources as possible, so that the 30 per cent provided by government would be a more substantial amount. Cattle already owed to the bank were included, as was land that was already being used for other purposes. The fact that this would in the long run also increase the share that the government should receive as a partner in the enterprise was not considered. Later projects had to be reformulated in more realistic terms, and the programme ended up contributing more than the stipulated 30 per cent.

Negotiations concerning technical assistance (for instance, who would provide it, but also what kind of cattle they should acquire, whether they should vaccinate or not, whether they should use artificial insemination) also sparked lively disagreements. One of the issues underlying these disputes concerned the interpretation of producers' interests. Some producers agreed with the programme officials' conception of long-term development for which efficient enterprises must be consolidated. To begin with, this entailed the acquisition of better breeds of cattle. But for other producers, the aim was to obtain cash in the short term – partly due to debts, their pessimism concerning their ability to consolidate an enterprise, and their conception of government aid as spoils to be taken advantage of. They thus bought old, poor-quality cows, and some even 'bought' their own cattle, using false documentation in order to pocket the funds.

Another issue was the nature of the enterprise. Commonly cattle entrepreneurs in the region use 'extensive' rather than 'intensive' methods, leaving the cattle to graze and reproduce without much investment in special varieties of fodder or labour. This allowed them to combine cattle-raising with other income-generating activities. They resorted to veterinarians only when a cow was sick or had difficulties giving birth. Vaccinations are used only when a generalized epidemic afflicts the region, and locals distrust artificial insemination, which they claim is costly. Artificial insemination entails more work, since cattlemen have to keep a close eye on the cows to predict their times of fertility, and then make sure they have semen at hand – which is also difficult since it has to be kept under refrigeration and electricity is unstable in the region. But officials believe that the enterprises should use intensive methods in order to be competitive in the market, and insisted on the need for systematic technical assistance. Few producers changed their practices, but technical assistance was accepted when FONAES offered to subsidize it in the initial stages. A small group was appointed, including two vets, an agronomist, an accountant and a social worker. The producers contributed a site for their office and put together an amount of money to pay for two computers and a stock of medicine to start a collective veterinary pharmacy. The agreement was that, after the second year, the producers themselves would pay 20 per cent of the staff salaries and gradually increase their contribution until the whole office was financed by them.

The third issue was of a more political nature. Some producers were not satisfied with the services provided by the technical assistance staff and claimed that they were incompetent. But more than that, they accused them of acting as representatives of FONAES and assuming positions of authority and control. The producers considered that the technical advisory group should be at their service. In other words, the producers should be the 'boss' and not the other way around. They used the language of the social aims of the programme, stressing the need for real change in the power relationships between the state and the producers to argue their case.

Encouraged by their allies in the region, who included the technical advisory group, regional FONAES officers interpreted the issue as a matter of corruption. They sought to undermine the influence of one of the most combative leaders by characterizing his groups as consisting of drug-dealers, thieves and vandals, and making reference to their previous participation in land invasions and struggles against the government, as well as to their debts to the bank. The accusation was indirectly aimed at the federal programme director, the implicit argument being that his group had made wrong decisions in selecting groups and that federal authorities should have no say in local decision-making.

It was important for the producers to clear their names, particularly with respect to the accusation that they were debtors and thieves. Local leaders countered such arguments by making sure their groups paid on time. Meeting the deadlines for the first payments was not always easy, since the enterprises were not successful enough to produce immediate gains. Producers had to resort to all sorts of sources for this: some borrowed money from relatives and friends, others sold a cow or two, others sold their wives' chickens or pigs, and many used money obtained from relatives in the USA. One of the leaders explained that it was important for them to maintain good relations with federal officials and that, by paying their debts, they opened up opportunities to receive greater support from the programme and the state - which, due to the economic situation the country is going through, has been a steadier source of income than cattle or crop production.

In the end, the technical group was dissolved and the producers allowed to select their own technical advisors and veterinarians. The battle was won by the cattle-producers. Some of them sought technical advice from local vets and friends, others established links with a parastatal research and experimentation centre, and a few pursued the contacts FONAES had helped them establish with specialized research centres in other states. However, it is clear that a number of them will continue to use traditional methods of cattle-breeding, thus under-using the resources they were granted and even eroding irrigatable land. It is quite improbable that they will resort to technical assistance.

On the other hand, programme officials accepted the suggestion that a trust fund should be formed from the money the groups should have reimbursed as FONAES' share of the dividends. The trust would continue financing the creation of enterprises and be controlled by the group members themselves. The issue of how the trust fund will function and who will control it is being discussed, and it is clear that none of those participating in the discussions, including the officials and producers, wants to be completely left out.

Thus, within the process of implementation of the programme, producers sought diverse spaces of negotiation to gain an edge and push forward individual and collective interests (including pillaging and money-grubbing as well as political aims and democratic endeavours), not only within the formal channels institutionally created for their participation, but also within a range of everyday contests and accommodations where particular interpretations of the terms of the relationship between the state and the producers were redefined. This was made possible by the interlocking of a diversity of interests, pertaining to both producers and government officials, which led to political alliances which 'empowered' particular forms of leadership.

Voice and Representation of the Poor in the Strife over Government Resources

The programme has not been a failure, nor has it been a complete success in the region. Some of its technical and social development aims were sacrificed in the negotiations that are intrinsic to participation. But participation takes place within arenas in which processes of mediation and of the negotiation and redefinition of interests are crucial features.

The voices of Lucía, Petra and Juan were articulated within the discourses available to them, which already entailed different scripts, adaptations and reinterpretations. On the one hand, their needs in terms of poverty alleviation were intertwined with a diversity of other interests, which included political and social commitments. Hence they quickly diverged from the 'voices' of other people living under similar circumstances. On the other hand, their particular histories and experiences influenced the ways in which their expectations for the future are framed, and thus the ways in which specific strategies for poverty alleviation can be pursued. This led to a fragmentation of voices and an erratic articulation of their interests.

Negotiations drew upon different representations of 'the poor's interests', which were mediated and redefined in the overlapping of domains of interaction. Institutional channels created for the 'participation of the poor' opened up access to a range of groups and individuals whose agendas differed. The crucial issue was how spokesmen were legitimized, how 'the interests of the poor' were formulated, and how they combined with other interests pertaining to regional and national actors. Lucía's, Petra's and Juan's 'retranscribed' voices were repeated within regional and national arenas, where they were reinterpreted and recontextualized to legitimize diverse interests and to secure spaces. As already mentioned, the boundaries between 'legitimate' and 'illegitimate' interests were fixed circumstantially. Political agency was required to defend or contest the validity and legitimacy of particular interests or issues. Political space for 'the poor' is necessarily inscribed within such socially restrained and repeatedly negotiated processes, which cross arenas of contestation at diverse levels of interaction and span both geographic and symbolic distances.

Notes

1. Quoted in Urquidi 1996: 161.

2. This became particularly acute with cabinet changes after President Zedillo took over.

3. The *ejido* is a socio-legal entity concerned with the administration of land and other collective properties. *Ejidos* were established under the 1920s land reform law that followed the Mexican Revolution. *Ejidos* consist of individual plots and generally include a communal grazing area. The term *ejido* is commonly used to designate the geographical site where its agricultural plots are to be found as well as the organization of members.

4. Which other left-wing organizations accuse of being linked to the ruling party.

Bibliography

Alarcón, G. D. (1994) 'La Evolución de la Pobreza en México en la década de los ochenta', in *La Pobreza, aspectos teóricos, metodológicos y empíricos*, Vol. 6, Mexico: El Colegio de la Frontera Norte.

Bovinik, J. (1994) 'Satisfacción de necesidades esenciales en México en los setentas y ochentas', in P. Pascual and J. Woldenberg (eds) *Desarrollo, desigualdad y recursos naturales*, México: Cal y Arena.

Dresser, Denise (1991) *Neopopulist Solutions to Neoliberal Problems: Mexico's National Solidarity Program*, La Jolla: Center for US–Mexican Studies, University of California, San Diego.

Gendreau, M. (1998) 'Tres dimensiones de la geografía de la pobreza', in *Los Rostros de la Pobreza: El Debate, Tomo II*, México D.F.: ITESO and Universidad Iberoamericana.

Pringle, R. and S. Watson (1992) 'Women's interests and the post-structuralist state', in M. Barrett and A. Phillips (eds), *Destabilizing Theory: Contemporary Feminist Debates*, Stanford, CA: Stanford University Press.

Urquidi, V. L. (1996) *México en la globalización. Condiciones y requisitos de un desarrollo sustentable y equitativo: Informe de la Sección Mexicana del Club de Roma*, Mexico: Economía Latinoamericana– Fondo de cultura Económica.

Valencia Lomelí, E. and R. R. Aguirre (1998) 'Discursos, acciones y controversias de la política gubernamental frente a la Pobreza', in *Los Rostros de la Pobreza: El Debate, Tomo I*, México D.F.: ITESO and Universidad Iberoamericana.

Villarreal, M. (1994) 'Wielding and yielding: power, subordination and gender identity in the context of a Mexican development project', Ph.D. thesis, Wageningen: Wageningen Agricultural University.

— (1998) 'Políticas de compensación social y la mujer campesina: negociaciones y candados en el caso de las UAIMs', in S. Zendejas and P. de Vries (eds), *Las Disputas por el México Rural*, Zamora: El Colegio de Michoacán.

5

Ambiguous Political Space: Chiefs, Land and the Poor in Rural Mozambique

Astrid Blom

In many African countries the institutional channels through which policies and decision-making can be influenced and challenged by the poor are often very limited, if not altogether absent. This is often seen as being closely related to the African state being distant, prebendal and neopatrimonial (Clapham 1993; Bratton 1994), leaving little space for the political demands of the poor in society. But as recent research has shown, a distant state does not mean a void at the local level (Bierschenk and Olivier de Sardan 1997). Moreover, it is necessary to look beyond formal institutional channels in order to determine access to decision-making for or by the poor.

This chapter will explore the existence of political space for the poor by discussing to what extent one particular type of actor, namely the chiefs, are being used to access political space in order to serve the interests of the poor. The chapter draws on fieldwork in the district of Angónia, which forms the north-east part of Tete province in central Mozambique. Mozambique is a good case of a country combining acute poverty with a state that is at a distance from the lives and localities of many of its citizens.

The chapter focuses on chiefs as actors and as the embodiment of customary decision-making institutions. Both 'chief' and 'customary' are complex terms. A chief refers to a leader who is part of a particular organization of power and authority. Historically, the organization of power prior to colonialization in Africa was characterized by different types of tribal organization exercising power over people in chieftaincies or larger kingdoms based on lineage affiliation. It may therefore be tempting to see chiefs as traditional or pre-colonial leaders distinct from modern, territory-based leadership. But as this chapter will show, such a modern–traditional dichotomy is not useful in relation to chiefs. The delimitation of a chief's constituency, privileges and obligations vary in space and time, and chiefly institutions are constantly being redefined.

As with the institution of chiefs, recent anthropological and historical research in Africa shows customs as constantly being produced, reproduced and negotiated. Again, a rigid modern–traditional dichotomy of African institutions is of little use.[1] These institutions are not static, but rather constellations of social interactions in which people move, acquire and exchange ideas and resources, and negotiate or contest the terms of production, authority and obligation (cf. Berry 1997: 1228). But neither are these institutions completely fluid and uncertain. There is a degree of durability and an implicit mutual understanding of a set of practices, obligations, norms and opportunities. Finally, even though institutions may guide social interaction, they cannot predict outcomes, nor do they determine people's behaviour: '(M)embership in social institutions creates opportunities for people to engage in negotiation and/or struggle, rather than guaranteeing outcomes (subsistence, identity etc.) or reproducing stable, consistent social relationships' (ibid.).

The central issue addressed in the following concerns the extent to which chiefs in the rural district of Angónia are using political space to serve the interests of the poor.[2] The analysis will focus on a particular type of political arena, the settlement of land conflicts. In order to understand the different interests involved in land conflicts it is useful to distinguish between access to land by users and control over land by the political authorities (Lund 1995: 10–11). The colonial and post-colonial states represent the formal political authority over land, while the chiefs represent what could be called the local political authority in Angónia. Conflicts are found not only between different users of land but also between users and the political authority or between different political authorities. It is the two former forms of conflict that have dominated post-war Angónia.

The Historical Context

Angónia, a northern district of Tete province, central Mozambique, comprises an area of 3,437 km^2 and a population of 245,000 according to the 1997 census. It borders Malawi and the majority of the population lives in relative proximity to the border area. Today there are eight top-level chiefs in the district. Below these there are three further levels of chief.

Before 1870 the Ntumba mainly inhabited Angónia. The political structure was highly decentralized, and various groups were headed by a number of hereditary chiefs called *mambo* and *mfumo*. Control over land was quite central to the power of chiefs at the time, not through interference in everyday land use and administration but through their ritual functions and their protection of the territory against strangers. The *mambo* was referred to as the 'land chief', constituting the link between the living people and the royal ancestors' spirits (Isaacman 1972). The tribute paid by people to the chiefs is described as constituting a recognition of the services provided by them, mainly the ritual duty to ensure the productivity of the land, and second to provide the land itself and protect it. The *mfumo* seems to have been a village headman who had a limited number of subjects under his authority and who passed on some tasks relating to land administration to the higher-ranking *mambo*.

In the nineteenth century groups of Ngoni left South Africa to conquer territories to the north. One such group conquered Angónia and settled there around 1870. This event significantly influenced political institutions in Angónia. The Ngoni came to control local political authority, and 'conquest chiefs' reigned at the top of the chiefly hierarchy. The supreme chief was the *inkosi*. The *nkosi* had (military) assistants below him called *induna*, also a position brought from South Africa. At the bottom were the headmen or *nhacuawa*. Some Ntumba chiefs continued as headmen, others were replaced with Ngoni, and new headman positions were established as new land was brought under cultivation. Usually, the lineage head that founded a new village would take control of the land and the position of chief. In some parts of Angónia this would be an Ngoni, in other parts an Ntumba. The authority of the chiefs was based not only on their hereditary positions and control over land, but also on physical coercion through a kind of police force.

Effective Colonial Control after the Turn of the Century

Not until the scramble for Africa in the late nineteenth century did the Portuguese try to exercise effective control over the interior of Mozambique and exploit its land and labour. Initially control was through private companies based on foreign capital (British, French or German), which were granted extensive rights over Mozambican territory. The Zambézia Company was established in 1892 and lasted for 38 years. Through Sena Sugar it turned Angónia into a labour reserve for their plantations and factories. Forced labour or *chibalo* and migration to the mines in South Africa and Rhodesia came to dominate the colonial experience in Angónia.

Control over the territory came to be exercised through collaboration with local chiefs. In principle the Portuguese government wanted to introduce direct rule in which 'the blacks' were to be assimilated into Portuguese civilization. However, in practice this proved to be difficult to implement, so as a first step the colonial regime collaborated with existing authorities in a kind of indirect rule (Osório and Rodrigues 1940). The collaborating chiefs became responsible for providing *chibalo*, collecting taxes and maintaining the infrastructure and the social order.

The Portuguese government tried to standardize the organization of chiefs. The title *régulo* (little king) was introduced all over Mozambique for the superior chief, and the territorial organization became based on *regedorias*.[3] The number of *regedorias* was reduced and *régulos* were given uniforms and regular salaries. One aim was to reverse the diminishing popularity of chiefs.

In Angónia the implications of collaboration with the colonial administration can be seen in the fact that today only four out of the eight top-level chiefs are the descendants of a chiefly lineage. The other four top-level chiefs are the descendants of commoners appointed by the colonial administrator. The colonial administration went on to create two more levels of subchiefs, called *nduna*, and *chewanga* as the population grew. By the late colonial period the chiefly hierarchy consisted of an *nkosi* at the top, then *régulo*, *nduna* and *chewanga*, with *nhacuawa* at the bottom as village headmen.

The colonial administration's attempt to influence chieftaincies was not always accepted locally. Some people fled to Malawi, and in some instances chiefs would try to protect people from *chibalo* despite harsh punishment. The *nkosi* himself resisted strongly the elimination of the superior chief level and incorporation into the level of *régulo*. Moreover the chiefs – the *nhacuawa* in particular – performed other tasks than those demanded by the district administrator particularly with respect to conflict settlement, religion and the distribution of land to newcomers.

While the distinction between *régulo* and hereditary local leader is crucial to bear in mind if we want to understand the post-independence fate of chiefs in Mozambique, the distinction is not so sharp in Angónia, as the Ngoni had suppressed Ntumba chiefly only a few decades before the Portuguese arrived. The notion of hereditary chief therefore embraced a range of chiefs, and both hereditary and administrative chiefs had to manoeuvre between serving the colonial regime and maintaining and protecting their constituencies.

Independence

The struggle for liberation led by the liberation front, Frelimo, began in the early 1960s but did not intensify in Angónia until the early 1970s. The struggle was concentrated in the northern part of Mozambique. It lasted for ten years, after which the colonial regime ended, not least due to the fall of the fascist regime in Portugal in 1974. Frelimo acquired governmental power in 1975.

Frelimo opted for its own Marxist strategy with a focus on the development of productive forces, modernization, and the leading role of the working class. Within agriculture a policy of collectivization was pursued with new state farms, cooperatives and communal villages, with the main aim being 'to eliminate the peasants' control of the means of production, especially land' (Filho 1997: 200)

Although land was nationalized, there is a sense in which there was a continuation with respect to land rights.[4] Officially smallholders still enjoyed usufructuary rights to the land they were cultivating and inheritance rights, but in practice the post-colonial state's agrarian strategy respected these no more than the colonial state it replaced.

In Angónia former colonial farms became a state farm, CAIA, and an attempt was made to create communal villages.[5] In many instances land was expropriated from smallholders or land expropriated by the Portuguese was not returned, but given to CAIA. Understandably this fuelled existing hostility towards the government linked to its failure to counter the collapse of the commercial sector and its introduction of a new local administration.

Frelimo found it was crucial that the colonial system of indirect rule and exploitation through *régulos* was replaced with a system based on socialist ideas. Chiefs and 'reactionary peasants' could not be accommodated within the revolutionary strategy. The latter should be proletarianized and chiefs were abolished in 1975. A new type of local administration was introduced with 'dynamizing groups' headed by a chairman. In 1977 Frelimo was turned into a Marxist-Leninist party and the dynamizing groups were replaced by a structure of party branches, still headed by the (party) chairman (Hall and Young 1997: 70). This new local administration was to constitute the vital link between Frelimo and the population. The chairman was selected by the village population but only with Frelimo's acceptance.

In Angónia, as in other parts of Mozambique, a relative of the former chief was sometimes selected as chairman, thereby sustaining the chieftancy informally. In some instances the former chiefs continued to work as leaders in local matters after 1975, usually because the new chairman chose to cooperate secretly with the *nhacuawa*. But the Frelimo regime was as brutal as its predecessor and most chiefs ceased to function after 1975.

Frelimo's nation-building project had some initial success in education and health, but not in agriculture. The policy of collectivization meant neglecting smallholder agriculture, which produced most of the agricultural output. Agricultural exports fell from 1975 onwards and the economic crisis intensified in the 1980s.[6] At the fourth party congress in 1983 Frelimo made major policy changes and soon after entered into negotiations with the IMF and the World Bank. In 1987 a structural adjustment programme was initiated, implying a policy shift from state control and planning to a market-oriented policy. As the policy of collectivization became less strict after 1983, commercial farmers were allowed rights to land, provided that they applied for a land title or an authorization and had approved production plans. In practice written titles tended to be preferred to oral testimonies concerning smallholders' usufructuary rights.

Control over land during the Frelimo period was highly centralized, and at village level the newly appointed leaders mainly had to deliver notifications from the government concerning collectivization, and so on. It was predominantly a one-way communication. Moreover, the new bodies lacked human, institutional and financial resources. The officials manoeuvred between two legal frameworks and worlds, the customary and the formal. Formal political authority over land was impeded by contradictory and unsuitable legislation, coupled with insufficient or absent land administration at all levels (Ferrao 1994). Most land transactions therefore took place between families without the interference of an external political authority.

War between Frelimo and Renamo

The war between Frelimo and Renamo broke out in the late 1970s and intensified in the mid-1980s. Renamo was strongly supported by external forces,[7] but even so the 'transformation of Renamo from a minor terrorist group into an army and, eventually, a large political party' (Filho 1997: 192) can be explained only with reference to the contradiction between Frelimo's modern Marxist policy and the interests of the smallholders in Mozambique. Renamo succeeded in taking advantage of the frustrations of the rural population, particularly in central Mozambique. The war lasted for 16 years, seriously devastating the countryside and leading to the displacement of about one-third of the population. In Angónia the war intensified in the mid-1980s and most of the population fled to Malawi in 1987.

The war also developed into a struggle for control over local government. One of Renamo's strategies was to make alliances with traditional authorities, including chiefs. Renamo would campaign for the reintroduction of 'true traditional' leadership and values. It would enter villages and demand reinstatement of the chief or a son of the former chief and promise to return power to chiefs after the war. Frelimo also tried to build up alliances with chiefs in return for protection, but Renamo came to control most of Angónia outside its capital Ulongue.

The Post-war Period

When the war ended in 1992, the Frelimo government was already changing its attitude towards the chiefs both out of necessity and in line with the more liberal policy. In 1993 and 1994 the district administration in Angónia, without being very specific, instructed the former chiefs to resume their old tasks, and their role remains a highly politicized issue. Six years after the peace agreement no clear government policy had emerged.

The politicization of the chief's role is illustrated in changes to the land legislation. A Reform Land Law was passed in July 1997 after two years of discussions.[8] While it is clear that so-called traditional authorities were central in the discussions over land issues, and that the 'local community' had become a key legal entity that could acquire a common title, the question of who represented the local community and the role of the chief was not addressed (Kloeck-Jenson 1998). Major NGOs and part of the Mozambican research community shared Renamo's position in favour of giving chiefs a central role in land management. Frelimo was much more sceptical for historical as well as political reasons. The legal distinction between a formal state authority and chiefly authority with respect to land issues therefore remains unclear, and chiefs have come to represent a type of semi-formal authority.

Political Authorities in Post-war Angónia

The rural population sees the chiefly institution as the main political administrative institution in rural Angónia. Today, chiefs are *de facto* in charge of tasks such as conflict resolution, diverse ceremonies, collecting taxes, keeping a population register, and mobilizing people for public works such as road maintenance and contributions to development projects.

The political community of chiefs is still constituted by a hierarchy of groupings, usually beginning with a matrilineal unit of four to five nuclear families called a *lomane*, headed by a *chefe de lomane*. Then there is the village of about 700 inhabitants headed by a *nhacuawa*, followed by a group of three to four villages headed by a *chewanga*. Further up the hierarchy is a larger group of about twelve villages headed by a *nduna*. Finally there is the top level of, on average, fifty villages headed by an *mfumo*.

Each chiefly level comprises a chief, a vice-chief, a secretary and a chiefly court consisting of the chief and his councillors or *alumusana*. These are most often elderly and influential people appointed by the chief. Connected to the chiefly court, and sometimes part of it, are two or three *mães*, elderly women who will lead investigations in cases of adultery, divorce, and so on. Many chiefs also express great respect for *mães* for their assessments of potential chiefly candidates. Decisions are reached through a consultative process involving discussions within the court and with the group of elders. The principle is to aim at consensus.

In terms of human and financial capacities, chiefs in Angónia possess very little. Few chiefs are literate but a secretary assists them. Written messages are widely used, and the *mfumo* usually keeps some written record of decisions and population numbers. Court facilities are practically non-existent, courts being located either in open air or in ruins. Chiefs, their assistants and councillors earn little income for their tasks. For instance, a *semane* is required for a case to be presented to the court, and after the solution of a case a payment is requested.[9] Incomes appear to be supplemented with bribes of various kinds.

Membership of the political community of a chief is primarily ascriptive, in that people are born as subjects of a certain chief. Should they move to a new territory, they remain under the same chief. However, there is an element of choice in that one can decide to 'adopt' a new chief by moving to his or her territory and explicitly stating the change.

This suggests a form of accountability in that subjects have the possibility of rejecting a chief in favour of another by being prepared to move or by mobilizing enough threats to move to have a chief dismissed. However, dismissing a chief – a *mfumo* in particular – is not easily done. Such a step threatens to divide a village in two. Most respondents felt that chiefs could in principle be dismissed, but that the responsibility lies with the chief's lineage.

How the present chiefs obtained their present positions varies. Those who were chiefs during the colonial period can claim a hereditary right to the position. The oldest son of the first wife of deceased former chiefs can also claim this right, but succession is not automatic. Other sons or daughters might contest succession rights and claim the position based upon a different interpretation of succession rules or with reference to the behaviour of the first-born son. As Comaroff and Roberts (1981: 37) write on the Tswana chiefdoms in Botswana: 'While status is *always* determined by birth, and authority is *always* contingent upon status, legitimate power *always* depends upon personal acumen and achievement, which cannot be inherited.'

The process in Angónia was far from straightforward. Other factors, such as party politics, revenge and internal power struggles, have influenced who became chief. One reason for these somewhat 'arbitrary' processes is that the mechanisms for checking whether the candidate is appropriate for a chiefly position have not been followed after independence. The wealthy and powerful Mr P. puts it this way: 'It is not true that the *mafumo* have been elected. Those who are *mafumo* now are so only because they have succeeded their father … There has to be a ceremony for the appointment. It is a big thing which is necessary. The government has to allow this to happen. All *mafumo* today are only protecting the position and keeping the seat warm.'

What constitutes the right procedures is, of course, subject to interpretation, but it seems that for the top-level chief the presence of all other *mafumo* and the district administrator is important. For the lower-level chiefs what seems important is the evaluation of their performance by the group of influential elders and their support for the candidate. Two reasons for the importance of government recognition among the top level chiefs are the historical links between the *régulo* and the colonial administration and the fact that chiefly positions came to be dominated by a well-organized political group of people. A third explanation is that this urge for state recognition is part of a struggle for resources and privileges, not least a permanent source of income and a more secure political status.[10]

Not only are the succession rights of particular individuals contested at times, but the actual decisions of chiefs are often opposed by the population. This is part of a more general trend in which new ideas and norms about freedom and democracy are challenging the authority of the chiefs. Experiences of democratic practices from refugee life in Malawi and elections in Mozambique have nurtured various ideas about democracy. The typical interpretation is that democracy means freedom and involves the right to do whatever you yourself want, including disobeying authority, whether local or state.

Although positions and decisions are contested, the chiefs continue to have support in their role in village-level public administration. In order to understand this, one has to understand how their power is based on customary village institutions involving general norms and ideas about leadership and reciprocity. A leader is not leader merely because of certain criteria of succession. A leader should earn the right to make decisions and to enjoy the privileges by acting as a protector and supporter of the community. The *nhacuawa* is a leader because he is seen as 'the head', 'the mother' and 'the protector' of the village.[11]

These customary institutions of leadership are embedded in the history of Angónia, but they cannot be seen as representing any kind of ancient, authentic, African authority: they have been redefined according to changing circumstances and balances of power. Drawing upon the ideas of Thompson (1991), one may see these customs of leadership as constituting resistance against the Frelimo's Marxist project and the brutalities of the war. This indicates not that the rural poor are reactionary but rather that their interests are best served at this point in time by defining custom as the chief's right to leadership, particularly in a situation that offers no alternatives. Today being a protector means making peace and friendship between the villagers – an important task in post-war Angónia.

The attitude of young men is illustrative of this point: 'It is not possible to elect a person from another family and set him up as leader. That would create conflicts between the family with roots in the *nhacuawa* or *mfumo* family and the new family. The first family would always be able to say that our position has been taken. And within the *nhacuawa* family people are never the same. There will always be one in this family who is capable of becoming a leader and then this person should be elected.'[12] The first priority is to prevent conflicts; change can be found from within the lineage rather than by replacing it.

One may ask why a chief would be interested in actively trying to protect the poor rather than allying with the rich and powerful. Chiefs do have their own individual strategies for maintaining a powerful constituency and alliances with influential people. This in some cases means letting the poor down. But a broader constituency is a route to prestige and power. More subjects mean a stronger chief and a chief will try many other options before suggesting that a family move out of his or her territory. Furthermore a large constituency increases material benefits in terms of tribute, fees, bribes, and so on. What is striking in Angónia today is the limited material benefits available to chiefs, particularly an uncorrupt chief. People have few resources, even in the more affluent districts, so the basis for extracting resources is limited. For instance, compared to the 1960s very few families today have cattle.

The chiefly institution in Angónia is not a stable or static institution; there is continuous contestation over the position of chief and the rules of engagement involving chiefs, and the roles of chiefs are often ambiguous and their authority not always respected, but the institution itself is rarely questioned. There is room for further negotiation and manipulation.

The formal state institutions constitute the other main political authority in Angónia. The district administration includes an executive council that consists of the district administrator and the directors of the line ministries, all appointed by the government. The district administration as such has the typical characteristics of local governments in a sub-Saharan African context, with extremely low levels of material and human resources and autonomy.[13] Below the district the state has a level called *posto administrativo*, with the same structure as the district administration but with fewer line ministries represented and even less capacity. Locality (*localidade*) is the level below *posto*, but in Angónia it has rarely constituted an effective administrative level.

Although interaction between the formal state institutions and the rural

population is almost absent, people still have an image of the state as a
body that should take care of problems such as the lack of drinking water,
schools and health centres. These expectations were probably fostered
during the refugee period, when the Malawian state provided basic necessities, but are also linked to the notion that the transition to democracy
should lead to material results. However, there is very little faith or trust
in the ability of the Mozambican state to provide anything.

The new opportunity to take part in the election of the government
through national elections has not changed this pessimistic outlook.[14] Competing political parties are not seen as trustworthy carriers of government
power. The political parties represented in Angónia include Frelimo and
Renamo. Frelimo tries to maintain a party structure, but it lacks a strong
base in the villages and there are very few resources available. The population views Frelimo as still closely connected with government, centralism
and poor results. Renamo has a handful of faithful officials, but to an even
greater extent lacks resources. Renamo enjoyed strong support in rural
Angónia during the war and in the 1994 national elections, and it tries to
maintain this support through close contact with the chiefs. In the western
part of Angónia the *posto administrativo* is facing problems that are seen as
being caused by Renamo trying to force the chiefs not to cooperate with
the government. So at both national and local levels the role of chiefs is
highly politicized. From the point of view of the population this does not
increase trust in political parties. Generally, people prefer to avoid party
politics.[15]

The linkage, albeit weak, between the state administration and the
population is through the chiefs rather than the political parties. But the
relationship is somewhat ambiguous due to the underlying political
struggles. On the one hand the government uses the chiefs whenever it is
considered convenient or necessary. There is thus a kind of *de facto*
inclusion of chiefs in parts of the public administration. On the other
hand, many parts of the public administration have little respect for the
authority of chiefs. The official understanding is that beyond the *posto
administrativo* level the state has no formal representation. Many questions,
such as the remuneration of chiefs, remain unsolved, adding to the political
controversies surrounding them. Some chiefs in Angónia have begun to
refuse to collect taxes, exploiting this ambiguous situation.

Returning to the question of political space, there are very few formal
institutional channels for the poor to access political decision-making. The
state does not provide any direct link between the rural population and
decision-making processes. Political parties are not considered to be a
possibility in terms of influencing decisions affecting people's lives.
However, chiefs may be seen to represent institutional channels, and even

though they must be seen as merely semi-formal, they can protect the interests of the poor.

Land Tenure and Poverty in Angónia

Identifying the poor in Angónia today involves, among other things, identifying the main sources of livelihood. While migrant work constituted an important source of income in the colonial period, its importance seriously diminished around the time of independence because the regional links with South Africa and Rhodesia were broken. Later the war led to an almost total loss of cattle among the rural population of Angónia. What remained as the main source of livelihood was agriculture.[16] Together with a relatively high population density, this has put high pressure on land.[17] Today, the majority of families are smallholders who produce maize mainly for self-consumption and sell some vegetables, beans or groundnuts at the local market. Agricultural methods are very simple, mainly based on the use of hoes and family labour.

Although permanent wage labour hardly exists today, another source of livelihood is the off-farm income earned through casual work, the so-called *ganho-ganho*. This is daily work paid in either maize or cash. For those who do not have enough land, in terms of either size or quality, *ganho-ganho* is the primary solution. But also for families not in crisis, *ganho-ganho* constitutes a source of income that is used to create a buffer against crises. Other types of off-farm income are limited to producing local beverages from maize, petty trading in Malawi and various handicrafts.

The better-off sector in Angónia is a small group of commercial farmers who produce maize for the market, primarily the market in Malawi, due to inadequate commercial networks and low prices in Mozambique. They have cattle, carts and maybe a tractor and a plough. Some have received from the government formal land rights over former state farm land and land that was originally taken by colonialists.

The importance of agriculture as the main source of livelihood means that access to land is obviously critical in Angónia. Today, opening up uncultivated and unclaimed land is not an option in the densely populated parts of Angónia. At the beginning of the twentieth century, when the founding lineage of a village, the first-comers, had taken over control of most of the land, they would donate land to families settling afterwards. Since the head of first-comer families often became the chief, this created a socio-political structure in which land and political power were both controlled by certain lineages. But as the villages grew and most land became divided between the different lineages, this control over land by chiefs diminished. In the 1960s chiefs no longer had to authorize land transactions, except in cases involving newcomers.

Most people have access to land through family, most often by marriage or to a lesser extent inheritance. These acquisitions of land follow customary institutions, not as rigid rules but rather as guidelines. There is quite a lot of room for flexibility, depending on the possibilities of the respective families of the couple and their overall relationship. Most people follow a matrilocal pattern originating from the *ntumba* practice. This means that the husband moves to the family of his wife when they marry, and they are given land by her family, staying for a few years, after which they may be given their own fields by her family. The matrilocal pattern does not imply that the woman owns the land like private property. Her brother or uncle, who is the lineage head, has a major interest in keeping the land within the lineage.[18] Land received from the lineage cannot be freely alienated: the lineage head must be consulted.[19] How long the rights to a piece of land can be claimed by a person or a lineage if the land has been left uncultivated is one of the many issues that can be negotiated or contested.

With population growth, fields have been divided several times and some are becoming too small for families to live on. But even small and rather exhausted pieces of land originating from your lineage are important because they ensure access to some land. One never knows who will show up and make claims on land that does not originate from your lineage.[20]

An option that might seem attractive to the outsider is to move to the western part of Angónia or the neighbouring district of Macanga, where land is plentiful. But this option seems less attractive to the people of Angónia. Moving to a new area where you would be a stranger, a *não-natural*, means being deprived of rights that are embedded in social relations, for instance within the lineage. The wealthy Mr H. says, 'If you move to another place you will have to follow the "laws of nature" there. To be *natural* is very important; everybody know that we are from here and my children also have rights.'

In the present situation identifying the poor and the better-off is to a large extent dependent on the social organization and the institutions embedded in it. There is a certain socio–economic differentiation between the so-called first-comer families and the rest. When they arrived in a virgin area, first-comer families would keep a large part of the land for themselves. Chiefly lineages or other first-comers are therefore in a slightly better position in terms of the amount of land they have access to than the commoners. Moreover, being related to such influential persons puts you in a stronger position in terms of other types of support. What is interesting, however, about this differentiation between chiefs or first-comers and others is that membership of the former type of family is not fixed. Family relationships, particularly more distant ones, are disputable and negotiable, and people may try to take advantage of this in order to secure access to land.

Another type of socio-economic differentiation is generational. Young families face greater difficulties in obtaining access to land than the older generations. Fields have become too small, and the opportunity to borrow land is becoming rarer because landowners want to avoid trouble, and usually prefer to secure their own descendants. Moreover, young people are somewhat excluded from decision-making processes since they are dependent on the older generation. In the village survey of Masumbe village, 79 per cent of young families could be considered poor, whereas this applied to 'only' 60 per cent of middle-aged couples.[21]

Another group of relatively poor are female-headed, single families or *solteiras* (including old widows) because of the high demands for manual labour in agriculture. A few decades ago a common practice was to arrange work parties, *dima*, to assist those who lacked labour at peak periods. Being part-time single was not unusual for wives during the colonial period because of male migration and *chibalo*. But this and other forms of collective work or mutual assistance have declined, and it is *solteiras* who suffer most from that. The disadvantage of *solteiras* is aggravated by the fact that the most common solution in times of crisis is to do *ganho–ganho* in the fields of others. The time when one can find such work is also the time when work should be done on one's own field. The result is a negative circle. The Masumbe survey showed that 95 per cent of *solteiras* could be considered poor.

The question of access to land also makes *solteiras* worse off. The labour demand would be less if the soil was of good quality, but in Angónia this is becoming a rarity. The poor, and *solteiras* in particular, are often left with the less fertile pieces of land and command fewer options for precautionary methods such as leaving fallow and using fertilizer.

To sum up, access to land, labour and favourable social relations are important factors in the production of wealth and poverty in Angónia. The groups that might be considered generally poorer than the rest are the *solteiras* and young families from non-influential families. But what is even more important to emphasize is that this does not imply that these groups are left with no options or room for manoeuvre, as we see when we turn to conflicts over land.

Land Conflict Settlement and the Social Practices of the Poor

Before the war, conflicts over land were not usual in Angónia. This picture radically changed as people returned after six to eight years in

Malawi around 1993. Some would find that their fields had been taken by others. Vegetation had grown up and obscured the boundaries between fields. Many members of the older generation had passed away, taking with them testimonies of rights in land. The number of people had grown and the need for land increased. Last but not least, old hostilities that had been dormant during the war or hostilities from the war could be played out over land conflicts. The arena was open for extensive and complex conflicts. In most cases these conflicts were handled by the chief as the third party.[22]

A typical case would be a conflict between different users over the location of boundaries between fields. In such cases the tenure rights were not challenged. Another type involved clashes between competitive tenure claims. At least two sorts of conflict took place here. One was between the right of first occupancy and the right of the user. The other was between the formal rights of commercial farmers and the customary rights of first occupancy.

In this section three land conflicts will be analysed in order to demonstrate some of the social practices the poor have been using in order to protect their land.

Case 1. Mr Nosi and Mrs Ama: conflict over boundaries

The middle-aged Mr Nosi has a wife in a neighbouring village, where they live. He is neither rich nor poor. He received a small field in his home village from his father where he has begun to cultivate some tobacco since the war. He encroached on a large part of the field of Mrs Ama, a poor old widow. Accompanied by her sons-in-law, Ama contacts the *chewanga* in her village and complains about the encroachment. A meeting is arranged between the parties and the *chewanga*. Mr Nosi claims that he is just using land he received from his grandparents. No solution comes out of this meeting. Then Mrs Ama goes to the *nduna*. Another meeting is arranged with all the parties and their witnesses. Like the *chewanga*, the *nduna* believes the testimonies that state that the field belongs to Mrs Ama, but Mr Nosi will not accept their decision and gets very angry. Then finally the case is taken to the *mfumo*. The *mfumo* sends out his councillors to the field and the boundaries are drawn according to the decision of the *nduna* following the testimonies made concerning the pre-war boundaries. Mr Nosi finally accepts that he has lost land he had previously cultivated. Mrs Ama gets her field back and is asked to pay the value of 120 kg of maize, part of which goes to Mr Nosi for the labour he has invested in the field.

This case between two smallholders shows how poor women like Mrs Ama do have access to the chiefly courts and can use them in order to protect their access to land. In these situations the poor have obvious interests in claiming the legitimacy of the customary institutions involving the chief, because there is no alternative and the chiefs do command some authority, which can be mobilized for their protection. Two points are striking, though. First, claiming does demand resources in terms of time and money, which may exclude the most destitute. Second, it was necessary for Mrs Ama to take the case all the way to the *mfumo* in order for Mr Nosi and his group to respect the decision, even though it was quite obvious. Had the situation been left as an intra-village struggle, Mrs Ama would probably have lost her field. This seems to indicate that the authority of chiefs is contested and certainly not absolute. The reason for accepting the decision of the *mfumo* may well be a fear of government interference, which may be much more arbitrary.

Case 2. Mr Zeque and Mrs Chani: conflict between competitive claims

Mrs Chani is a younger woman with six daughters. Her first husband died during the war. Her present husband is in charge of a maize mill, but does not contribute to the household. Mrs Chani lacks land, which is even more pressing because her daughters are approaching the age of marriage. She has a *munda* and a *dimba*, both of which were previously cultivated by her maternal grandmother.

Mr Zeque is an *influential* man of Ngoni origin and related to the *chewanga* family. In 1996 his daughter was getting married so he told Mrs Chani that he needed the field she was cultivating. Mr Zeque claimed that the field originally belonged to his lineage because his father had lent it to Mrs Chani's family around 1950.

Mrs Chani's *maternal* uncle complained to the *chewanga* and later on to the *mfumo*. Due to testimonies and advise from an elder, both chiefs decided that the field belongs to Mrs Chani because her family has cultivated it for so long, and the field was given to her back in 1950. But Mr Zeque refuses to give back the field. He has been elected as chairman and has a strong position in the village. Mrs Chani cannot see how she can get back the land, probably because she does not have the means to take the case to the *posto administrativo*.

While discussion during the hearings revolved around finding out under what conditions a field was transferred in 1950, this is in fact a case of a clash between the right of the first occupant versus the right of the user, in this case after over forty years of cultivation. The chiefs and their councillors argue that use right should in this case have a priority over the right of the first occupant, but their decision has been ignored because Mr Zeque is a strong and influential man.

This type of case has been quite common in post-war Angónia. Transfers of land made in the 1950s and even back in the 1940s are being contested on the grounds that land has to go back to the original owner, the first occupant. Generally this is to the disadvantage of the poor because those families who can claim right of first occupancy are typically the powerful and influential families, not the poorest.[23] This type of claim was being made in 38 out of 71 cases, and in 19 cases reclaiming land was successful. This does indicate a certain concentration of land, but the chiefs are not necessarily supporting this type of claim. Chiefs do sometimes take into consideration the need of the parties just as much as they are considering customary rules. The courts may attempt to suggest a compromise that will ensure the poor party access to land even if, according to custom, they should lose the land. Bonds of familiarity may be emphasized in order to encourage a decision which favours the vulnerable part. A *nhacuawa* says: 'E's mother had received land from S before the war ... [but] you see E and S are directly related and so I explained to E that it would be good if he could give a field to his cousin, S's son, because he himself already had three fields.' In another case a *nhacuawa* says about a case where an old *dimba* loan was reclaimed, 'We advised K that now that P's family had previously borrowed the *dimba* for a long time whether it would then not be the best solution to divide the *dimba* [to let both have some]. But K rejected this proposition because P had insulted him. P should have asked politely first.'

Chiefly courts may in this way try to protect the poor, but they are far from being always successful. Still, the data indicate that the poor are not always the losers. Just to give a vague indication, out of 43 cases 44 per cent were won by the poor party. This indicates that chiefs and customary institutions can be used as a channel through which poor people's access to land can be protected.

Tensions between the right of first occupancy and the right of the user are growing stronger as the pressure on land increases. Chiefs find it increasingly difficult to find land for those who are in need. Therefore there is a growing tendency for user rights to be given precedence over rights of first occupancy. This is a critical point where a process of institutional change in customary land tenure is taking place through struggles over land.

Case 3. Mr Toni and a group of ten smallholders: a conflict between the formal rights of the commercial farmer and the customary rights of the first occupant

Some land that had been taken by Portuguese settlers and later on became part of a state farm had been granted to commercial farmers. Mr Toni was one such farmer. He had been an employee of the Frelimo government and in 1984 he received 75 ha of land and received an authorization from the governor as legal proof of his use rights.

After the war ten smallholders complained that they wanted back the land the *colonos* had initially taken from them. Other farmers had made the same type of demand on former state farm land to other commercial farmers. These cases had been very violent. The group allied with the *nhacuawa* and the chairman in the area, who took the case to the *mfumo*. The group were said to be affiliated with Renamo, and it is suggested that it is the transition to democracy that has encouraged them to demand their former rights. Mr Toni contacted the DDAP (district director of the Ministry of Agriculture and Fisheries) where the case was settled. The decision of the DDAP was that Mr Toni should give back 20 hectares of his land to the smallholders. Mr Toni accepted out of fear.

This case is a clash between the right of a formal grant of land concession by the government and the customary right of first occupancy. Contrary to what is the general picture in Mozambique, Mr Toni's written proof of formal land rights proved to be weaker than the oral testimonies of the smallholders, even in a decision made by the formal state administration. To understand this result, one must take into account the politicized nature of the case. Mr Toni supported Frelimo and was therefore weak in this area, which was heavily influenced by Renamo. But the conflict was also politicized by new democratic aspirations. People are no longer physically oppressed by an authoritarian state, and democracy is perceived as being an opportunity to make your own demands and claims. This is a general tendency that does not apply only to clashes between formal rights and first occupancy rights.

Apart from party politics, other means have been used, such as violence in this case. While the chiefs may represent an institution through which the poor can also seek to protect their access to land, people use a range of other measures in their struggle for land. The use of violence has been very widespread in post-war Angónia, and linked to it are the issues of poisoning or witchcraft. Because these measures have been used, the mere threat of using violence or witchcraft has affected the outcome of land conflicts.[24]

The general understanding within the formal state administration is that cases involving commercial farmers will have to be dealt with by DINAGECA, the formal state authority, on the basis of the formal land law. But evidence shows that these cases involve both the state and the chiefly authority, sometimes in contradiction, sometimes in collaboration. This institutional and legal ambiguity opens up a space for individuals trying to manipulate their way in accessing more land.

These three cases have indicated various practices available to the poor in trying to protect their interests in terms of access to land. Even though the position of chiefs may be highly ambiguous, the chiefly institution in itself can be used to protect the poor.

Political Space for Poverty Reduction in Angónia

This chapter has explored the political space of the poor in Mozambique and the extent to which chiefs in the rural district of Angónia are being used to access political space in order to serve the interests of the poor. This exploration has been carried out through a historical analysis of political authorities in Angónia, by a contemporary institutional mapping and by studying access to land and land conflicts as an approach to understanding the production of poverty and of political space for the poor.

In terms of formal institutional channels, there are very few for the poor in Angónia. Since independence the Mozambican state has not been able to establish an administrative structure that could ensure smallholders access to services and resources such as land. Generally the central state has no recognized formal links to the rural population, and political parties do not constitute a direct channel for the poor to use to influence political decisions.

Strictly speaking, chiefs do not constitute a formal institutional channel. However, they can be seen as representing a kind of semi-formal channel, which at this point in time is the primary channel through which the poor may try to protect their interests. This is not least due to the course of events during the Frelimo–Renamo war, which opened up a political space for chiefs at several levels.

From a national perspective some linkages, from poor people through chiefs to the national political arena, have been created through intermediaries such as NGOs and the opposition party, Renamo. The issue of whether chiefs can be seen as the representatives of the smallholders – that is, the poor – has been widely debated nationally. It represents a kind of opening up of political space for the chiefs, but it can also be seen as an indirect channel for the poor to voice their concerns. It can therefore be described as a political space for the poor, even if the actual relationships between chiefs and different rural groups are much more diverse and ambiguous than reflected in the national debates. It therefore remains a weak channel for influencing political decisions at the national level.

Political space also has to do with discourses that define poverty alleviation as a legitimate political goal. Here the study seems to indicate that talking about the poor and assisting the poor does take place in Angónia. There is a sense of who can be considered the poor, and why. Chiefs are, however, not seen as responsible for alleviating poverty. They are talked about as protectors of the poor, but not as being actively engaged in development and poverty alleviation. This may be because the discourse on poverty and the poor developed during the years when many Angónians were refugees in Malawi, and where the Malawian state and other external agencies were taking care of people's needs.

The third dimension of political space are social practices through which the poor can obtain access to political decision-making, which is where the role of the chiefs is most obvious. The chiefly institution does constitute a channel for local conflict settlement. This provides the poor, at least in principle, with a chance to influence decisions. The chiefly courts and the procedures surrounding conflict settlement do function, even though they are continuously contested. The contestation of succession rights and of specific decisions does not necessarily undermine the chief institution as such. On the contrary, it contributes to its reproduction.

In terms of outcomes of land conflicts, there is no clear conclusion as to whether the chiefs are 'pro-poor' or not. On the one hand the poor groups do try to have their interests served, by supporting the chiefs, arguing their case well, revitalizing family ties, using violence or witchcraft, and so on. And they do emphasize the reciprocity inherent in the chiefly institutions in order to obtain protection. On the other hand, the role of chief is ambiguous, and chiefs are dependent on alliances and the support of powerful groups. Thus chiefs are not simply protectors and representatives of the rural poor. However, an institutional arena exists that allows some political space for the poor through the chiefs.

The study seems to suggest some general points concerning the chiefs. First, the chiefs and chiefly institutions cannot be relegated to being part of a 'traditional' static social sphere distinct from the 'modern' civil society of NGOs, grassroots organizations, and so on.[25] Certainly history is crucial in understanding the role of the chiefs, as is demonstrated also by Mamdani (1996), but chiefs should be understood as representing contemporary and highly dynamic political institutions. They are constantly being redefined according to changing circumstances and power struggles at various societal levels. Second, the study supports a point made by, for instance, Lemarchand (1992) and Ferguson (1998), namely that a rigid separation between state and civil society including the chiefs is neither desirable nor possible. Chiefs in Angónia cannot be seen simply as part of a local social sphere where people interact independently of the state. Rather, chiefs move in and out of the state sphere over time. This also questions the notion of the distant state. From a formal point of view the central state is weak and absent in terms of village-level administration. But chiefs in Angónia do in certain ways act as the representatives of the state.

This leads to a few comments relating to policy based on this study. Coming to grips with rigid dichotomies such as traditional and modern, state and non-state, when dealing with the future role of chiefs seems crucial, particularly when considering 'pro-poor' policies. The policy debate in Mozambique seems to have suffered from these dichotomies. Moreover, there is a need to define a policy in relation to the chiefs that has both a short-term and a longer-term perspective. In the short-term perspective one has to recognize that chiefs constitute an important part of local public administration, at least in certain parts of rural Mozambique like Angónia. Often there will be no alternatives to these 'traditional authorities'. The study has shown that the chiefly institution may embody certain 'pro-poor' elements that might be used more explicitly in future policies. Rather than establishing new organizations at village level, existing ones should be built upon while at the same time taking their weak capacities into account. Chiefs, as well as their assistants and councillors, may be used in the transitional phase towards decentralization and democracy – a phase that may turn out to be very long – even if in the long-term perspective chiefs may not continue to play a key role in local administration.

Postscript

After this chapter was written, the Frelimo government passed a decree on 15 June 2000 stating that community authorities or *autoridades comunitarias*, defined as traditional chiefs and other leaders recognized as such by their respective local communities, should be consulted by the local state bodies in a number of areas such as land use, employment, food security, housing, public health, education and culture, peace, justice and social harmony, civic education, environment, and transport and communication (*Mozambique Bulletin*, issue 25, AWEPA, ed. J. Hanlon). This policy change seems to be linked to the results of the national elections in December 1999 in which Frelimo won only a very narrow victory. The opposition coalition Renamo–UE won the majority in six out of eleven provinces. Rather than power-sharing, the Frelimo government seems to opt for some kind of alliance with chiefs. But even if the decree means a change in the legal framework for chiefs in Mozambique, it remains to be seen whether it will change the profound scepticism within the Frelimo government and party at various levels towards the so-called traditional authorities.

Notes

1. See Comaroff and Comaroff 1992; Feierman 1990; Moore 1986; Ranger 1992.

2. The chapter is based on ten months of fieldwork during 1997 in the district of Angónia. The fieldwork included the collection of data on 71 land conflicts.

3. Those who were appointed *régulo* were either a former hereditary chief, a relative of the former chief, or a common man favoured by the colonial administrator.

4. Officially there is a distinction between peasants or *camponeses*, and commercial farmers or *privados*. In this chapter smallholder refers to a semi-subsistence farmer not using permanent labourers while a commercial farmer produces for the market using permanent labour, machinery, and so on.

5. Five communal villages were created by 1982 and 12 out of a total of 18 *aldeamentos* (villages created by the Portuguese) continued as informal villages (Coelho 1993).

6. Hall and Young 1997: 108. See Torp 1990 for an analysis of economic development after 1975.

7. Renamo was established from three sources: the Rhodesian government, who wanted to create a counterinsurgency unit; former Portuguese and Mozambican soldiers from the colonial army, who had fled to Rhodesia after 1975; and Frelimo dissidents. When Rhodesia obtained independence in 1980, support for Renamo was taken over by South Africa, which wanted to destabilize the frontline states to protect its apartheid regime. From 1980 Renamo slowly began to develop a political profile (Hall and Young 1997: 131).

8. Under the new law land is not privatized, but the possibility of the state to expropriate land has been restricted, and testified oral proof is now considered as strong as written titles. The law has yet to be implemented.

9. The price of a *semane* ranges in value from 3 to 20 kilos of maize sold on the local market; a settlement varies between 20 to 150 kilos of maize.

10. Alexander (1997) found a similar tendency in Manica Province.

11. Power based on a promise of nurture and parental care is not confined to Angónia; see Schatzberg 1993.

12. Group interview with younger men, Masumbe, 4 September 1997.

13. A process of government decentralization has been initiated, but as of 1997 it remains an urban phenomenon and has not affected the work of the DA in Angónia to any significant degree. The DA includes the following line ministries: agriculture and fisheries (DDAP); education; health; public works; culture, sports and youth; and commerce and industry. The DDAP is the strongest institution due to its donor assistance. This mainly comes from the Danish Development agency, Danida. Others agencies are the UNDP, the Mozambican NGO Foundation for Community Development, and the American NGO World Vision.

14. National elections were held for the first time in 1994.

15. The poor turnout of 15 per cent at the local elections showed this general trend (Hanlon 1998).

16. There are two types of land, *munda*, the dryland field where maize and other crops are grown, and *dimba*, the wetland fields where vegetables are grown. The latter is important for monetary income and a second annual crop.

17. In 1960 the average population density in Angónia was 24 per km² (Matos 1965: 24). In 1983 it had increased to 54 per km² (CEA, 1983: 3) and in 1997 to 71 per km² (National Census 1997; Administrator of Angónia, personal communication). In 1960 and 1983 Angónia district also included the neighbouring district of Tsangano.

18. The Ngoni brought virilocal residence from South Africa, where the man takes his wife to live with his own lineage, which pays a bride price or *lobolo* to the wife's family. The couple receive land from the husband's father, and if the husband dies, the children belong to his family. This practice never became widespread in Angónia. Today, a few wealthy and powerful families practice virilocal residence and define themselves as 'the proper Ngoni'. Instead a mixed practice of *chitengua* has evolved, where the man asks permission to take the wife to his family but pays no bride price.

19. But land cannot be considered family land because the receiver has full rights over its use. The lineage has a kind of 'right of preference in all proposed alienations' (Matos 1969: 220).

20. Another option is to borrow land, which is quite common in Angónia today, even if the borrower is in a highly insecure position. The purchase of land is illegal since land belongs to the state, but an informal land market does exist. People will try not to pay for what they can get for free, but sometimes poor people find selling off part of their land the only option left.

21. The survey covered only 68 families, so the percentages should be treated with caution. However, the same trend was found by Åkesson (1996) from a survey in another Angoni village. The poverty criteria used comprised shortage of land, periodic lack of food, regular selling of casual labour, poor health, old age and lack of social capital. The ranking was done through a combination of self-evaluation, evaluation by the village chief and the village teacher, and listing available economic, social and human capital.

22. Studies of land conflicts in Angónia in 1993 and 1994 confirm this observation; see Myers et al. 1994.

23. The reason for this tendency to contest use rights by claiming first occupancy rights seems to be the generally high pressure on land and open spaces in terms of political authority left after the war, but it is also due to the fact that during repatriation the government told returnees to 'return to their place of origin'.

24. Violence or the threat of it was used in 35 out of 71 cases. Almost everyone would say that post-war land conflicts have led to killings by using either *catanas* (knives), or drugs and witchcraft brought from Malawi. Even if this is difficult to verify, it proves that fears of violence and witchcraft are very effective in Angónia. Another means used to affect the outcome of a case is bribing the chiefs, which seems to be on the increase.

25. See, for instance, how this common conception is applied by Bratton 1989.

Bibliography

Åkesson, J. (1996) *A participação nas actividades de extensão agrária*, Tete: Danida.

Alexander, J. (1997) 'The local state in post-war Mozambique: political practice and ideas about authority', *Africa*, 67, 1: 1–26.

Berry, S. (1997) 'Tomatoes, land and hearsay: property and history in Asant in the time of structural adjustment', *World Development*, 25, 8: 1225–41.

Bierschenk, T. and J.-P. Olivier de Sardan (1997) 'Local powers and a distant state in Rural Central African Republic', *Journal of Modern African Studies*, 35, 3: 441–68.

Bratton, M. (1989) 'Beyond the state: civil society and associational life in Africa', *World Politics*, 41, 3: 407–30.

— (1994) 'Neopatrimonial regimes and political transitions in Africa', *World Politics*, 46: 453–89.

CEA (1983) *Famílias Camponesas de Angónia no Processo de Socialização do Campo*, Centro de Estudos Africanos 83/2, Maputo: Universidade Eduardo Mondlane.

Clapham, C. (1993) 'Democratisation in Africa: obstacles and prospects', *Third World Quarterly*, 14, 3: 423–38.

Coelho, J. P. (1993) 'Protected villages and communal villages in the Mozambican province of Tete (1968-1982)', Ph.D. thesis, Bradford: University of Bradford.

Comaroff, J. and J. Comaroff (1992) *Ethnography and the Historical Imagination*, Boulder, CO: Westview Press.

Comaroff, J. and S. Roberts (1981) *Rules and Processes, the Cultural Logic of Dispute in an African Context*, Chicago: University of Chicago Press.

Feierman, S. (1990) *Peasant Intellectuals*, Madison: University of Wisconsin Press.

Ferguson, J. (1998) 'Transnational topographies of power: beyond "the state" and "civil society" in the study of African politics', in Henrik Secher Marcussen and Signe Arnfred (eds), *Concepts and Metaphors: Ideologies, Narratives and Myths in Development Discourse*, Roskilde: IDS Occasional Paper No. 19.

Ferrao, V. (1994) 'State land apparatus in Mozambique', in R. Weiss and G. Myers (eds), *Second National Land Conference in Mozambique: Briefing Book*, Madison: University of Wisconsin Land Tenure Center.

Filho, A. S. (1997) 'The political economy of agrarian transition in Mozambique', *Journal of Contemporary African Studies*, 15, 2: 191–218.

Hall, M. and T. Young (1997) *Confronting Leviathan: Mozambique since Independence*, London: Hurst and Company.

Hanlon, J. (1998) *Mozambique Peace Process Bulletin*, 21, 1, July.

Isaacman, A. (1972) *Mozambique: the Africanisation of a European Institution: The Zambesi Prazos, 1750–1902*, Madison: University of Wisconsin Press.

Kloeck-Jenson, S. (1998) 'Locating the community: local communities and the administration of land and other natural resources in Mozambique', in *Proceedings of the International Conference on Land Tenure in the Developing World*, University of Cape Town, 27–29 January.

Lemarchand, R. (1992) 'Uncivil states and civil societies: how illusion became reality', *Journal of Modern African Studies*, 30, 2: 177–9.

Lund, C. (1995) 'Law, power and politics in Niger', Ph.D. thesis, Roskilde: Roskilde University.

Mamdani, M. (1996) *Citizen and Subject*, London: James Currey.

Matos, M. L. (1965) *Notas sobre o Direito de Propriededa de Terra dos Povos Angoni, Acheua e Ajaua de Província de Moçambique*, Lourenço Marques: Memórias do Instituto de Investigação científica de Moçambique, 7, série C.:1–127.

— (1969) 'Portuguese Law and Administration in Mozambique and their Effect on the Customary Land Laws of their Tribes of the Lake Nyasa Region', Ph.D. thesis, London: University College London.

Moore, S. F. (1986) *Social Facts and Fabrications: Customary Law on Kilimanjaro, 1880–1980*, Cambridge: Cambridge University Press.

Myers, G. et al. (1994) *Security, Conflict and Reintegration in Mozambique: Case Studies of Land Access in the Postwar Period*, Madison: University of Wisconsin Land Tenure Center, LTC Research Paper 119.

Osório, J. de C. and J. F. Rodrigues (1940) 'Integração dos actuais régulos na obra administrativa nas colónias de Angola e Mozambique', *Congresso do Mundo Portugues*, 15: 545–61.

Ranger, T. (1992) 'The invention of tradition revisited', in T. Ranger and O. Vaughan (eds), *Legitimacy and the State in Twentieth-Century Africa*, London: Macmillan.

Schatzberg, M. (1993) 'Power, legitimacy and "democratisation" in Africa', *Africa*, 63, 4: 445–61.

Thompson, E. P. (1991) *Customs in Common*, London: Penguin.

Torp, J. E. (1990) *Mozambique: Politics, Economics and Society*, London: Pinter.

6

Speaking with Space: Displacements and Claims in the Politics of Land in Zimbabwe

Amanda J. Hammar

Drawing on case-study material from a remote communal area in the north-western district of Gokwe North in Zimbabwe, this chapter examines the dynamic relationship between discourse, power and space in the politics of land displacements and claims in the Communal Lands of Zimbabwe. It shows how successive states, both colonial and post-colonial, have engaged in space-ordering practices that have been aimed simultaneously at terri-torial control and asserting political authority, and how various discursive strategies and practices have been employed to transform space, place and environment to such ends. It also shows, through a particular case of eviction in north-west Zimbabwe, how situated actors construct the spaces and places of their everyday lives, and how they engage with the state in competition over land and authority. In this sense, we see that power is neither monolithic nor mono-directional.

The chapter concludes that discursive practices are critical, albeit not determinate, in both shaping and reflecting the political space for claims over land and land authority in Zimbabwe over time, *and* as part of the strategies of different social actors in making use of such space.

Land, in both its material and symbolic dimensions, has been central to politics in Zimbabwe throughout its history and on all social and spatial scales. The dramatic political events that have unravelled since February 2000, leading up to and following the parliamentary elections in June 2000, have demonstrated once again its extraordinary powers to unify some and divide and devastate others. Despite this, a wide consensus exists across the political and social spectrum of the profound need for land reform and fair land redistribution. However, President Mugabe's representation of the invasions as a spontaneous movement against sustained neo-colonial oppression in the form of white farmers has convinced few but his strongest supporters and allies.

Prior to the crisis that erupted in 2000, the late 1990s had already seen the central state begin to intensify its efforts to revitalize the land reform and resettlement process. This was linked in no small way to the state's declining legitimacy and the build-up to the general elections due in 2000. Official documents and debates on land reform produced between 1997 and 1999 had begun to emphasize the combined principles of poverty reduction, increased productivity and equity, but little progress was achieved on the ground. Frustrations were high and pressures were mounting from many quarters, not least from an emerging and impatient black elite constituted by black commercial farmers, black investors, and agricultural graduates (Moyo 1999). At the same time, the state was faced with a mushrooming of informal land self-provisioning activities during this period by the land-hungry, including war veterans, whose narratives of political justice, retrieving lost ancestral lands and the need for a 'land acquisition revolution' echoed those being used by state actors themselves, including the president.

The focus of many of the land invasions prior to 2000 was on farms in large-scale commercial farming areas assumed by the land activists to have been listed for designation and acquisition. (The subsequent occupations of over fifteen hundred farms by mid-2000 was not limited by such criteria.) Receiving less focused attention in both the media and in official land policy deliberations are the interrelated and widespread phenomena of independent migrations, forced displacements and competing land claims occurring both *across* and *within* the Communal Lands themselves. The present chapter is concerned with these phenomena, and particularly with the significance of discursive strategies and practices used by key and often competing social actors to establish and defend their sense of belonging and entitlement to land during successive processes of migration and displacement.

Colonial Invasions and Translations

The first wave of conquest north of the Limpopo river began in the 1890s with the search for gold and land. Modernist notions of progress and imperialist codes of morality, religious doctrine and even aesthetics (Ranger 1999) were drawn upon both to justify European penetration of African lands and to establish colonial structures of power and authority over 'conquered' territory. One of the initial tactics of the early settler state in assuming its authority over land was through its mapping of 'spheres of influence' over given spaces by various ethnic groups and specific traditional leaders. Palmer gives the example of the settlers' deliberate exaggeration of the magnitude of territorial control of the powerful Ndebele chief, Lobengula, noting that 'the advantage of such a pretence was that any

concessions which could be wrung from Lobengula would cover as large
an area as possible' (Palmer 1977: 10). This is echoed by Worby (1994) in
his analysis of colonial ethnoscaping in north-western Zimbabwe. He
describes how the invention of macro-ethnicities was a way of 'creatively
enlarging political realms' over which the colonial state could assert its
jurisdiction. In this sense, Worby argues, Cecil Rhodes and his colleagues
'imagined political relations between the tribal entities they invented in
order to extend the compass of their own conquests' (1994: 377). Such was
their confidence that they renamed the former areas of Mashonaland and
Matabeleland 'Rhodesia'.

Having invaded and appropriated prime mineral and farming lands by
both force and guile, the colonial settlers were to spend the next eight
decades manoeuvring resources and discourses in various ways so as to
counter opposition, both internal and external, and to consolidate and
perpetuate their strategic spatial, economic, political, social and moral
authority and control. Conservationist discourses, which overlaid racist
and segregationist attitudes towards Africans, played an important role in
this process. For example, by the 1920s, official alarm was high concerning
the rates of deforestation precipitated by the timber requirements of intense
mining operations in the colony. As McGregor (1995) notes, this was linked
to regional and Empire-wide scientific debates on the relationship between
forests, hydrology and climate, which, even if misled, provided grounds for
state intervention. As a result, conservation legislation was introduced
intensively from the late 1920s onwards to contain the impending 'disaster',
although enforced against indigenous and settler farmers in ways that clearly
favoured the latter.

The colonial state drew substantially on this kind of conservationist
logic to legitimize its attempts to construct organized landscapes, from its
initial creation of Native Reserves through decades of segregationist and
exclusionary land legislation whose implementation it facilitated through
evictions, enforced settlement patterns and prescribed agricultural practices. Further justification was provided by the scientific classification of
agro-ecological zones that would make certain types of farming – and
hence only certain types of farmers – 'suitable' for given natural regions,
a practice that in effect naturalized racial and class hierarchies by writing
them on to the landscape itself. However, in the post-Second World War
period, the need for political stability, for an expanded supply of food for
the colony due to the 'tobacco rush', for more secure labour for secondary
industrial growth, and for increased African spending power to absorb
output forced the state to rethink its strictly exclusionary approach to
African agriculture (Phimister 1986).

One consequence was the introduction of the notorious Native Land

Husbandry Act of 1951, which insisted on individualizing land holdings and communal grazing in the communal areas and enforcing 'good husbandry practices' under threat of dispossession (Phimister 1986). Its modernizing plans to 'revolutionize' land tenure patterns in the reserves failed dismally, however, and the policy was abandoned in the early 1960s, but not before it had displaced thousands of African farmers from productive lands.

'Inventing' and Perpetuating the Communal Lands

Discourses of tradition and modernity have functioned repeatedly as moveable assets for colonial and post-colonial states in demarcating territories, constructing domains of authority over land and people, and establishing or supporting practices of inclusion and exclusion with respect to both resources and rights.[1] Nowhere has this been more consistently demonstrated in Zimbabwe than in the creation and perpetuation of the so-called Communal Lands (interchangeably called Communal Areas) where the country's poor rural majority continue to be concentrated. They were originally constituted by the colonial state as Native Reserves in the mid-1890s, recast by the illegal regime of Ian Smith in the late 1960s as the Tribal Trust Lands and renamed the Communal Lands soon after independence in 1980, and their terminological history and administrative application have consisted of continual spatial and social myth-making.

In his recent work, Mamdani (1996, 1998) analyses such forms of colonial segregation in terms of a distinction between 'ethnic space' and 'civic space', and correspondingly between 'natives' (subjects) and 'settlers' (citizens). He correlates these spaces with the emergence and maintenance of two types of political identity recognized by the colonial state in equatorial Africa – namely ethnic/native and civic/settler identities. These, he argues, became the basis for ethnic and civic forms of citizenship in the post-colonial era. The civic sphere encompassed citizens with individual rights, protected by civil laws enforced by the central state. Initially such rights were the preserve of the 'civilized' settlers, and natives were entirely excluded. Instead, their identities were defined (for them) in terms of an assumed belonging to an imagined ancestral, ethnically discrete territory. According to colonial discourse, rights and obligations in this sphere were defined as group rights determined by custom. These were then encoded in 'customary' laws which, in this logic, necessitated their own brand of local state enforcement and administration, or what Mamdani refers to as the Native Authority.

While the previously racially enclosed civic space was eventually opened out, at least in principle, to include civic rights for all citizens of the country, the ethnic space (associated territorially with the Native Reserves) remained, conceptually if not in reality, an exclusive zone for natives or 'indigenous' citizens, where 'customary' practices, identities and belonging were expected to prevail. In Zimbabwe, for example, the colonial Land Tenure Act of 1969 'made the newly-created office of State President "responsible for ensuring that ... the Tribal Trust Land is used and occupied exclusively by tribesmen"'(Cheater 1990: 201). Yet, as Mamdani (1998) suggests further, within ethnic spaces land entitlements were often related to definitions of insiders and outsiders: on the one hand authentic indigenous inhabitants, and on the other non-indigenous strangers, *mzungu*, 'restless people who will not stay in one place'. Building on these assumptions, from the 1920s onwards the colonial state introduced 'customary' laws into these so-called Communal Areas, which included a decentralized system of hierarchical, patriarchal land-allocation authorities that cascaded from chief to headman to kraalhead.

Much of the literature has been especially concerned with demonstrating the inappropriateness of the term 'communal' when applied to actual forms of land-holding and land use practice, whether during the pre-colonial, colonial or post-colonial periods (Holleman 1969; Cheater 1990; Doré 1993; Moyo 2000). Most cultivation and household accumulation and reproduction practices within the Communal Lands exhibit clear forms of private ownership in ways that dispel any lingering myths of homogeneity and egalitarianism (Cousins et al. 1992). This is not to say that there are *no* communal or collective resources or practices in these areas. As Cousins (1993) notes, 'communal' tenure in southern Africa denotes a system of combined property rights and obligations. These provide households within a defined socio-spatial group with rights of use over certain parcels of land for cultivation and residence, while simultaneously giving them collective rights of access, as part of this defined group or 'community', to common land for grazing, firewood, water and building materials.

The main point here is that both colonial and post-colonial states have reinforced in different ways an *image* of non-commoditized land (de-commoditized in resettlement areas) and subsistence-based agriculture – of ethnic space, if you will. Together with conservationist, nationalist and modernization discourses, this has been used to legitimize continued state control over the land-spaces and populations that fall within the Communal Lands, and to institutionalize differential treatment of Communal Lands 'subjects' as distinct from other 'citizens' elsewhere.

Shifting Land Authorities

Paradoxically, and by no means unambiguously, traditional authorities and their continuing reinvention have been intrinsic to successive states' attempts to reach into and control the Communal Lands in different ways over the past century. Assertions of such authority characterized the early colonial state's project of regulating landholding and land use in the Native Reserves. The post-1965 illegal Rhodesian state swung between removing and reinstating the chiefs, but finally decided through the Tribal Trust Lands Act of 1979 to define them as the 'sole "tribal authority" whose consent every "tribesman" required in order to "occupy or use land for agricultural or residential purposes"' (Cheater 1990: 201).

The role of traditional authorities in relation to land had a different meaning and focus for the nationalist political parties and armies of the liberation struggle that led to Zimbabwe's independence in 1980. In this context, a reinforcement of the authority of the powerful ancestral land spirits (*mhondoro*) through the spirit mediums became a critical strategy in the liberation struggle (Lan 1985), as well as in more localized land conflicts (Spierenburg 1995). It gave greater moral and spiritual weight to the struggle through its emphasis on the injustice of colonial appropriations, not just of land but of *ancestral* land.

Since independence, state policies and legislation concerning the nature and scope of traditional authorities in both their judicial and land-allocation roles in the Communal Lands, have themselves swung from one extreme to another. The 1982 Communal Lands Act officially removed most of the administrative powers of chiefs and headmen, making way for the proposed new forms of decentralized 'democratic' institutions in the form of village- and ward-level development committees and elected district councils. Unofficially, however, there was a strong reluctance on the part of some state and political actors to abandon the traditional authorities (Alexander 1995), many of whom had provided crucial nationalist support during the struggle, and whose ongoing political support would remain critical in the largely rural constituencies. Despite an intensification of the decentralization process in the late 1980s and early 1990s, the strong representation by chiefs on the highly select Land Tenure Commission was a telling sign of their revived political significance. The promulgation of the Traditional Leaders Act in 1998 indicated a further extension of this trend.

There is a clear logic of self-preservation in the post-colonial state's recognition of a role for chiefs and other traditional leaders for the foreseeable future. The ruling party's declining legitimacy in rural areas is partly linked to the very uneven successes to date in establishing an alternative system of governance in rural areas, despite many years, dollars and words invested to develop effective, decentralized, democratically elected local structures. In such a political climate, the collective lobbying power of chiefs has gained strength. In addition to their role in the Land Tenure Commission, they have formal representation both in the Rural District Councils and in Parliament, and have been consulted by the president on matters of national importance. Not surprisingly, there are growing fears – borne out by recent Supreme Court rulings that reversed gains in women's inheritance rights – that this trend will reinforce traditional patriarchal practices, not least in relation to land, that further marginalize women, the young and the already poor (Alexander 1995; Goebel 1999).

Post-independence Transitions and Dispositions

Following increases in agricultural production levels in the early 1980s, and high public-sector investments in social services and infrastructure with a range of positive downstream effects, severe macro-economic and fiscal constraints in the late 1980s precipitated a major shift in Zimbabwe's overall economic development strategy, which included the adoption of a structural adjustment programme in 1990. These reforms emphasized, amongst other things, deregulation, export-led growth in place of import-substituting industrialization, significant reductions in public-sector spending, and increased efforts towards decentralization. These represented a clear ideological retreat for the government.

In the 1990s the consequences of policy changes, together with a series of devastating droughts, poor public-sector financial management and an increasingly corrupt political leadership had serious impacts on both urban and agrarian socio-economic landscapes. The decade was marked by reduced public sector expenditures, increased pressure on rural local authorities to raise revenue, a growth in land conflicts, particularly in marginal areas with an increase in evictions, growing poverty, expanding urban and agricultural unemployment and extremely high rates of AIDS. Throughout, there has been persistent land scarcity and insecurity exacerbated by the commodification and alienation of commonage and familial land and an inadequate land resettlement programme. The growth of independent land seizures in the late 1990s, drawing upon discourses of nationalism, political justice and indigenous rights, is therefore not so surprising.

Related discourses are evident in the state's own land-claiming and displacement strategies. In the late 1990s, moves towards the compulsory acquisition of commercial farms by the state intensified. On this subject, the president's and ministers' public speeches frequently invoked the rhetoric of rightful claims to such lands by 'sons of the soil' who had lost 'our ancestral lands', and made various populist calls for a 'land-acquisition revolution'.[2] Yet despite assurances that the new land reform proposals would address skewed income distribution through 'removing the imbalances in land ownership',[3] the proposed reforms gave strong weight to the selection of progressive farmers for resettlement.

Contradictions have also characterized the state's discourses on gender and land. At independence, the contribution of women to the liberation struggle was widely acknowledged, and, in line with the socialist sentiments of the ruling party, a number of legislative and administrative mechanisms were put in place to expand and protect women's civic rights. However, this did not go so far as to challenge or reverse women's access to and rights over land in the context of the Communal Lands, where patriarchal 'customary' laws and practices prevail. In these areas, women's entitlements to land are secondary and remain largely dependent on men. While new inheritance laws have come into being that entitle women to inherit 'property', they do not include rights to inherit land in the Communal Lands.

Returning now to discourses of conservation and environmental sustainability, as noted earlier these have been intrinsic to both the colonial and post-colonial states' control over land-space and land use. As elsewhere in Africa, the project of state-formation and nation-building in newly independent Zimbabwe precipitated attempts by the new state to construct structures of feeling around given territories at different spatial levels: national, provincial, district, ward and village. These processes were partly facilitated through the creation of institutions and procedures associated with defined politico-administrative boundaries. Within this context, land-use planning, with its assumptions about sound, modern environmental and agricultural practices, provided one of the key technical justifications for introducing such fundamental expressions of state formation and control as villagization, especially in the early period after independence.

As Munro (1995) has observed, the deep intrusions into everyday life that villagization entailed were an attempt to reorient the settled social practices and social identities of rural people away from traditional forms of authority towards forms of political authority consistent with a modern nation-state. Together with other agrarian policies and practices, this was also a way of maintaining control over local resources and agricultural production in the Communal Lands and elsewhere. However, the effectiveness of such reorientations and controls has been neither even nor consistent, especially with diminishing public-sector funds and central state capacity. On the other hand, new forms of intrusion and attempts at control are beginning to emerge with the growing assertiveness of the Rural District Councils, combined with increased pressure on them to generate their own revenue.

Over the past decade, following the popularization of CAMPFIRE,[4] wildlife has become one of the most accessible and lucrative resources that can be tapped by councils to generate such revenue. (This applies mostly to districts that are entirely or partially located in marginal agro-ecological zones, most of which border game-rich national parks or are traversed by game corridors.) Although the bulk of the revenue from such activities as safari-hunting and trophy sales is intended for the 'producer communities' who have to live with the daily disadvantages of large game in their areas, councils are entitled to a substantial 'management fee'. Frequently, the percentage has been increased or funds have been diverted to other, more pressing council projects.[5]

Local Versions and Inversions

Parallel to the meta-discourses, both national and global, that have helped shape various states' efforts at space-ordering and related land claiming and displacement practices are the dynamic 'local' discourses linked to situated historical, material and social conditions within particular localities. The increasing land invasions taking place in the late 1990s – prior to the mass wave of occupations after February 2000 – provide one example of how the discourses of national-level politicians were simultaneously appropriated and challenged by local non-state actors. The earlier invasions were being undertaken by land-poor activists (including disaffected ex-combatants and the urban unemployed), the majority of whom were economic and environmental refugees from densely over-crowded, infertile and under-resourced Communal Lands.

Narratives of political justice, ancestral belonging and appeasement of the dead were interwoven by some of the land invaders to justify their claims to occupy white-owned farms. In the words of one such land activist as far back as November 1998:

> Our forefathers were pushed from this area to make way for the white settler farms. To us this is the big home-coming and we feel very much at home ... We went to war for land. Now we were being haunted by guerrillas who perished during the struggle because we had not got the land. I had my first night of good sleep here in the open because the souls which had been haunting me had been pacified.[6]

At that time, threats of arrests by the police, and even violent evictions, seemed to provide little deterrent for the settlers, who continually returned to the sites from which they had been removed. Many saw themselves as having no alternative, given their desperate economic circumstances. For some, as one police officer observed: 'Invading communities regard it as martyrdom to be arrested for land problems.' In general there has been a deep frustration at the slow rate of resettlement and the perceived unfairness of earlier land redistribution programmes. These are seen to have concentrated benefits on wealthy black landowners, state-land managers, politicians and so-called 'capable' farmers (Moyo 2000).

Research and media coverage during the 1990s provide countless tales of groups of households establishing fields illegally on grazing lands in resettlement schemes, on privately owned commercial farms, or in wildlife 'buffer zones' on the periphery of Communal Lands. There are also reports of people grazing their cattle in national parks or on commercial farms. Moyo (2000) cites numerous examples of land self-provisioning activities in Communal Lands in different parts of the country, frequently facilitated through illegal land sales by kraalheads, headmen, chiefs and councillors, and involving anything from 30 to 3,000 so-called squatters. A more recent phenomenon is that of urban residents in over-crowded cities like Harare buying land illegally in nearby Communal Lands.

The state was caught largely unprepared, and its erratic and often heavy-handed responses to the 'illegal' occupations exposed capacity constraints, contradictions and political fault-lines within its own ranks, which together underpinned many of the tensions evident in its land reform policies and implementation practices. Such inconsistencies allowed different local versions and inversions of land entitlement, ownership and authority to continue. At the very least, this began reshaping the political space for local land claims. It also demonstrated, as Moore (1998: 347) has noted, that while land claims are deeply localized and territorialized in nature, they 'are never simply local, sealed off from an outside beyond'.

The 'Making' of Gokwe North District

In 1993, Gokwe North came into existence as one of Zimbabwe's 57 administrative rural districts, the result of splitting up the much larger single district of Gokwe into north and south. This was the year in which the partly administrative, partly political Rural District Councils (RDC) Act of 1988 finally began to be implemented. But it could just as well denote the beginning of a sixth 'wave of conquest' to add to the five that Worby (1992: 558-9) identifies in his extremely rich study of Gokwe:

> The invading 'Red Army on Motorcycles' [Agritex workers] represents perhaps a fifth wave of conquest to wash over Gokwe. The first was led by Chireya, who tricked the autochthonous inhabitants out of their salt, their wives and their land, but couldn't seize the power to make it fertile. The second was led by the *indunas* of the Ndebele, who accepted tobacco from people they called the *VaShangwe* as a sign of subordination and peace. The

colonial conquest that followed not only extracted tribute and labour, but more profoundly, established a different language of agrarian discipline and practice and made possible the re-imagination of relations of power and identity. It was under the aegis of the colonial state that the fourth 'conquest', that of the *Madheruka*, took place. The late colonial and post-colonial regimes took the spatial journey of the *Madheruka* into the land of the *VaShangwe* as an allegory of the journey from the backward past into the progressive present and future.

The RDC Act aimed at establishing a single type of rural local authority by amalgamating two previously separate types of council, District Councils and Rural Councils, which served the Communal Lands and the mainly white large-scale commercial farming areas respectively.[7] This involved a re-mapping of territory that not only demarcated new administrative boundaries, but also achieved the double act of asserting new levels of *localized* control over land-space (for example, by empowering the RDC as both the 'appropriate' land-allocation and land-conservation authority), while simultaneously reasserting the power of the *central* state over territory and people (given that the RDCs are far from autonomous from the centre).[8]

The Act was also geared towards deepening the process of decentralization through a far greater devolution of power and resources to elected local authorities. It is therefore hardly surprising that its implementation has been characterized by deviations and delays, but international pressure for a reduction in public-sector spending and the promotion of democratization and good governance has caused the process to speed up.

Historically, much of Gokwe, especially those areas in the north-west, now part of Gokwe North, were considered extremely remote. Some suggest it was perceived as being 'off the map' from the point of view of native policy (Worby 1994: 388), so that it escaped some of the intrusions of the colonial state that were experienced elsewhere in the country. Remoteness (distance from centres of production and administration), together with the specific geographical and demographic features of the district, have played an important role in the evolution of land-occupation patterns in Gokwe. Characterized in colonial texts as 'hot, malarial lowlands', the area was widely affected by tsetse fly infestation. As a result, much of Gokwe was relatively sparsely populated until the early 1950s, by which time tsetse eradication programmes had had some success. At this point it began to be used as a site of relocation for groups of Africans forcibly displaced due to various colonial land, agricultural, water and mining policies and programmes.

For example, soon after the Second World War large numbers of African farming households – some of whom became the migrant outsiders known as *madheruka* in Gokwe (Worby 1994) – were evicted from good-quality lands in different parts of the country, which were appropriated by the state and given as 'rewards' to white ex-servicemen. Around 1956/7, there was large-scale displacement of Tonga communities from their homes along the banks of the Zambezi River due to the construction of the Kariba Dam, some of whom were moved into the north-western parts of Gokwe. In addition, consistently from the 1930s to the 1970s, numerous evictions and land squeezes were perpetrated as a result of segregationist legislation relating to land apportionment (1930), land husbandry (1951), and land tenure (1969). These resulted in gradual flows of migrants into the district. From the 1970s onwards, greater success with tsetse control in northern Gokwe meant that livestock could now be kept, which opened up previously underpopulated areas for habitation. The liberation war disrupted and distorted rural migration as a whole, but from independence onwards, and increasingly in the 1990s, growing land hunger in many parts of the country intensified the demand for land,[9] leading to an expansion of spontaneous migrations into and within Gokwe North (Cumming and Lynam 1997).

A number of interrelated spatial factors (real and assumed) made Gokwe a suitable foil for the displacement and appropriation projects being undertaken elsewhere by the colonial state. This included images of it as an empty space waiting to be filled, its peripheral position (at that time) relative to the country's political economy, and its inherent status as 'ethnic space' (Mamdani 1996), far removed from the civic entitlements of citizens in more 'developed' and 'modern' environments.

Despite the fact that much of the land is officially considered agriculturally marginal and unsuited to either large or small-scale commercial farming, let alone subsistence agriculture (Cumming and Lynam 1997), some parts of the district have exhibited phenomenal success in small-scale commercial cotton-growing. At the same time, here as elsewhere in Zimbabwe, land has become available through the expansion of informal land markets, involving sales of land disguised as 'allocations' by either traditional and/or elected local leaders.

Locating Vumba

Vumba is located some 150 kilometres' drive north-west from Gokwe district centre (itself 300 kilometres from Harare). It lies in the south-western corner of a triangle of territory bounded by Chizarira National Park to the west and Chirisa Safari Area to the southeast. It is a hard place to pinpoint on official maps, since it is defined formally as part of a larger administrative ward (overlapping a chiefly domain) called Simchembu. Yet

'Vumba' does exist as an identifiable place in some official sense as denoted by such institutional (state) markers as Vumba Primary School and a newly constructed clinic. The inhabitants are a mixture of Tonga-, Shona- and Ndebele-speaking people, whose combined presence inscribes on to the landscape the diverse but interrelated histories of two major waves of migration into the area over the past half-century.

In more recent years, Vumba has become the focus of intense conflicts over land and authority, gaining a certain colloquial notoriety as 'DRV' (the Democratic Republic of Vumba), evoking images of war and resistance, in this case directed primarily towards the state. Such images and their discursive reproduction reflect, but also affect, local processes of place-making and identity-formation, which have implications for the ways in which different actors formulate and operationalize either their land-claiming or displacement strategies.

Hand-drawn maps of Vumba made by residents interviewed about their experiences of eviction in 1997 reveal an important relationship between naming, place-making and historical struggles over landscapes/land-spaces (Myers 1996; Harvey 1996; Moore 1998). Village settlements established by the more recent settlers (a mixture of Shona- and Ndebele-speaking families who migrated into the area between the late 1980s and early 1990s) were given such names as *zvichemo zvavanhu* (people's grievances), *dzivareshungu* (a pool of desire), *chawasarira* (why we were left out), *zvido zvavanhu* (people's choice), and *masimba evanhu* (people's power). These names, the kernels of rich and often painful stories in themselves, reflect a more general combination of despair, hope and militancy among these settlers, sentiments that become more comprehensible through an investigation of their individual and collective stories of displacement and the quest for secure land, water and livelihoods. By comparison, the villages of earlier Tonga settlers (following their forced removal from the Zambezi Valley in 1956/7) were given less combative and, ironically, more modernist Tonga names such as *lusumpuko* (development) and *molali* (moral).

Such naming of places by the people who inhabit them, combined with their detailed narratives of displacement and migration, exemplifies 'the agency of historical tales' that not only shape the images people have of themselves, but also make their identities and the conditions of their lives and struggles more widely visible to others.[10] Yet equally significant is the naming by *outsiders* of places and spaces (as well as things and people), as noted earlier with reference to colonial ethnoscaping (Worby 1994), but also with direct relevance for land displacements and claims in present-day Vumba, and elsewhere in Zimbabwe.

Narratives of Displacement, Migration, Adaptation and Belonging

In Vumba, the place-making effects of naming are reinforced and embellished through insider narratives of displacement, migration, adaptation and belonging.[11] These are used in many ways to counter the discourses and actions of successive states and their local allies that have displaced, or threatened to displace, more vulnerable social groups with impunity. These narratives, individualized and often contradictory, but in some way representative of a shared moment in time/space, are distinguished here in terms of the two key waves of migration referred to above. Although occurring at different historical junctures (in the late 1950s and late 1980s respectively), under unique circumstances and with particular effects, they resonate with one another on certain levels and have become layered over and into one another as part of Vumba's constantly transforming social, cultural, political, economic and ecological landscape.

With regard to the first wave of settlers, one of the oldest Tonga residents in Vumba, who arrived with his chief and community around 1957, recounted the tale of their forced displacement from the Zambezi Valley with a mix of bitterness, boldness and resignation. To him, the move was at first unimaginable but no choice was given, 'only instructions'. The hardships and suffering were severe, as many have testified, especially when compared with their previously independent and relatively plentiful lives along the banks of the Zambezi River.[12] In facing the hardships, the only legitimate channel at the time through which the traumatized community could make sense of and express anger over the disruption of their former world was through the medium of their ancestral spirits.

After men from the community were shown land in Vumba, and forced to build temporary shelters to prepare for their impending removal, they were taken back to the valley while roads were built:

Then we were brought back here in lorries with our possessions. But soon people started to die. Snakes were coming into people's homes. They started to get headaches, and by 9 p.m. they would die. To step on the tracks of the snake caused death.

We had to think hard about what to do … We had to consult *n'angas* to explain what was happening. The elders sent me to a *n'anga*. He explained to me that we had made a mistake with the migration. We should have brought with us a little soil from the Zambezi Valley to the new place. This was what was causing death to us. After that, we had to take a small clay pot from our old home and we inserted it into the soil. But then came a lion and it uncovered the pot from beneath the soil and cracked it, and threw it aside. The ancestral spirits were angry at our removal from the Zambezi. We were instructed then [by the *n'anga*] to pay a hoe to our ancestral spirits, to apologize for not knowing [the proper way of moving from our old homes]. This was done in a ceremony of elders only. After that the death stopped. And then we were free. Anyone could choose to go and settle where he wanted. There was no council when we came here. We didn't know of that.[13]

The absence of either a council or any pre-existing traditional authority at that time, and the freedoms this entailed, contrasts sharply with narratives from a wide spectrum of Vumba residents concerning the intrusive and often brutal space-ordering and governance practices of the current Gokwe North Rural District Council. In fact, following the eviction of around one hundred and forty households from Vumba in late 1997, the council became so unpopular that many of its officers, including the local councillor, feared going into the area. The council is particularly reviled and mistrusted by those who were directly affected by the eviction, which included a few Tonga settlers but primarily targeted second-wave migrants settled in a 'buffer zone' close to the national park boundaries.

These later settlers in Vumba are a mixture of Shona- and Ndebele-speaking families who migrated into the area over the past decade, with the majority arriving between 1989 and 1994. Many recall the multiple migrations, forced or voluntary, during their own or their parents' lifetimes, invoking sedimented memories of state victimization and marginalization, both colonial and post-colonial, that they share with their Tonga neighbours. Many left areas where the land and water supplies were too sparse and the soil too tired to support their families. Through such tales of desperation, they call upon a deep pool of historical injustices related to the inherited land inequalities. In addition, a number of households had been active in supporting the nationalist liberation struggle. Most came after hearing that there was fertile land available in Vumba, and almost all claim to have followed what they understood to be the correct or even 'legal' procedures for accessing land. Certain settlers who had been threatened with eviction from another part of Gokwe claimed that they were actively encouraged, even directed, by the council and the provincial governor at the time to go and settle in the Simchembu/Vumba area.

Multiple, Simultaneous Land Authorities

Some of the local Tonga leadership in the area formally acknowledge their role and responsibility in allocating land to the new settlers. Speaking at a public meeting in Vumba in late October 1998, the VIDCO (Village Development Committee) chairman from 1991 described the usual procedures as follows:

No one can resettle without the responsibility of the area. We were allocating the land – Muthunthuli, Kambajo [the kraalheads] and myself – after following the documents they [the new settlers] brought with them. After showing them the land, they had to go back to the chief and to the councillor and finally to the council. That's where they were given 'removal' letters.

Disputes over the legitimacy of competing land-allocation authorities are fundamental to claims and counter-claims by the second-wave settlers (constituting the majority of evictees/returnees) and council respectively over the settlers' 'rights' to continue occupying their homes and fields. In attempting to prove that the 1997 eviction was unlawful, the evictees will have to prove that the land was properly allocated to them, 'factual' evidence of which is hard to produce.

According to the assertions of most second-wave settlers interviewed in late 1998, they had conscientiously followed the correct land-seeking procedures on entering Vumba. (The first-wave settlers gained access to land through self-allocation.) They had approached and consulted various combinations of local leaders, both 'traditional' and 'modern', considered in one way or another to be 'owners' of the land. In addition, in a large number of cases the council was apparently visited by the land-seeker in order to confirm official permission to relocate to Vumba from elsewhere. This practice constitutes a type of inter-district immigration control, whereby the council's formal stamp and a signed 'letter of removal' are required to allow a resident of one district to transfer to another. However, the involvement of the council is usually the last stage in a much longer process of negotiation, during which the physical allocation of a particular plot of land is made by either the kraalhead or the VIDCO chairman, or sometimes both together.

For well over half the second-wave migrants interviewed, some form of cash payment was made to those assisting the migrant household in acquiring a plot of land. Amounts varied wildly from 60 to 2,500 Zimbabwe dollars. There seemed to be no strict pattern as to how much a household would be charged as a fee or at what stage in the process, this practice being illegal according to all official discourses. Nor was there any clear correlation between the size of plot (varying from 3 to 42, but averaging between 18 and 24, acres) and the amount of money paid.

Over the past two decades, as well as during previous eras, as discussed earlier, the state has demonstrated its ambivalence with regard to this issue, treading a delicate line between the outright exclusion of traditional authorities and their full inclusion. In practice, it has failed to reconcile its own formal structures of land administration (a role increasingly delegated to the RDCs) with the traditional roles and functions of chiefs, headmen and kraalheads. The persistent hedging on the issue of land-allocation authority in the Communal Lands becomes very apparent when examining three cross-referring pieces of legislation: the Communal Lands Act of 1982, the Rural District Councils Acts of 1988, and the Traditional Leaders Act of 1998. In combination, these laws ensure that a resolution of this question remains conveniently out of reach, allowing for the widest possible range of interpretations and a degree of discursive flexibility that feeds into sedimented layers of competition over land and power.

Shifting Land Values, Reshaping Boundaries

Despite what has been described by some second-wave settlers as initial encouragement by the authorities to settle in Vumba, the RDC is said to have later 'changed its story'. With support from a number of interested stakeholders, the RDC began to redefine key land-spaces and boundaries in Vumba and hence reconfigure entitlements to land. This mirrored shifts elsewhere in the country concerning changing land values and land uses (Moyo 2000), as well as the growing influence of a global conservationist discourse. In Vumba, these interests were focused around the potential for wildlife-based tourism in the area, including both ongoing large game hunting and the possibility of establishing a safari lodge along the Busi River at the most western edge of Vumba.

Establishing a luxury safari camp along the Busi river, to be implemented in line with CAMPFIRE principles, appealed to an interesting cross-section of parties: the Rural District Council, the CAMPFIRE Association, a private hunting safari operator, several environmental NGOs and donors, and several allies among some of the local Tonga leadership. The project ideas fitted in with discourses on conservation and environmentally sustainable development. In this case, however, an initial funding proposal submitted to USAID by the council was turned down after participants at an environmental workshop in 1995 undertook a field visit to Vumba and were allegedly met with threats of violence by some settlers.

Following the council's eviction of these same settlers in late 1997, discussions about the project resumed between the RDC, potential investors and one of the larger environmental NGOs. On the basis of this, a socio-economic feasibility study of the Busi site was commissioned in 1998 by the RDC to assess its tourist development potential and its 'social acceptability'. (By this stage, the majority of evictees had returned to Vumba on instruction from the courts, after successful legal appeals.) While the study's findings on the former issue were reasonably conclusive and optimistic, the report indicated, if somewhat obscurely, the need to resolve internal conflicts over land use and settlement patterns in the area before proceeding with more substantial investments in the project (Geckoconsult 1999).

The Buffer Zone: 'A Place where People End'

For many years, under the rubric of CAMPFIRE, first Gokwe District Council and then Gokwe North Rural District Council had given a hunting concession covering vast areas of land to a private safari hunter. Income from hunting licenses and actual trophy fees constituted a significant proportion of the council's locally generated revenue. However, this began to decline as new settlers and their cattle moved into areas previously rich in game, thus shrinking the space available for lucrative hunting. Faced with increasing financial pressure as decentralization intensified, the idea of establishing a safari lodge in Vumba represented an important alternative source of income. This was boosted by positive examples of similar ventures elsewhere in Zimbabwe and further afield in the region. However, any attempt at either sustaining or increasing the level of hunting or following the (non-consumptive) safari lodge option would necessarily imply the displacement of a number of households.

Rather than negotiate the resettlement and/or compensation of those who necessarily would become development displacees, the council focused instead on wielding its technocratic authority by emphasizing the need for a 'buffer zone' along the borders of Chizarira National Park and Chirisa Safari Area. Buffer zones are viewed in current conservationist discourse as vital to 'protecting the integrity' of the national parks (Neumann 1997) and the council has been quick to identify itself with this discourse and represent itself in terms of responsible ecological stewardship. But while this exclusive band of territory is still *de facto* part of the Communal Lands, it precludes local residents from access, control or use of the land-based resources within it, while allowing full access to wildlife resources to the safari operator. In effect, a good number of Vumba's residents were evicted from the buffer zone in 1997. Some evictees believe the safari operator persuaded the council to evict people from Vumba. This may exaggerate the white safari operator's personal powers of influence, but in other ways it astutely recognizes the alliance of interests between the council and private capital relative to the revenue-generating potential of eco-tourism.

When people in Vumba were asked what the buffer zone was or what it meant to them, many said they didn't know precisely, only that 'it is a word that assaults us'. Both the first-wave Tonga settlers and those that came later said that it had not been there when they came to Vumba, but was subsequently introduced by the council. For one person it simply meant 'no farming inside it'. For another, 'it's why our homes were burned'. For yet another it meant 'a place where people end'.

Settlers or Squatters? The Power of Naming

Parallel to its reconstruction of space, the RDC began renaming selected households settled on the edges of Vumba (especially but not only in the buffer zone) as 'squatters', in order to justify the dispossession of their land-based entitlements and rights. But as one of the affected evictee leaders noted: 'People were shown land, only to be shown it belongs to the animals. Then they had to call us squatters. How can a man be a squatter if he followed the right procedures to get land?' Wildlife use represents one of the most lucrative sources of local revenue for RDCs as a whole, and the anticipated revenue from a prospective eco-tourism venture such as the Busi safari lodge is central to the motivation of the council to evict the settlers. As noted earlier, RDCs are entitled to a management fee for administering CAMPFIRE projects, but in practice they have much wider control over the use of these funds (Murombedzi 1992). No such benefits accrue to the council from marginal subsistence farming or even from successful cotton production for the market, which engages most second-wave migrants and increasing numbers of first-wave settlers. Similar conflicts between agriculture and wildlife are emerging as a major feature of the politics of land in present-day Zimbabwe.

In its narratives of the 1997 eviction, the council played down this conflict, drawing instead on technocratic logic and legal discourses to justify its actions against the evictees. In this regard, defining the settlers as illegal squatters had the dual effect of undermining their legitimacy both in formal, legal terms (as 'civic' citizens with rights to land and livelihood), and in 'customary' terms (as 'ethnic' subjects, with socio-cultural claims to the soil). According to Zimrights, the human rights-based organization involved in defending and supporting the Vumba evictees, throughout the council's applications to the courts for the eviction order, it consistently focused on the illegality of the settlers' occupation of the territory now defined as a buffer zone. Section 12 of the Communal Lands Act states that communities having certain basic rights interfered with – including the right to life and livelihood, to shelter, to education, to health, and so on – should be consulted and agree to an offer of alternative land. Compensation should be paid for structures and improvements made, and land quality should also be taken into account. In the case of squatters, such rights would necessarily fall away.

It is somewhat ironic that the council should appeal to discourses of participation, conservation and environmental sustainability – so popular in developmentalist circles – in order to generate donor support for a 'community-managed' eco-tourism project at the very site at which the lives and livelihoods of substantial sections of the targeted community have been disregarded and destroyed.

'The Day of Burning'

In September and October 1997, Gokwe North Rural District Council, officially through the police but allegedly assisted by councillors, council staff and hired hands, violently evicted approximately one hundred and forty households from selected parts of Vumba.[14] Allegedly without much direct warning, huts and granaries were burned and some people were said to have been beaten, before lorry-loads of evictees and their scattered possessions were abandoned at the local business centre some 40 kilometres away. Many families spent up to five months there, without adequate food, shelter or clean water, resulting in far-reaching health problems and further destruction of their remaining property. Many of their livestock were either destroyed during the eviction or were lost in other ways during their absence. A few families were able to relocate temporarily within Vumba with the assistance of neighbours and friends. For most households, an entire growing season was lost.

In the meantime, an evictee committee began to organize some form of short-term emergency relief through agencies such as the Red Cross. But more significantly, through already established networks of legal and human rights support garnered during the previous years of their resistance to the council, they began applying to the courts to reverse the eviction order. Here appeals to global discourses of justice and universal human rights have played a key role. In February 1998, following protracted legal appeals and negotiations managed jointly by lawyers from Zimrights and several of the most active leaders of the evictee community, the courts ruled (partially) against the council's actions. This was mainly on technical grounds due to the incorrect issuing of the summons. Nevertheless, the evictees were ordered by the courts to return to Vumba. Undeterred, the RDC immediately began processing another set of eviction orders.

The main leader of the evictee committee has played an especially important if complicated role in the whole process. A man in his early seventies, he is extremely articulate, well-educated, politically shrewd and actively committed to resisting the injustices he believes have been perpetrated by the council against him and his fellow evictees. However, for the council he has come to symbolize a threat to their authority in Vumba. Simultaneously, he is perceived by some of the local Tonga leadership as wanting to replace them, even wanting 'to become chief'. He has also been accused by some of his fellow evictees of conducting his own brand of exclusionary practices. This became a point of intense conflict in the case of his distribution of farm inputs to fellow evictees as part of a short-term emergency support package he had initiated to assist evictees to retrieve their lost livelihoods. His list of eligible evictees was found to contain many 'errors', and many of those correctly listed received nothing.

With regard to the story of the eviction itself, I had heard the bare bones of it in Harare early in 1998. Six months later, the dry details of the first distant telling paled in comparison with the immediacy of hearing individual's narratives of what many called the 'day of burning'. While sitting beside burned homes that had been painstakingly rebuilt, or being shown the charred remains of grain beside the skeleton of a once-full granary or the blackened clothing and kitchen utensils that had not been replaced for lack of money, vivid details of the eviction and its aftermath were recounted in a disarmingly matter-of-fact way. Contrasting this were the detached, technocratic tones of RDC staff, or the self-assured political rhetoric of the council chairman when interviewed about the eviction. Despite their active involvement in the event, they used more abstract language to describe or justify it. They referred constantly to those evicted as 'squatters', and to their illegality, lawlessness, lack of respect for the local leadership, and the fact that 'the majority of these people are not indigenous'.

Insiders and Outsiders, and Scripts of Belonging

The council's choice to play the ethnicity card and make such a clear distinction between insiders and outsiders in Vumba provides them with a useful hook on which to hang their justifications for the eviction. Undoubtedly, there *are* various tensions within the area between some of the older Tonga residents – in particular some of the more powerful local leadership – and the newer mixture of Shona and Ndebele settlers (who even today are considered foreigners or *madheruka* by some). However, lines of commonality and solidarity between the different waves of settlers were also evident in Vumba, although these varied in strength between different factions as pre- and post-eviction conflicts unfolded.

In general, clusters of homesteads in Vumba are distinguished between Tongas and 'others', in part linked to the historical sequencing of migration, although there is a degree of intermarriage across ethnic divides. People from all 120 households interviewed in a baseline survey in late 1998 seemed prepared to acknowledge differences among themselves with respect to language, spiritual beliefs, ritual practices, farming methods, and so on. Tonga, Shona and Ndebele households all noted that the second-wave migrants owned and ploughed with cattle and were therefore able to cultivate larger areas more productively. By contrast, most Tonga households had previously farmed using hand-held hoes, but had now begun to adopt more 'modern' methods. For some Tonga households, however, the arrival of modernity was accompanied by what they perceived as arrogance and a challenge to existing patterns of (Tonga) authority in the area. As one of the younger kraalheads in the area commented: 'The newcomers looked down upon the local people as though they were primitive. They took themselves as highly educated. They wanted to take the prominent leadership in the area. They even wanted to take the position as kraalhead.'[15]

According to this kraalhead, there seemed to be no objection to the original allocation of land to the newcomers. It was rather that they were seen to be too independent of, and disrespectful towards, the traditional power structures. At the same time, although they were initially welcomed for acting as a human buffer against problem animals such as elephants that destroyed crops and sometimes people, their continued presence would mean denying the original, indigenous settlers the benefits of the proposed Busi river safari lodge project. In fact, the kraalhead went so far as to state quite bluntly: 'We prefer animals.' (This same man acts as a problem animal control officer for Vumba, under CAMPFIRE. As such, he receives a fee for reporting large, dangerous game in the area, which is subsequently destroyed either by the Department of National Parks and Wildlife or by a contract hunter.)

This extreme view was not widely expressed by other Tonga residents. An older kraalhead talked much more sympathetically about the evicted households and the second-wave migrants in general. For him, 'these are also my people, because I received them and gave them land to cultivate'. But he also recognized their value in protecting people and crops from destructive wildlife: 'Since we settled here from the Zambezi, elephants have been the main problem. They caused us poverty. The Shona were brought, like a fence. We are now able to grow our crops. So I really hate the council's deeds about the eviction.'[16] The proposed pegging of a game fence in the area by the council (acting simultaneously as a foot and mouth disease control fence), although hotly contested because of its implications for limiting grazing and for further evictions, may weaken this particular line of solidarity.

Among the evictee leadership there is greater wariness of and animosity towards some of their Tonga counterparts, whom they suspect of betraying them to the council. But this is tempered by the voices of ordinary households, who are less confrontational and who seem to feel more at ease with their Tonga neighbours. This is based in no small measure on common experiences of displacement, marginalization and exclusion by successive states.

Most of the recent evictees from Vumba, including Shona, Ndebele and the few Tonga who were affected, are deeply sceptical about being included as a part of Zimbabwe. Many spoke of betrayal by the state, by Mugabe, by the council. They saw the council in particular as 'spoiling development in our area'; as 'making trouble, even causing war'. But rather than expressing defeat as a result of their eviction – in spite of its devasta-ting social and material effects – they appeared instead to have gained political strength, clarity and confidence in asserting their claims to land, if not in Vumba itself then elsewhere.

An out-of-court settlement between the evictees and the RDC in 1998 initially appeared to have secured the promise of alternative land elsewhere (in the same or neighbouring wards), to resettle households that would still have to be moved to make way for the safari lodge. The basis of the agreement was that evictees would be allowed to cultivate and harvest their crops during the 1998/99 growing season, but by the end of August 1999 would move to new plots shown to them by the end of January 1999. However, by mid-1999 the agreement had fallen apart entirely, in part because the council limited its offer to only a portion of the households affected by the previous eviction, namely those whom the council had defined as legitimate claimants. This was unacceptable to the evictee leaders, who were bidding for alternative plots for *all* affected households. In addition, they were pushing for compensation for the extensive losses caused by the eviction before they would agree to move elsewhere. A stalemate ensued. But so great was the council's frustration that in November 1999 it once again attempted to evict the most troublesome of the evictee households.

Conclusion: Reshaping the Political Space for Land Claims in Zimbabwe

At an exhibition of Chiko Chazunguza's paintings in Harare in Sep-tember 1998, several of his works had explicit 'land-grabbing' themes, with titles such as 'Come Let's Go Grab and Self-Settlement'. His ironic use of golf-flags to represent literal 'stakes' in the land by the landless evoked some of the complex class, race and spatial underpinnings of Zimbabwe's ongoing land disparities and struggles. His work reiterated how much the politics of land and land claiming is embedded in everyday images and discourses, in both rural and urban settings, while foreshadowing the massive land invasions of large-scale white commercial farms that followed the constitutional referendum in February 2000. Land continues to be central to political, economic, social and cultural relations at every level in Zimbabwe. Today it determines the country's potential for either economic growth and political stability or spiralling decline and deepening divides.

Repeatedly since independence, the state has initiated policies and programmes to address issues of land reform and redistribution, often coinciding transparently with the waxing and waning political credibility of the ruling party. However, slow rates of resettlement, inconsistencies and lack of transparency in settler selection and allocation practices, contradictory political statements, and generally poor public feedback had previously undermined confidence among a range of land stakeholders. Towards the end of the 1990s attempts were being made to reverse this trend, especially in bureaucratic circles. A new policy drive towards reform and resettlement was initiated in 1997, with a three-pronged focus on productivity, equity and poverty reduction and a greater emphasis on 'stakeholder participation'.

By early 2000 little progress had been made on implementing the new, widely promoted Land Reform and Resettlement Programme outlined in 1998. Despite their own role in producing delays and distortions within this process, President Mugabe and senior politicians in the ruling party would subsequently capitalize on such delays to launch yet another election campaign that simultaneously put land reform at centre stage and masked their own complicity in its failure. Yet although the tactics used by the ruling party to promote or even orchestrate the land invasions after February 2000 were crude, violent and clearly unlawful, one cannot ignore the fact that there had been a steady growth in spontaneous migrations and informal land invasions occurring within and across all land tenure categories during the previous few years.

At the same time, reflecting some of its own internal pressures relating to structural reforms, new expressions of land bidding by the state itself have been under way for some time. One of the consequences of this has been an increase in both the extent and violence of forced removals of so-called squatters from land in which the state has had a particular interest, as the Vumba case has demonstrated. Such involvement of the state in land-claiming disputes has been particularly acute in the more marginal Communal Lands, where potential returns from wildlife have become a critical and deeply contested source of revenue for competing stakeholders, and especially for Rural District Councils in alliance with other interested parties. This mirrors related trends in the commercial farming sector (Moyo 2000).

This adds a new twist to the political space in which the most marginalized, land-poor farmers can make bids for land in order to establish or improve their livelihood possibilities. On the one hand, we have witnessed an opening up of opportunities for the land hungry, partly through new land policy reforms that ostensibly give weight to poverty reduction, partly through Mugabe's intensified political support, and partly through the discursive strategies and organizing practices of independent land-poor activists themselves. On the other hand, the elected rural local authorities, which should in principle represent and serve the interests of all their rural constituents including the most economically and socially marginalized, are in fact now beginning to compete with some of them for land-based resources.

However, what I have tried to do in this chapter in tracing both historical and contemporary manifestations of land displacements and claims in Zimbabwe through the optic of discursive practices is to shift the perspective from which land is viewed. My intention has been to look at land less as a static or finite 'political good' struggled over by winners and losers, and more as fluid currency in deeper processes of space-, place- and state-making. These are processes through which, as Moore (1998: 351) notes, 'social spaces are formed, reproduced and reworked through situated cultural practices'; spaces 'saturated with power relations' (ibid.) in which difference and otherness are produced (Harvey 1996). They are processes linked not only to material struggles, but also to struggles over authority, identity, memory, mobility and belonging. The complexities that are revealed through such an approach are extremely difficult to unravel, let alone plan and legislate for. Yet it seems imperative that we begin this task if current and future land reform policies and programmes are to be anything more for the land-poor than hollow words in abstract space.

Notes

1. See Robins' (1998) discussion of how the 'Great Divide' between tradition and modernity, artificial yet instrumental, has functioned within development discourses in general and in post-independence Zimbabwe in particular, to both support and challenge strategies of accumulation by different social actors. Yet this is clearly not only a strategy of the state.

2. See *The Herald*, 20 February 1997 and 17 October 1997.

3. 'Land Reform and Resettlement Programme Phase II: a policy framework', Government of Zimbabwe, Draft, July 1998.

4. CAMPFIRE (Communal Areas Management Programme for Indigenous Resources) is a national programme that supports the 'responsible community management' of natural resources – especially but not only wildlife – and so entitles local communities to derive income from the proceeds of wildlife-based and other similar activities. The local council, as the local conservation authority, is empowered to act as broker and part-beneficiary for CAMPFIRE activities.

5. Literature on CAMPFIRE includes Alexander and McGregor 2000; Child 1995; Derman 1995; Dzingirai and Madzudzo 1999; Murombedzi 1992.

6. *The Herald*, 17 November 1998.

7. The Rural Councils were significantly better resourced and had greater autonomy in general than the District Councils. Gokwe was an exception in having no large-scale commercial farming areas, hence there was no Rural Council with which the former District Council had to amalgamate. The district was split in two instead, resulting in two new, separate Rural District Councils, Gokwe North and Gokwe South.

8. This redefinition of RDC authority over land, together with the pressure on councils to generate revenue, has precipitated serious conflicts over land and natural resources in numerous Communal Lands across Zimbabwe.

9. My own research in Vumba confirms that insufficient land and water for cultivation and decreasing soil fertility were primary 'push' factors for those migrating to the area over the past decade. Stories of the availability of land for settlement from both government officials and informal sources were a strong pull factor.

10. This paraphrases Basso 1984, quoted in Harvey 1996: 265.

11. 'Insider' here refers to an actual resident of Vumba. However, an insider–outsider discourse also operates within Vumba, among its residents, linked to the historical sequencing, cultural composition and socio-economic differentiation of the two major waves of in-migration. See also the earlier discussion with reference to Mamdani 1998.

12. Songs sung by the Tonga grandmothers in Vumba recall their eviction 'from the place where we used to eat watermelons, meat, fish and many delicious foods' (translated by K. Mudenda, Vumba, October 1998).

13. Interview conducted in Vumba, 25 October 1998.

14. A precise figure for the number of households evicted has been impossible to obtain. The council gives figures ranging from 71 to 78. Leaders of the evictees initially talked of 200 but later reduced the number to 140. Although there are logistical reasons for such discrepancies, they are also obviously linked to competing interpretations and representations of the scale of injustice and possible future claims for compensation.

15. Interview, Vumba, 27 October, 1998.

16. Interview, Vumba, 26 October 1998.

Bibliography

Alexander, J. (1995) 'Things fall apart, the centre can hold: processes of post-war political change in Zimbabwe's rural areas', in T. Bhebhe and T. Ranger (eds), *Society in Zimbabwe's Liberation War, Vol. 2*, Harare: University of Zimbabwe Publications.

Alexander, J. and J. McGregor (2000) 'Wildlife and politics: CAMPFIRE in Zimbabwe', *Development and Change*, 31, 3: 605–27.

Basso, K. (1984) '"Stalking with stories": names, places, and moral narratives among the Western Apache', *Proceedings of the American Ethnological Society 1983*, Washington, DC: American Ethnological Society.

Cheater, A. (1990) 'The ideology of "communal" land tenure in Zimbabwe: mythogenesis enacted?', *Africa*, 60, 2: 188–206.

Child, G. (1995) *Wildlife and People: the Zimbabwean Success. How the Conflict between Animals and People became Progress for Both*, Harare and New York: Wisdom Foundation.

Cousins, B. (1993) 'Debating communal tenure in Zimbabwe', *Journal of Contemporary African Studies*, 12, 1: 29–39.

Cousins, B., D. Weiner and N. Amin (1992) 'Social differentiation in the communal lands of Zimbabwe', *Review of African Political Economy*, 53: 5–24

Cumming, D. H. M. and T. J. P. Lynam (1997) *Landuse Changes, Wildlife Conservation and Utilisation, and Sustainability of Agro-ecosystems in the Zambezi Valley. WWF Final Technical Report, Vol.1*, August, prepared for the European Commission, Harare.

Derman, W. (1995) 'Environmental NGOs, dispossession, and the state: the ideology and praxis of African nature and development', *Human Ecology*, 23, 2: 199–227.

Doré, D. (1993) 'Land tenure and the economics of rural transformation. A study of strategies to relieve land pressure and poverty in the communal areas of Zimbabwe', Ph.D. thesis, Oxford: Linacre College, University of Oxford.

Dzingirai, V. and E. Madzudzo (1999) 'Big men and CAMPFIRE: a comparative study of the role of external actors in conflicts over local resources', *Zambezia*, XXVI, i: 77–92.

Geckoconsult (1999) *The Gokwe North Tourism Project Feasibility Study: Report on the Social and Institutional Acceptability of the Project*, Harare: WWF.

Goebel, A. (1999) '"Here it is our land, the two of us": women, men and land in a Zimbabwean resettlement area', *Journal of Contemporary African Studies*, 17, 1: 75–96.

Harvey, D. (1996) *Justice, Nature and the Geography of Difference*, Oxford: Blackwell.

Holleman, J. F. (1969) *Chief, Council and Commissioner: Some Problems of Government in Rhodesia*, Assen: Royal VanGorcum and London: Oxford University Press.

Lan, D. (1985) *Guns and Rain: Guerrillas and Spirit Mediums in Zimbabwe*, Berkeley: University of California Press.

McGregor, J. (1995) 'Conservation, control and ecological change: the politics and ecology of colonial conservation in Shurugwi, Zimbabwe', *Environment and History*, 1, 3: 257–80.

Mamdani, M. (1996) *Citizen and Subject: Contemporary Africa and the Legacy of Late Colonialism*, Princeton, NJ: Princeton University Press.

Mamdani, M. (1998) *When Does a Settler Become a Native? Reflections on the Colonial Roots of Citizenship in Equatorial and South Africa*, inaugural lecture as A. C. Jordan Professor of African Studies, University of Cape Town, 13 May.

Moore, D. S. (1998) 'Subaltern struggles and the politics of place: remapping resistance in Zimbabwe's eastern highlands', *Cultural Anthropology*, 13, 3: 344–81.

Moyo, S. (1999) *Land and Democracy in Zimbabwe*, Monograph Series No. 7, Harare: SAPES Books.

— (2000) *Land Reform Under Structural Adjustment in Zimbabwe: Land Use Change in the Mashonaland Provinces*, Uppsala: Nordiska Afrikainstitutet.

Munro, W. (1995) 'Building the post-colonial state: villagization and resource management in Zimbabwe', *Politics and Society*, 23, 1: 107–40.

Murombedzi, J. (1992) *Decentralization or recentralization? Implementing CAMPFIRE in the Omay Communal Lands*, CASS Working Paper no. 2, Harare.

Myers, G. A. (1996) 'Naming and placing the other: power and the urban landscape in Zanzibar', *Tijdschrift voor Economische en Sociale Geografie/Journal of Economic and Social Geography*, 87, 3: 237–46.

Neumann, R. P. (1997). 'Primitive ideas: protected area buffer zones and the politics of land in Africa', *Development and Change*, 28: 559:82.

Palmer, R. (1977) *Land and Racial Discrimination in Rhodesia*, London: Heinemann.

Phimister, I. (1986) 'Discourse and the discipline of historical context: conservationism and ideas about development in Southern Rhodesia 1930-1950', *Journal of Southern African Studies*, 12, 2.

Ranger, T. O. (1999) *Voices from the Rocks: Nature, Culture and History in the Matopos Hills of Zimbabwe*, Harare: Baobab; Oxford: James Currey; Bloomington: Indiana University Press.

Robins, S. (1998) 'Breaking out of the straitjacket of tradition: the politics and rhetoric of "development" in Zimbabwe', *World Development*, 26, 9: 1677–94.

Spierenburg, M. (1995) *The Role of the Mhondoro Cult in the Struggle for Control Over Land in Dande (North Zimbabwe): Social Commentaries and the Influence of Adherents*, Harare: University of Zimbabwe, CASS Occasional Papers NRM Series.

Worby, E. (1992) 'Remaking labour, reshaping identity: cotton, commoditization and the culture of modernity in northwestern Zimbabwe', Ph.D. thesis, McGill University, Canada.

— (1994) 'Maps, names and ethnic games: the epistemology and iconography of colonial power in northwestern Zimbabwe', *Journal of Southern African Studies*, 20, 3: 371–92.

7

The Limitations of Political Space in Burkina Faso: Local Organizations, Decentralization and Poverty Reduction

Lars Engberg-Pedersen

> Si tu ne fais pas de la politique, la politique va te faire.[1]
> *Mossi saying*

Local organizations and decentralization are two phenomena that have attracted considerable attention in recent years. They are both seen as important measures in adapting national politics and developments to the specific conditions of a locality. They are supposed to facilitate the communication of local knowledge and interests to a wider forum, and above all, they are believed to be prerequisites for economic and political development.

The aim of this chapter is to address the constraints and opportunities provided by national and sub-national politics and state administration through the impact these have on the actions and orientations of local organizations. These constraints and opportunities create a 'political space' that delimits the scope of activities that local organizations can undertake. Similarly, the availability of financial resources, the development discourse and the cultural characteristics of the locality influence the kind of activities that local organizations consider.

Political space is created in the interaction between the state and social actors of various kinds. It denotes the limits to conceivable and legitimate political discourses and activities, and it describes some basic issues regarding political processes, such as political identity, the role of the state, the organization of politics, and so on. As mentioned in the introduction to this volume, the state should not be conceived as a monolithic body with coherent and uniform policies. Nevertheless, it does play a major role in Burkina Faso as a uniform social actor because of its dominant position in organizing the country's economic development and in determining the legality of political processes.

In the present context political space will be analysed with respect to poor people and poverty reduction. The argument is that the poor themselves, and local organizations on their behalf, have very few possibilities to improve their conditions through political action. Local organizations can provide social services and stimulate production, but the scope for influencing state actions, political decisions or policy-making is severely restrained. Given the contemporary process of democratization and decentralization, this may seem surprising. Why is political space limited at a time when democracy and decentralization have been major notions in development discourse, when national and local elections are being carried out, and when any politician seeking support needs to emphasize popular participation and poverty reduction? Why is no competition between political ideologies, ideas and development perspectives emerging? Why are discussions of social inequalities, political rights for the poor and processes of marginalization almost non-existent?

The aim of this chapter is therefore to discuss these questions by clarifying the nature of political space in Yatenga province in Burkina Faso. The discussion begins with a section on recent political developments and the process of decentralization in Burkina Faso. This should provide an idea of the nature and extent of the democratization taking place. Second, I address the character of local organizations, their activities and their involvement in political affairs in Yatenga. In this context 'local organizations' means associations (*groupements*) and NGOs. Associations are characterized by their undertaking activities that are supposed to benefit their members. They consist typically of peasants and sometimes of herdsmen and artisans. NGOs are supposed to serve a particular target group to whom they are, however, seldom accountable, and they are sometimes staffed by graduates and other trained personnel. The distinction between associations and NGOs is often quite blurred, but the important factor is how the organization relates to poor people. Numerous other organizations exist in Yatenga, such as projects, field administrations, regional societies and unions, but the focus is directed towards the NGOs, in particular those based in Yatenga.

Third, political space and the organization of political life in Yatenga are discussed. The political as well as social histories of the province go some way in providing an understanding of the nature of political space, which is nevertheless also strongly related to politics at the national level. So far, the process of decentralization has had only a minor influence on political processes in the province.

Political Change and Decentralization

Since independence in 1960, civilian and military governments have succeeded one another in Burkina Faso, but generally without much bloodshed. The relatively calm atmosphere in which national politics has taken place is exemplified by General Lamizana, who took power in 1966 and, after four years of civilian rule, again in 1974, only to win fairly democratic elections for president in 1978. Apart from the military and a few prominent politicians, the two main social actors in bringing about changes of government have been the unions and the students at the university in Ouagadougou. More often acting in response to deteriorating living conditions than from ideological convictions, they have sometimes been able to force the government of the time to resign. Other social actors, such as peasants and the opposition parties, have seldom influenced the course of events to any noticeable degree.[2]

After two military coups of a transitional nature in 1980 and 1982, a quite extraordinary government came to power in 1983. Captain Thomas Sankara, the leader of this military government, promulgated an ideology of revolution and self-sufficiency, and revolutionary defence committees and popular tribunals were created all over the country. An investment programme for rural development, socio-economic infrastructure and human resources was launched,[3] and austerity measures to reduce state budget deficits were introduced, as well as a campaign against corruption and laziness among civil servants (Kafandi 1990: 125–6; Savonnet-Guyot 1986: 179–91; Speirs 1991: 100–1). A kind of self-imposed economic adjustment was initiated (Savadogo and Wetta 1992), which goes some way towards explaining why no structural adjustment agreement was signed with the World Bank until 1991. However, Sankara challenged most of the social groups that had hitherto profited from national politics. Employment in the public sector was cut down; salaries were reduced; agricultural producer prices were increased leading to a rise in food prices in the towns; and trade unions, political parties and customary authorities were marginalized (Speirs 1991: 101–3). Even the rural population, whom Sankara had favoured through the price policies, were perplexed and upset by his quite unambiguous claim that all land was the property of the state (Otayek et al. 1996). Officially, the claim is still in force, although it is seldom implemented because of opposition from the rural population.

Sankara's assassination in 1987 ended this period of radical change from above. Captain Blaise Compaoré took over and adopted a softer line towards trade unions and customary authorities, and food prices in the towns were lowered (Speirs 1991: 105). Following internal and external pressure, a change to civilian rule and a multi-party system was prepared. Although

Compaoré indicated his intention as one of introducing democracy as early as 1987, the process did not gather speed until his New Year's speech of 31 December 1989. During 1990 the revolutionary movement, the Front national, held a major congress on the matter, a commission produced a draft version of a constitution, and a national conference agreed to a slightly revised version of the constitution (Kiemde 1996; Sawadogo 1996). The ground was prepared for three elections during 1991–92 when a new constitution was adopted, Compaoré elected president, and a national assembly set up.

How should one explain this fairly dramatic change in the organization of the political regime? External reasons are easy to discern, such as the wave of transitions to democracy in Africa (see Bratton and Walle 1994); the increased concern among donors concerning human rights, popular participation and good governance; and the breakdown of development visions other than liberal democracy and capitalism. However, the internal factors are no less interesting. Sankara had challenged the most powerful social groups, which normally profit from good relations with the government. In order to improve relations and get the political regime back in working order Compaoré had to accept some sort of popular influence. Also, he did not benefit from Sankara's general popularity for getting things done and for reducing corruption and idleness. Moreover, the Burkinabé were not used to indefinite military rule. Apart from during Sankara's regime, the history of political rule in Burkina Faso is one of civilian governments rectified by military intervention with the explicit intention of returning to civilian rule eventually.

Nevertheless, the revolution of 1983–87 had been so pervasive that an immediate transition to democracy was difficult to imagine. The revolutionary project did not tolerate competing political visions or multiple agents interacting: 'son achèvement supposait l'inscription autoritaire de la société dans la sphère de l'État et le monopole de la parole politique légitime' (Otayek et al. 1996: 10). Thus the transition to liberal democracy in 1991–92 took place against the background of an authoritarian regime with an ideology clearly emphasizing the role of the state as the leading agent in the development process. And it took place because the subsequent military government had very little legitimacy to build upon.

Public enthusiasm for the democratization process has, however, been limited. For instance, Compaoré had no opponents at the presidential election, and only 25 per cent of the electorate went to the polls. Furthermore, Compaoré's political party (Organization pour la Démocratie Populaire–Mouvement du Travail, ODP–MT, later renamed Congrès pour la Démocratie et le Progrès, CDP), won 78 out of 107 seats in the National Assembly in 1992 (on a turnout of 35 per cent), and 101 out of an increased number of 111 seats at the elections of May 1997 (turnout 44 per cent), meaning that debate was again removed from the party political arena. The unions, the students and an increasingly critical press seem to constitute the only opposition.

Although the administrative division of the country has changed repeatedly since independence, decentralization and the devolution of authority to locally elected bodies have seldom been high on the agenda. While specific reforms have been undertaken at least four times (Jacob and Margot 1992: 18), the number of administrative units has tended to increase between the reforms. In 1974, an ordinance established ten regions and 44 districts, but the latter figure rapidly increased to 76 in 1979 and 107 in 1982 (Cabanis and Martin 1987: 25). However, devolution has been resisted by bureaucrats in the centralized state, a lack of financial resources and a lack of educated personnel (ibid.: 24–7).

Prior to 1974, there had been 83 rural local governments, which were financially autonomous and elected through direct and universal suffrage (ibid.: 28–9). Furthermore, their budgets were financed primarily from the collection of local taxes and were considerably larger than the budgets of present-day administrative structures covering a similar geographical area. These rural local governments nevertheless ran into political and administrative trouble and were abolished in 1974 (Jacob and Margot 1992: 19).

The present administrative division was created in 1983–85 and confirmed in 1989 and 1993 (GOB 1989b, 1993). It originally consisted of 30 provinces, some 300 departments, at least 33 communes divided into sectors and more than 7,500 villages, in 1996 15 additional provinces and a similar number of communes in the provincial capitals were created (H. S. 1996). Some new departments were also established during the 1990s. In the rural areas the department, headed by a prefect and comprising at least five villages and 10,000 people, is generally the administrative level closest to the population. In addition, a person responsible for administrative affairs is supposed to be elected in every village (GOB 1993).

State administration is deconcentrated in two ways. Each line ministry has field administrations at various levels. Hauts Commissaires and prefects belonging to the Ministry of Home Affairs (Ministère de l'Administration Territoriale et de la Sécurité) are supposed to coordinate and monitor state interventions as well as all other development activities in the provinces and departments respectively. According to the legal texts, the Hauts Commissaires and the prefects enjoy substantial powers, but they are often bypassed by the technical ministries, not the least in the case of donor-financed projects. They dispose of too few resources in order to be in charge of and coordinate local development (Jacob and Margot 1992: 59–60). All in all, the state has come fairly close to the people administratively speaking, but it has certainly stayed very centralized and distant with respect to attitude and the provision of services.

According to the constitution adopted in 1991, the provinces and the communes are regarded as local government entities, whereas the departments, communal sectors and villages are deconcentrated units. In reality, however, the provinces have not functioned as local governments, since no elections have been held for the provincial councils. On the other hand, in 1995 councils were elected in 33 communes, leaving decentralization an urban phenomenon. In 1993 a Commission Nationale de la Décentralisation (CND) attached to the Premier Ministère was established and had as its primary task the preparation of legislation for decentralization. Its proposals were adopted by the National Assembly in 1998, the major points being to establish rural communes in the departmental capitals with elected councils and mayors, to specify the distribution of competences between decentralized and deconcentrated units, to clarify the financial basis of the provinces and communes, and to indicate a timetable for the implementation of the decisions. The establishment of elected councils at the provincial level is reiterated, and elections at this level are required within five years from the adoption of the set of laws (GOB 1998a, 1998b, 1998c, 1998d).

Prior to the presentation of the laws, the CND had worked on extending decentralization to the countryside. The suggestion was to create Collectivités Locales de Développement (CLD) encompassing five to fifteen villages according to the preferences of the villagers themselves, not least as to whether they should agree to invest money and effort in developing socio-economic infrastructure in their area. These units were to lie within existing departmental borders and were not to be imposed 'from above'. Thus people could choose not to create a CLD, and the sustainabililty of those created should rest with the villagers themselves (see GOB n.d.; Laurent 1995).

However, these ideas about rural decentralization were abandoned after strong criticism; instead, the suggestion concerning rural communes was put into the set of laws that are supposed to guide decentralization. Apart from the somewhat distanced provincial level, there are currently no suggestions as to how rural areas outside departmental capitals are to benefit from the decentralization. There is seemingly very strong hesitation in political and administrative quarters about involving the rural population more strongly in political processes.

Two reasons for this situation might be suggested. First, the Burkinabé state is very centralized, and most civil servants and political leaders consider it to be the agent that is supposed to control and direct national development. Thus the idea of devolving important decision-making powers to illiterate peasants is not very appealing and may even be considered irresponsible by some. Decentralization in urban areas is probably less frightening, since the level of education and the political culture there are much more in agreement with those of the ruling elite.

Second, the democratic system of elections has proved to be quite useful for this elite, since it provides ample support and unquestionable legitimacy, not least internationally. An evolution of rural decentralization along the lines suggested by the CND might endanger the ruling elite's control of politics throughout the country, generating 'pockets of political protest'.

It is tempting to draw a parallel with Mahmood Mamdani's discussion of decentralized despotism and the legacies of late colonialism (Mamdani 1996). He argues that the bifurcated colonial state has not been dismantled thoroughly in contemporary Africa. The difference between direct and indirect rule in late colonialism was not just a difference between modes of intervention – it was also a difference with respect to the understanding of the societies in which the interventions were carried out. Direct rule was applied in urban areas and had the purpose of excluding the indigenous peoples from civil society and civic rights, whereas indirect rule was enforced in rural areas and 'was about incorporating natives into a state-enforced customary order' (ibid.: 18). This customary order was, moreover, understood as collective, not individual, and as traditional, not based on personal rights. With independence, deracialization tore down urban exclusion from civil society, but only under a few radical regimes was an attempt made to detribalize rural customary authorities too.

Sankara's regime was one of these radical attempts to turn rural power structures upside down, but it was clearly too short-lived to bring about substantial change. When subsequently Compaoré needed to ensure a social basis for his government, he could hardly go on alienating customary authorities. Although these have not regained their erstwhile strength, rural areas are obviously marked by the colonially enforced customary order, which entailed the fusion 'in a single person [of] all moments of power: judicial, legislative, executive, and administrative' (ibid.: 23). As a result, rural political life has not been democratized, and the lack of decentralization in rural areas tends to reinforce the bifurcation of the state.

Finally, an important characteristic of the process of decentralization in Burkina Faso should be mentioned, namely that the elections of municipal council members take place on a partisan basis. Only political parties can run for election, which has the distinct disadvantage that one has to be involved in 'politics' to become a member of local government. Independent candidates and local lists with a particular affiliation to the locality are not allowed. This has also the consequence that local politics is strongly related to national political processes, and that local elections form part of national partisan struggles rather than being influenced by concerns for local development.

Local Organizations in Yatenga

Yatenga[4] is a relatively densely populated province with on average 50 persons per km[2] outside the provincial capital, Ouahigouya, which has some 50,000 inhabitants.[5] The population today mainly consists of Mossi, but a few Peulh are scattered around the province. Migration to the two large cities in Burkina Faso, Ouagadougou and Bobo-Dioulasso, and to Côte d'Ivoire and Ghana is a particular important feature of Yatenga. It is said, although it is probably an exaggeration, that one-third of the Burkinabé in Côte d'Ivoire come from Yatenga, which has no more than one-fifteenth (667,000) of the country's population. Rainfall in Yatenga averages some 500–600 mm and has been declining for a number of years. The number of rainy days have also declined, making the timing of the rain crucial (Atampugre 1993: 11–12; Dugué 1990). Land degradation is said to be a significant problem in Yatenga. It is difficult to document, but people talk about the previous existence of forests where today one can hardly see a shrub (Atampugre 1993). Degradation is primarily ascribed to declining precipitation, to increasing numbers of people and animals, and to inappropriate use of natural resources (GOB 1989a; Wardman and Salas 1991). On the whole, the widely shared impression of Yatenga is one of a resource-poor, heavily populated province with little agricultural potential.

The province has a large number of organizations compared to the rest of the country. According to an inventory made by the Direction Régionale de l'Economie et du Plan in 1997, some 26 NGOs are working in Yatenga. One source estimates that, in 1992, the number of NGOs in Burkina Faso reached 166, of which 59 were national NGOs (Piveteau 1996: 186). Based on these figures and a plausible assumption that the number of NGOs did not change much between 1992 and 1997, the 'density' of NGOs in relation to the size of the population is more than twice as large in Yatenga as in the country in general. Similar figures do not exist with respect to associations, but a reasonable suggestion would be that the proportion of associations in Yatenga compared to the rest of the country resembles or surpasses that of NGOs. Moreover, it should be mentioned that the largest NGO in Burkina Faso, FUGN (Fédération des Unions des Groupements Naam), a federation of village associations with important international connections, is based in Ouahigouya.

The following information is based on a questionnaire survey of 28 local organizations and interviews with leading members of twelve organizations, three of which were not covered by the initial survey.[6] The twelve organizations are all Burkinabé NGOs with their headquarters or an important branch in Ouahigouya. I will start by describing the organizational landscape, including activities and resources, and then enter into a discussion of the relationship between the NGOs and political life. It should be mentioned from the outset that the distinction between the various types of local organization is much more blurred than the categorizations indicate. For instance, NGOs do not always work primarily for the benefit of their target groups – their main purpose may be to provide employment opportunities for their founders. Thus the distinction between an NGO and an association is often quite fluid. The term NGO is also somewhat misleading, since it is generally used to denote organizations such as Oxfam and BRAC, which can in no way be compared with the organizations discussed here. In Burkina Faso most of the NGOs I shall be describing are called Associations, and they are much less 'professional' than the above-mentioned NGOs. Below, I will return to a discussion of some characteristics of Burkinabè NGOs.

The 28 organizations and their main activities are listed in Table 7.1. The distinction between the various fields of activity is not absolute. For example, instruction in agricultural techniques covers more fields. Soil conservation, sheep- and goat-breeding and vegetable gardening are the main activities with respect to agriculture. Social action covers especially activities in support of women, but some organizations also work with orphans and disabled people. It should be noted that all the organizations interviewed are located in Ouahigouya. Thus the activities of the associations in particular are not representative of similar organizations in the rural areas.

It can be concluded from the table that agriculture is by far the primary

TABLE 7.1 Local organizations and their major fields of activity

	Associations	NGOs	Total
Number of organizations	15	13	28
Agriculture, animal husbandry, etc.	14	8	22
Education	0	7	7
Health	1	3	4
Social action	3	6	9
Drinking water	0	2	2
Infrastructure	0	0	0
Petty production	2	1	3
Commerce	3	2	5

field of activity. The proportion of associations working with agriculture is astonishing, considering that they are based in an urban area. One may speculate that this is due to some sort of risk-aversion strategy, whereby town dwellers seek to have access to agricultural production in order to supplement their urban activities. Only a minority of the associations are involved in any other activities. This may reflect the fact that people do not value this kind of activity or that they expect the state to take charge of it (cf. Piveteau 1996: 191). Both explanations are probably relevant, but the strong orientation towards income-earning activities indicates where people are prepared to invest their energies.

In addition to agriculture, education and social action are also important fields of action for the NGOs. It is surprising that they are not very concerned about health and drinking water, which are generally areas of highly valued social services. Again, it may be that the state is expected to take charge of these fields of action, but the need for capital investment might also prevent some NGOs from undertaking this kind of work. To some extent the figures hide the fact that some NGOs are little more than well-organized associations, whereas others control significant resources, as is evident from Table 7.2.

Human, material and financial resources are not evenly distributed among the different organizations. It is no wonder that the level of education of the staff or the leading members is relatively low in associations and higher in NGOs. However, it is interesting to note that 93 per cent and 60 per cent of associations have leading members with, respectively,

TABLE 7.2 Local organizations and their resources

	Associations	NGOs	Total
Number of organizations	15	13	28
Including graduates	1	5	6
Including persons with ten years in school	9	13	22
Including persons with six years in school	14	13	27
Having motorized transport	3	8	11
Having computer or photocopying machine	0	3	3
Control of more than 5 million CFA*	1	7	8
Control of more than 2½ million CFA*	8	9	17
Receiving assistance from donors	15	11	26

Note: * The financial resources are used for investments, services, salaries and administrative expenditure. CFA: Communauté Financière d'Afrique, the currency used in 'French' West Africa.

at least six or ten years of schooling. Compared with adult illiteracy rates of 91 per cent for women and 71 per cent for men in 1995 in Burkina Faso (see World Bank 1997), this indicates that the 'organizational game' is played mainly by the minority of people who have received a formal education and who speak French.

Most NGOs are in great need of transport and office equipment. Without donor assistance, they cannot come to possess cars, motor cycles, computers or photocopying machines. Thus the material evidence of financial support and relations to donors is quite evident and classifies NGOs. None of the associations has office equipment, which probably troubles them less than the lack of transport.

It is also noteworthy that all associations receive financial assistance. One may speculate whether they would exist had it not been for that support. The fact that quite a number of them control resources that are significant in a Burkinabè context is related to the presence of an EU project seeking to provide income opportunities for the young people of the area in order to prevent out-migration. That all associations receive grants from donors is all the more noteworthy considering that some NGOs do not. Although associations live and die according to the dynamics of the group and one should be careful not to over-interpret the recent creation of the associations surveyed, there is little doubt that the availability of EU funds contributes to explaining the existence of these organizations. Conversely, the existence of NGOs having no financial support indicates that donors are not always easily accessible and that some NGOs compete more successfully than others in the market for development assistance. Furthermore, it is quite clear that few funds for organizational activities are available in the province, as all resources for investment originate outside the province and, to a large extent, outside the country. All in all, these local organizations are heavily dependent on donors.

Turning more explicitly to the NGOs in Yatenga, they seem to be fairly vague with respect to defining target groups for their activities. Three of the 13 NGOs surveyed mention the poor or marginalized groups, and two others work specifically with the handicapped and orphans. The remaining eight NGOs identify the rural population, women and village associations as their target groups. Some NGOs have close relations with a particular area, and they function primarily as representatives of this area in the provincial capital, looking for resources to channel back into their homeland. No organization presented even an embryonic analysis of poverty, inequality and the social conditions for marginalization. The only widely recognized acknowledgement of inequality concerns women, whom many NGOs target, at least at a rhetorical level. Improving the conditions of women seems to be a discursive necessity if an NGO wants to present itself as serious and obtain access to funds. Indeed, bringing up poverty is often dismissed with the reply that everybody is poor, which can be related to the further observation that the notion of poverty is relatively absent from general discussions of development in Burkina Faso.

The lack of target groups and of an understanding of the situation of poverty is one reason explaining that none of the NGOs acts as a mouth-piece or a pressure group on behalf of the marginalized parts of the society. There is very little acknowledgement of, or sympathy for, the idea of taking issues to politicians or to the municipality in order to put pressure on them to improve the conditions of particular groups. Even NGOs with clearly defined target groups in Ouahigouya (for example, orphans and the disabled) concentrate on supporting these groups directly without involving the political system. They do not perceive themselves as having a role in political discussions concerning the conditions of their target groups, and they tend to focus on solving problems rather than on preventing their emergence.

Leaders of some NGOs state clearly that they try to avoid the politicians as much as possible: 'Nous ne nous adressons jamais aux hommes polit-iques.' They prefer to maintain a distinction between development and politics. NGOs and associations are concerned to create development through activities with the population, whereas politicians are involved in politics which, according to the NGO leaders interviewed, has nothing to do with development. The distinction is, of course, impossible to uphold in reality, but it is a discursive fact in the sense that many NGO leaders believe in and prefer a separation between their work and the political sphere. They shy away from politics because this domain is understood as a scene of hegemonic dialogue and almost unrestrained power struggle. 'La politique' is perceived to have very little to do with social progress or different development visions.

NGO leaders offer two explanations for this reluctance to become involved in politics. First, leaders would be compromised in the view of their target groups and members if they addressed politicians either to obtain financial support or to influence policies. Those opposed to the ruling party would start to mistrust leaders associating with the politicians in power. The rift between the ruling party and the opposition is seemingly so great that any interaction with one of them immediately places a person in a suspicious light in the view of others. It is impossible to stay neutral in this conflict, as you are seen as being in opposition if you are not explicitly in favour. Any interaction with politicians will stress this, and it is therefore perceived to be a risky business by the leaders.

Second, NGO leaders fear being exploited or harassed by politicians, and they do not trust them. If an NGO turns to the ruling party, is promised support for the construction of a school, for instance, and eventually nothing materializes, the target groups and associations expecting the school are likely to turn their back on the NGO and to argue that it is the leaders who have profited from the affair. Leaders also fear that politicians will take the credit for their work if they maintain close relations with the political world. Finally, the funds available at the municipality are regarded as politicized by some, though not by everybody, meaning that in order to access such resources one must subscribe to the ruling party. In short, NGO leaders are nervous of becoming implicated in political struggles by interacting with politicians, in case this distances them from members and target groups.

Nevertheless, some NGOs are strongly involved in politics. NGOs are sometimes created by a dynamic and outstanding individual who is already a well-known politician or who has entered political life on the basis of being an NGO leader. In the former case, the politician profits from having an independent group of followers, which is crucial in Burkinabè political life, but access to resources is also a reason for creating an NGO. As one observer puts it: 'Tout le monde sait que les bailleurs de fonds s'adressent aux associations.' In the latter case, an NGO leader may wish to increase his (or her) influence and to obtain contacts, since these are very important in securing funds. NGO leaders repeatedly said that the way to get activities financed is to do a good job and have good contacts. It is not very important which side you belong to politically, but being in politics will increase the number of relationships. For instance, a couple of NGOs have profited from the twinning arrangements between Ouahigouya and a number of French towns. These arrangements are conducted by politicians, and, by associating with them, some NGOs have established contacts with French NGOs. This indicates that it is more important to associate with the ruling party, since the opposition has markedly fewer opportunities for facilitating such contacts. However, once the contact is established, it is important to appear to be 'outside' political life, since donors like effectiveness and dislike politics.

As indicated by the Mossi saying introducing the chapter, those NGOs that seek to steer clear of politics are to varying degrees involved in it. Even though an NGO officially claims to be apolitical, its leaders cannot be so. In the relatively limited environment of Yatenga, the political inclinations of the leaders are known to most people, and adversaries tend to infer that the political sympathies of the leaders are shared by members and target groups of the NGO. This leads to interesting organizational strategies such as having leaders from both sides and sending people known to support the ruling party to contact civil servants whenever the organization has to deal with the public administration.

NGOs belonging to the opposition tend to feel that it is very difficult to interact with the public administration. Whenever they attempt to apply for funds, ask for an authorization or use official channels to contact a donor, they claim that the administration often blocks or delays their demands. 'Notre administration est pourrie,' as one leader expressed it. One NGO, which sought to disseminate a particular agricultural technique useful in very degraded areas, applied an original strategy partly to obtain some room for manoeuvre vis-à-vis the state. According to one of its leaders, members went 250 kilometres to the home town of the president, Blaise Compaoré, to demonstrate this technique to him. In 1995–96 they cultivated 3 hectares of his land using the technique, and the following year cultivated another 17 hectares. According to the leader, since the technique was labour-intensive, it meant making quite an effort, both to demonstrate the usefulness of the method and to establish a relationship to the president. Being on good terms with the president, who is said to be very satisfied with the work, is believed to protect the NGO against harassment and to facilitate its activities in Yatenga.

However, it is not only in relation to political life and the public administration that NGOs have to manoeuvre. Several leaders interviewed pointed to the competition existing between NGOs. One organization, which has established tree plantations around Ouahigouya, claimed that other organizations display these plantations to donors as their own work. The secretary of another NGO said that a senior civil servant at provincial level had withdrawn official recognition of the NGO because his own organization was working in the same domain. The NGO had managed to solve this problem by obtaining nationwide official recognition in Ouaga-dougou. Leaders from a third NGO argued that they were unable to obtain funds from a certain public commission with credit facilities because large NGOs with representatives in the commission opposed it. Whether or not these are accurate descriptions of particular events, they reflect a sense of competition and power struggle among NGOs. There is clearly a strong desire to be the only organization within a particular field and to be able to count numerous followers. One very large NGO claims to have 600,000 members all over the country, and another claims it has 37,000 adherents, even though it does not control any financial resources. There is little doubt that these figures are exaggerations and that they disguise the reality of NGOs' presence and practices in the villages. There is evidence that people may experience very little contact with an NGO once they have joined an association created by an NGO (Engberg-Pedersen 1996). Thus NGOs devise strategies to compete not just for financial resources, but also to a large extent for followers.

Political Space and the Organization of Politics

Historically, Yatenga has been a stronghold of the political party called Rassemblement Démocratique African (RDA). The leader of this party, Gérard Kango Ouédraogo, was president of the National Assembly in the period of civilian rule in 1978–80, and belongs to an older generation of politicians who were active before the series of military regimes in the 1980s. These politicians are sometimes seen as negligent and as the reason for the military takeover in 1980 (Otayek 1996: 48). However, some still mention Gérard Kango Ouédraogo as one of the influential people in Yatenga.

The atmosphere between the RDA and the CDP, the president's party, is very tense. At the National Assembly elections in 1992 and in 1997 and at local elections in 1995, the CDP tried to wipe out the RDA in Yatenga to demonstrate that its power also exists at the provincial level. One of the leading figures of the CDP put a great deal of effort into the election campaigns in Yatenga. Apart from a partisan conflict, the struggle has been interpreted as one between young people's wish to be recognized and the older generation attempting to retain power and prestige, and between modern, post-independence politicians and the old guard of the in-dependence period (cf. Loada and Otayek 1995; Otayek 1996). The public administration has increasingly become implicated in the confrontation between the two parties. It is said that the CDP to a large extent controls the administration, that civil servants who do not support CDP are marginalized, and that pressure has been put on primary schoolteachers, among others, to join CDP support groups. It even seems that prefects have unlawfully refused the RDA the right to hold electioneering meetings in their departments (H. S. 1997).

The recent political history of Yatenga has also been characterized by confrontations between antagonistic parties. After the Second World War the RDA, with a social basis in customary chiefs and traders, argued strongly in favour of independence. It was opposed by a French lieutenant and his movement, consisting primarily of Burkinabè ex-servicemen who were eager to maintain a close relationship with France (Ganne and Ouédraogo 1996: 219). The conflict between customary chiefs and ex-servicemen was also acute after independence in 1960, when the national political regime under Maurice Yaméogo launched an attack on the customary chiefs, which the ex-servicemen tried to profit from. Later, in the late 1960s and early 1970s, a strong conflict emerged inside the RDA between Gérard Kango Ouédraogo, who had captured the leadership of the party, and a group of 'Indépendants'. When Gérard Kango become prime minister in 1970, he used his position to favour his followers in Yatenga, which created serious and violent conflicts with the Indépendants. According to some, it seemed as if he wanted to control his own backyard ('rester seul maître dans son fief' (ibid.: 224)).

Thus Yatenga has been the scene of heated political clashes for a long time, which one NGO leader described by referring to the way in which every community and social entity has become divided into two: villages had two chiefs, religious communities had two imams, and so on. However, things have changed, he argues: now people can cooperate, and tensions have decreased. This view is supported by others (ibid.), but there is little doubt that the dualism and antagonism of past politics influence the present. It is said that politics is in people's blood in Yatenga; as one observer described it: 'Ici la politique est en permanence.' Furthermore, some villages are still divided into two conflicting parties organized around different lineages and often also around different external partners, such as NGOs, the extension service, and others (Engberg-Pedersen 1997).

Nevertheless, political confrontations now tend to be in decline, at least between elections. The creation of the municipality in Ouahigouya has contributed to a more relaxed atmosphere, according to one town councillor, since the leaders of the two parties now see each other on a regular basis. In this sense decentralization may contribute to a greater degree of understanding between the different social groups in a locality, although the opposite is far from inconceivable. The creation of the municipality must be viewed as a new platform for exercising political power in Yatenga, and the position of mayor is especially a focal point for political struggle. The present mayor, Bernard Lédéa Ouédraogo, is the founder and leader of the FUGN (Fédération des Unions des Groupements Naam), a large NGO organized on top of the Naam movement. He entered politics within the ruling party and was chosen as its candidate for mayor. By entering politics as a member of the CDP and thus dissociating himself from members and target groups belonging to the opposition, he clearly ran the risk of undermining the unity of the FUGN. Several observers argue that he has weakened his influence by abandoning his independent position as an NGO leader.

Most of the NGO leaders interviewed saw the election of the mayor as an internal CDP decision strongly influenced by the national level. Officially it is the town council that elects the mayor, but in reality the decision was seen as having been made by a few CDP leaders. It was especially the national influence that many, but not all, interviewees stressed ('Il n'y a pas un choix ici qui n'est pas influencé par Ouaga,' 'Tout vient de Ouagadougou,' 'C'est à Ouaga qu'on décide les choses les plus importantes comme le choix du maire'), and by mentioning Ouaga some were also referring to the president. The national level is not only thought to influence the nomination of people to important positions, it is also believed to account for much of whatever socio-economic dynamism is found in Yatenga ('Si les choses accéléront au niveau central, on pourra voir plus de choses ici'). Thus, according to one observer, the municipality cannot be blamed if things do not change rapidly.

The national level also influences political struggles and rivalries in Yatenga in a less direct way. Being on good terms with the leading figures in Ouagadougou makes one difficult to criticize ('Si on a une corde en haut, on n'est jamais attaqué'), which goes some way in explaining the organizational strategy mentioned above of establishing a relationship with the president. According to some people, an internal opposition to the mayor has emerged recently in the CDP precisely because it is felt that he is not wholeheartedly supported by the centre.

Contrary to the national political elite, customary chiefs, religious leaders and local organizations in Yatenga are not believed to influence the choice of mayor in any way. Customary chiefs and religious leaders may be consulted on important decisions in order to pay them the respect due to them, but they are not likely to be able to change decisions, and the influence of local organizations on the choice of mayor is nil, according to respondents. It seems that very few social actors outside the inner circles of the ruling party are able to affect the nominations of important people. Until now, decentralization and the creation of the municipality have not changed decision-making processes substantially or included greater numbers of provincial actors in decisive discussions.

All in all, the political space for poverty reduction seems to be significantly circumscribed in Yatenga. First, the institutional channels for accessing policy formulation and implementation are confined to an elected town council in the provincial capital, to national elections and to a co-ordinating body at the provincial level (Cadre Technique Provincial de Concertation du Yatenga). All elections are organized on a partisan basis and, as mentioned, independent candidates belonging to the province are not allowed to stand at municipal elections. This evidently gives a national flavour to local elections, which become the playground of national political parties and their struggles. The ongoing process of decentralization has not reached rural areas, and the rural poor have no opportunities to access local political discussions through elections. Moreover, the history of Yatenga and people's perceptions of politics sketched out above indicate that elections have little to do with choosing between competing political orientations or with the needs and interests of marginalized groups.

With respect to accessing the state administratively, the provincial coordinating body may constitute an opportunity for the poor. This body is supposed to coordinate state and non-state organizations working in development in Yatenga. The various local organizations are expected to report on their activities, and meetings are held regularly under the auspices of the Haut Commissaire. Accordingly, it is formally an administrative body with no political authority, but as politics in the form of local government is a recent phenomenon, it has been and continues to be an influential forum. While the body may be useful in disseminating information about government policies and the activities of other organizations,[7] it does not seem to provide an opportunity for raising issues, setting the agenda or controlling resource allocation. On the contrary, the leaders of several organizations said that they felt accountable to this body rather than the reverse and that they had no say in its deliberations. This tallies with the generally hierarchical and centralized nature of the Burkinabé state.

Second, few talk about the poor in Burkina Faso. 'Les pauvres' are conspicuously invisible in the sense that they do not figure prominently in development discourses on target groups or the social configuration of rural areas. Projects, field administrations and NGOs are essentially concerned about having organized counterparts or, to put it more correctly, organized recipients in the villages. A few NGOs, primarily in Ouahigouya, direct their activities towards orphans and disabled people, but most NGOs are quite vague regarding their beneficiaries. Thus an understanding of rural dwellers as socially differentiated is not very widespread and has little consequence for development interventions.

A notable exception is the relatively widespread concern with gender and the acknowledgement that women have special problems, are extremely burdened, and should participate more in decision-making at all levels. Development discourse in Burkina Faso emphasizes this issue, and most NGOs take it into consideration in their activities. Many women are organized in associations, and some NGOs deal exclusively with 'female activities', as they are called. To a large extent, the gender issue has been turned into a question of activities for women rather than a discussion of unequal and exploitative relations between the sexes. 'Female activities' have become a field or sector like education and health, and a gender perspective is seldom integrated into activities that are not directly aimed at women. Despite this shortcoming, women as a broad, undifferentiated, but generally marginalized social category do figure in the development discourse.

One reason why poverty is a little-discussed notion has to do with its associations. To be poor is shameful, and nobody would like to be described as such or to use such a characterization of oneself in an attempt to improve one's living conditions. Poverty is used only in a very general sense: for example, Burkina Faso is a poor country, or the rural population is poverty-striken. As it is discussed in the global development discourse, poverty is an outsider's concept that has little resonance in Burkinabè society. The global discourse identifies the poor as the 'key' beneficiaries of government policies and as rightful political agents precisely due to their poverty. This is not how 'the poor' are understood in Burkina Faso, and the whole international concern with the poverty orientation of policies and projects is therefore not particularly useful in this context.

Third, the poor have few social and political practices for influencing decision-making processes, and the organization of decision-making in village associations and NGOs does not facilitate the influence of the poor. Leaders decide quite independently of their members, and target groups in general do not participate much in NGO planning processes (Engberg-Pedersen 1996; Piveteau 1996). Thus, there is little chance that the poor – that is, families with few able-bodied adults, few animals or farm implements and little land – can put pressure on local organizations to steer their activities in a pro-poor direction.

How should one try to explain this situation? Why is political space relatively limited in Yatenga? What factors contribute to the ruling party's control of political life in the province? Why are social actors in Yatenga neither able nor willing to counteract the limitation of political space? Three general features of social life in the province provide some clues to an understanding of these questions.

First, historically there has been a strong tradition of organizing in Yatenga. At the village level, a well-established tradition ensured some years ago that young people of the same age worked together in the fields of others. The idea of this custom was to help farmers in a difficult situation and to educate young people to value cooperation with fellow villagers. Although the custom is becoming less widespread it is still considered important, and the Naam movement has its ideological roots in it (Ouédraogo 1990). The strong social hierarchy, in which village and land chiefs and other leaders are able to unite people for the 'common' good, also facilitates cooperation, albeit of a guided nature (Engberg-Pedersen 1997). The strong inclination for organizing and cooperation is, moreover, reflected in the large number of associations and NGOs at both village and provincial levels mentioned above. It is possible to gather many people for a cause, and social identities are to some extent formed on the basis of the groups people belong to.

With these practices of organizing, one might expect greater attempts to influence political discussions. This is not the case, because organization and cooperation typically concentrate on executing decisions rather than making them. Collective efforts take place within clearly defined limits and with almost predetermined aims, and they seldom involve processes of deliberation. Accordingly, organizing practices do not automatically equal political practices or efforts at promoting particular collective interests, as some of the literature on social capital seems to imply (cf. Putnam et al. 1993).

Second, leaders are very influential. Decision-making is highly centralized at most levels in Yatenga, and followers often accept their leaders' decisions rather uncritically. At the village level, a leader's influence depends not only on political affiliations, but also on the position of the leader's family in the pre-colonial kingdoms and in present-day social hierarchies. Significant status within this Muslim society constitutes another important basis for influence. While the status of the family and political relations are important, an ability to organize and enthusiasm are also necessary qualities in becoming a leader.

Potential candidates struggle a lot to become leaders, and once in position they strongly oppose competing associations. This struggle has to be explained in both political and social terms, since being a leader is not always associated with significant material benefits. The impetus for the struggle is power and prestige, which are associated with having numerous followers.

Since people seldom object to leaders, replace them or dispute their decisions, leaders have substantial leeway to use the organizations they head for their own purposes. Leaders are mainly constrained by their need for people to carry out their decisions, when they have to accommodate to the views and sentiments of members or villagers (Engberg-Pedersen 1997). In other cases, such as when an association receives bags of maize in return for labour input in project activities and the bags need to be distributed, leaders can typically decide independently. At the same time, politically or economically resourceful organizations such as projects, NGOs and the state work mainly with organized villagers, meaning that the leaders of village associations play the role of 'gatekeepers', with considerable scope for action.

Leaders of associations and NGOs in Yatenga therefore have an independent power base vis-à-vis the political parties. They sometimes control numerous followers, which makes them interesting in the context of competitive party politics because they can influence people's choice on election day. Consequently, the partisan struggle is often directed towards these leaders, and it would be erroneous just to subordinate the various associations and NGOs in Yatenga to the partisan struggle between the CDP and RDA.

Third, there is pre-colonial, colonial and post-independence experience with intervention from outside. The nature of the interventions has varied a lot, but the question of adapting to profound economic, social and political changes coming from outside has always been present. Originally the Mossis conquered the area in the fourteenth century, settled down and all but merged with the people who lived there. Then the French arrived and intervened at arm's length, but in a no less profound way, in seeking to extract resources primarily in the form of labour. Today the state and foreign projects are officially more benign, but they are also seeking to change people's way of living in a dramatic way.

This has contributed to what one informant called 'la stratégie de la dérobade' (the strategy of evasion). Although certainly very interested in the various benefits accruing from projects and NGOs, people protect themselves against the different implicit social and political consequences of the interventions. Most interventions would have profound implications for social organization, for shared understandings of the world, and for widespread values in rural areas if they were implemented in full (ibid.). This calls forth the strategy of evasion, which indicates that the different village associations, in addition to being instruments for obtaining access to project and NGO resources, are regarded by villagers as a kind of socio-political buffer against the surrounding world.

This point of view should no doubt be mediated by the fact that rural dwellers do not comprehend interventions in a homogeneous way. Whereas some (such as the young) may be eager to promote social change, others (such as the old) seek to reduce the speed of change. Village associations are a focal point in divergent strategies, and their activities need to be understood in this light.

The strong practices in the collective implementation of activities, the large scope left to leaders, and the strategy of evasion due to the long history of outside interventions are three significant characteristics of Yatenga that contribute to explaining the limited political space for poverty reduction in the province. While the two last features clearly work against the influence of marginalized groups, the first might be conducive to this. However, this is not the case, partly because people's organizing practices are focused around the implementation, not the deliberation, of activities, and partly because village associations are organized around chiefs and other leaders, not according to socio-economic categories. Apart from women, who are often united in female associations, people in precarious conditions never organize to improve their lot.

Conclusions

The argument in this chapter is that political space for poverty reduction in Yatenga is fairly circumscribed. This is a reflection of both macro and micro issues in the sense that institutional channels for accessing policy-making have been provided only to a limited extent by the colonial power

and various post-independence governments, that the prevailing development discourse in Burkina Faso does not identify poor groups and poverty
as a major concern (although women's marginalized status is recognized),
and that the rural population in general and the poor in particular have
few social practices influencing decision-making at any level in Yatenga.

The limited political space does not mean that no poverty reduction
efforts take place. Although this chapter has concentrated on the organizational landscape in Yatenga, there is little doubt that many NGOs have
provided goods and services for the benefit of the population in general.
Schools, health clinics, water supply, vaccination pens, farm implements,
and so on have been provided in great numbers in most parts of the
province. Intangible goods such as useful agricultural techniques and some
natural resource management principles have also been disseminated. One
may, however, question whether the poor have benefited from these
improvements. Some of the goods and services provided can be exploited
only by families with certain resources. For instance, it is necessary to have
cattle in order to benefit from vaccination pens; a family needs to control
sufficient labour power to be able to send its children to school; and money
is needed to buy the medicine that the doctor in the health clinic prescribes
or to buy cereal from the 'corn bank',[8] even though these are sold at a
reduced rate.

A careful historical analysis is needed to elaborate a thorough explanation of the limited political space in the province. In the present
chapter, only some important issues, such as the relationship between state
and population, Yatenga's history of intrusions and the power of leaders,
have been touched upon. The economic situation of the province is another
crucial issue. The vulnerability of large segments of the population and
the limited economic opportunities in the province are especially likely to
influence the nature of political space. As long as few people or organizations have an independent and secure resource base for entering politics,
it is doubtful whether a political space for poverty reduction can emerge.

In conclusion, it is worthwhile highlighting a few implications for the
nature of politics and processes of democratization. First, the practices of
extensive organization and centralized decision-making in Yatenga have
contributed to the formation of political identities that subordinate villagers
to leaders. As we have seen, villagers conform to a large extent to the social
groups to which they belong and seldom publicly criticize or defy their
leaders. Indeed, leaders are supported without much consideration: 'On
vote son père.' Villagers seek to exploit opportunities arising from economic
change, but they are quite reluctant to express political demands for
improvements. To a high degree they do not understand themselves as
having an important part to play in political discussions and decision-

making in collective matters, and consequently they do not exercise much pressure on leaders or politicians. In this sense the well-established practice of organizing in Yatenga has not led to the political mobilization of the poor or other segments of the rural population.

Second, politics is a power struggle, and it is dangerous. The support of the ruling elite, whether in the village, at provincial level or nationally, may secure economic or other advantages, since this is a part of the relationship between leaders and followers. As an NGO leader expressed it: 'Finance ceux qui sont derrière toi - c'est ça qui compte. C'est la politique ici.' If you do not support the elite, you are not only incapable of profiting from the goods and services it might provide, you also risk being harassed in various ways. This is one reason why both the leaders and the population at large tend to support the ruling elite at any given moment, and consequently there is very little outspoken opposition. If any significant opposition were to arise, it would be likely to emerge within the ruling party, and only when a change of leadership had become possible. Leaders at all levels manoeuvre to position themselves in the power struggle, and the conversion of opposition leaders to the ruling party is not unusual in Burkina Faso.

Yatenga is partly an exception to this description, since political confrontations are so very entrenched. But although opposition and profound disputes are part of the province's history, this does not mean that politics is no longer a question of giving and receiving support between leaders and followers. Thus the general point is that the atmosphere in which political discussions and processes take place does not contribute to the open criticism of the policies pursued or to poverty reduction being strongly advocated.

Third, ongoing democratization and decentralization have not changed much seen 'from below'. The rural population especially does not distinguish greatly between political parties and the state, although the former may come round and seek support once in a while. While Mamdani's discussion of decentralized despots is provocative ('To the peasant, the person of the chief signifies power that is total and absolute, unchecked and unrestrained' (1996: 54)), there is little doubt that the 'strategy of evasion' reflects an uneasiness, to put it mildly, of the rural population vis-à-vis external agents, be they prefects, politicians, NGO leaders or others. External agents are basically not civil servants or project employees or NGO workers but first and foremost powerful persons who have connections and who are able either to improve people's living conditions or to make matters worse. Thus the creation of liberal democracy with elections does not change much or open up a political space for the expression of demands and needs. Politics and politicians constitute what is probably the last resort when people go about seeking ways of coping with crisis and hardship.

Notes

1. 'If you don't do politics, politics will do you.'

2. Claudette Savonnet-Guyot (1986: 149–91) provides a thorough description of changes of government from 1960 to 1985.

3. Despite the rhetoric, 80 per cent of the finance of this programme was supplied by external sources (Speirs 1991: 101), which indicates the extremely limited options for the Burkinabè state to initiate development activities.

4. When the 15 additional provinces were created in May 1996, Yatenga Province was divided into three; Yatenga, Loroum and Zondoma. The latter two provinces are 'under construction', and since most of the available information and socio-economic history of the area refer to the old province, 'Yatenga' in this chapter refers to the pre-1996 province.

5. This figure covers the commune of Ouahigouya. All population data are based on provisional results from the 1996 census.

6. The fieldwork on which the study of the organizations is based was carried out in 1997–98.

7. However, organizational competition does not easily allow for the exchange of information. This came out clearly when one organization sought to obtain access to my interviews in order to gain knowledge about the activities of two other organizations.

8. 'Corn banks' are quite widespread in Yatenga. They buy cereals after the harvest when prices are relatively low and sell them again to villagers at a reduced rate in the period before the next harvest (la soudure). In bad years the price difference between the periods prior to and after the harvest may exceed several hundred per cent on the 'open' market.

Bibliography

Atampugre, Nicholas (1993) Behind the Lines of Stone: The Social Impact of a Soil and Water Conservation Project in the Sahel, Oxford: Oxfam.

Bratton, Michael and Nicolas van de Walle (1994) 'Neopatrimonial regimes and political transitions in Africa', World Politics, 46, July: 453–89.

Cabanis, André and Michel L. Martin (1987) 'L'administration locale en Haute-Volta de 1962 à 1983', in F.-P. Blanc et al. (eds), Administration et développement au Burkina Faso, Toulouse: Presses de l'Institut d'Etudes Politiques de Toulouse.

Dugué, P. (1990) 'Les stratégies des paysans du Yatenga (Burkina Faso) face aux propositions d'aménagement des terroirs villageois', Les Cahiers de la Recherche Développement, 26 June: 1–14.

Engberg-Pedersen, Lars (1996) 'Cooperation, confrontation and change: changing decision-making institutions in four villages in Burkina Faso', Ph.D. thesis, Copenhagen: Institute of Organization and Industrial Sociology, Copenhagen Business School, and Centre for Development Research.

— (1997) 'Institutional contradictions in rural development', European Journal of Development Research, 9, 1: 183–208.

Ganne, Bernard and Moussa Ouédraogo (1996) 'Filières commerçantes et évolutions politiques: chassés-croisés à Ouahigouya', in R. Otayek, F. M. Sawadogo and J.-P. Guingané (eds), *Le Burkina entre révolution et démocratie (1983–1993): ordre politique et changement social en Afrique subsaharienne*, Paris: Editions Karthala.

GOB (Government of Burkina Faso) (1989a) *Rapport de synthèse et d'analyse des expériences pilotes de gestion des terroirs villageois*, Ouagadougou: Ministère du Plan et de la Coopération.

— (1989b) *Zatu No. An-VII 010/FP/PRES portant organization et modalités de l'Administration du Territoire au Burkina Faso*, Ouagadougou: Président du Front Populaire.

— (1993) *Loi No. 003/93/ADP portant organization de l'administration du territoire au Burkina Faso*, Ouagadougou: Assemblée des Députés du Peuple.

— (1998a) *Loi No. 040/98/AN portant orientation de la décentralisation au Burkina Faso*, Ouagadougou: Assemblée Nationale.

— (1998b) *Loi No. 041/98/AN portant organization de l'administration du territoire du Burkina Faso*, Ouagadougou: Assemblée Nationale.

— (1998c) *Loi No. 042/98/AN portant organization et fonctionnement des collectivités locales*, Ouagadougou: Assemblée Nationale.

— (1998d) *Loi No. 043/98/AN portant programmation de la mise en oeuvre de la décentralisation*, Ouagadougou: Assemblée Nationale.

— (n.d.) *Etat des lieux du processus de décentralisation au Burkina Faso*, Ouagadougou: Premier Ministère, Commission Nationale de la Décentralisation.

H. S. (1996) 'Les quinze nouvelles provinces', *L'Indépendant*, 30 April, pp. 6–7.

— (1997) 'Législatives au Yatenga', *L'Indépendant*, 8 April, pp. 11–12.

Jacob, Jean-Pierre and François Margot (1992) *Relations entre l'administration locale et les organizations locales au Burkina Faso*, Geneva: Institut Universitaire d'Etudes du Développement (IUED).

Kafandi, Talata (1990) 'Burkina Faso: August 1983 – the beginning of delinking?', in A. Mahjoub (ed.), *Adjustment or Delinking: The African Experience*, Tokyo: United Nations University Press.

Kiemde, Paul (1996) 'Réflexions sur le référendum constitutionnel et les élections présidentielle et législatives de 1991 et 1992', in R. Otayek, F. M. Sawadogo and J.-P. Guingané (eds), *Le Burkina entre révolution et démocratie (1983–1993): ordre politique et changement social en Afrique subsaharienne*, Paris: Editions Karthala.

Laurent, Pierre-Joseph (1995) 'Les pouvoirs politiques locaux et la décentralisation au Burkina Faso', in Cahiers du Cidep, Louvain-la-Neuve: Centre International de Formation et de Recherche en Population et Développement.

Loada, Augustin and René Otayek (1995) 'Les élections municipales du 12 février 1995 au Burkina Faso', *Politique Africaine*, 58, June: 135–42.

Mamdani, Mahmood (1996) *Citizen and Subject: Contemporary Africa and the Legacy of Late Colonialism*, Princeton, NJ: Princeton University Press.

Otayek, René (1996) '"Voter, ca veut dire quoi?" Sur les élections législatives du 24 mai 1992', in R. Otayek, F. M. Sawadogo and J.-P. Guingané (eds), *Le Burkina entre révolution et démocratie (1983–1993): ordre politique et changement social en Afrique subsaharienne*, Paris: Editions Karthala.

Otayek, René, Filiga Michel Sawadogo and Jean-Pierre Guingané (1996) 'Introduction: du Burkina, du changement social et de la démocratie', in R. Otayek, F. M. Sawadogo and J.-P. Guingané (eds), *Le Burkina entre révolution et démocratie (1983–1993): ordre politique et changement social en Afrique subsaharienne*, Paris: Editions Karthala.

Ouédraogo, Bernard Lédéa (1990) *Entraide villageoise et développement: groupements paysans au Burkina Faso*, Paris: L'Harmattan.

Piveteau, Alain (1996) 'Les ONG favorisent-elles le développement agricole?', in R. Otayek, F. M. Sawadogo and J.-P. Guingané (eds), *Le Burkina entre révolution et démocratie (1983–1993): ordre politique et changement social en Afrique subsaharienne*, Paris: Editions Karthala.

Putnam, Robert D., Robert Leonardi and Raffaella Y. Nanetti (1993) *Making Democracy Work: Civil Traditions in Modern Italy*, Princeton, NJ: Princeton University Press.

Savadogo, Kimseyinga and Claude Wetta (1992) 'The impact of self-imposed adjustment: The case of Burkina Faso, 1983–9', in G. A. Cornia, R. v. d. Hoeven and T. Mkandawire (eds), *Africa's Recovery in the 1990s: From Stagnation and Adjustment to Human Development*, New York: St. Martin's Press.

Savonnet-Guyot, Claudette (1986) *Etat et sociétés au Burkina. Essai sur le politique africain*, Paris: Karthala.

Sawadogo, Filiga Michel (1996) 'L'élaboration de la Constitution de la Quatrième République', in R. Otayek, F. M. Sawadogo and J.-P. Guingané (eds), *Le Burkina entre révolution et démocratie (1983–1993): ordre politique et changement social en Afrique subsaharienne*, Paris: Editions Karthala.

Speirs, Mike (1991) 'Agrarian change and the revolution in Burkina Faso', *African Affairs*, 90: 89–110.

Wardman, Anna and Lucio G. Salas (1991) 'The implementation of anti-erosion techniques in the Sahel: a case study from Kaya, Burkina Faso', *Journal of Developing Areas*, 26, October: 65–80.

World Bank (1997) *World Development Report 1997: The State in a Changing World*, Washington, DC: World Bank.

8

Where Local Organizations do not Work: Problems of Poverty Reduction in Tamil Nadu, India[1]

D. Rajasekhar

Growing numbers of the poor and the alleviation of poverty have been concerns of successive Indian governments since independence in 1947. The policy response of the government shifted from capital-intensive growth-oriented strategies with assumptions of trickle-down in the 1960s and the 1970s to the launching of nationwide anti-poverty programmes in the late 1970s and 1980s. Since 1991, macro-policies have been introduced aimed at growth with equity, linking the economy with global markets, a reduced role for the state, the privatization of development (by involving NGOs in development work) and decentralization in administration. During the last five decades, a number of local organizations have been created, administration has been decentralized and space provided for NGOs so that macro-policies can be implemented, the interests of the poor can be represented and a broad-based development, poverty alleviation and reduction can be made possible. A positive impact of these developments is that the proportion of people living below the poverty line declined, especially from the 1970s onwards, due to agricultural growth. However, the number of absolute poor increased and those crossing the poverty line remain vulnerable.

In this context, the distinction between poverty alleviation and poverty reduction becomes very pertinent. Poverty alleviation is the short-term improvement of the capital endowment of the poor. Poverty reduction is the long-term elimination of the poor's dependence on social relations, and of vulnerability with respect to changes in their environment (Engberg-Pedersen 1998). Thus, while agricultural growth and better access to markets can alleviate poverty, the involvement of the poor in development efforts becomes crucial in poverty reduction. Further, as Lars Engberg-Pedersen and Neil Webster stress in this volume, 'poverty reduction requires the generation and facilitation of opportunities for the poor and organizations working on their behalf to exert an influence on political and

economic processes' (see Chapter 1). Poverty reduction also requires building the capacity of the poor through the provision of knowledge and
information so that they can identify needs, articulate their rights, gain
access to resources and change the terms of engagement with other organizations. If NGOs are defined as those organizations that facilitate the
implementation of development programmes for the poor, then they are
the ones that can work on behalf of the poor in India, generating and
facilitating opportunities for them to exert an influence on political and
economic processes.

There is a widespread belief (and acceptance) in India that, being small
in scale, flexible, innovative, participatory, focused on development and
relatively independent, NGOs are more successful in reaching the poor
and in poverty reduction. This has contributed to the increasing popularity
of NGOs with the government and external aid agencies, and their rapid
growth. Notwithstanding the charges of corruption and lack of accountability and public transparency with respect to some NGOs, the last ten
years has also witnessed improvements in their credibility and legitimacy.

With growing numbers and increased funding, the NGOs have been
able to create a vast social infrastructure. It is estimated that there are
20,000 NGOs active in rural development in India today.[2] If we assume
that each of these NGOs is working in ten villages, the NGOs together
would be covering half the villages in India. If we assume that each NGO
has five trained workers, the number of qualified persons engaged in rural
development would be large. A majority of NGOs have formed people's
organizations at village level and provided education and training to the
people in various issues, and most of them work with marginalized groups
such as women, *dalits* (depressed castes) and Adivasis (tribals). This social
infrastructure provides ample opportunities for NGOs not only to provide
services but also to enable the poor to access the resources of the government and to become involved in *gram panchayats* (village-level local
government) to improve their capacity as *gram panchayat* members and
make *gram panchayats* pro-poor and people-centred, thus representing the
interests of the poor in decision-making bodies at various levels.

The emergence of NGOs as important development actors in India
implies that one might hope that more attention might be given to the
needs and concerns of the poor in policy formulation and implementation.
This raises a number of questions. What has been the experience of NGOs
in generating and facilitating the possibilities for the poor to exert an
influence on political and economic processes? How are their intervention
strategies designed? Are the intervention strategies based on poverty as
viewed from a historical perspective? Are they based on the condition and
severity of poverty across different villages and different poverty groups

within a village? Have they succeeded in enabling a political discourse to develop in which poverty and poverty reduction are significant issues? Have they facilitated social and political practices among the poor so that decision-making, agendas, policy and programme implementation can be influenced at the local level?

These questions are analysed here using the results of mapping exercises on poverty and local organizations[3] in the project area of SHARE (Self-Help Association for Rural Education). SHARE is a membership-based organization (but registered as an NGO) working for the empowerment of its women members through an income-generation activity in about forty villages in a block[4] in Vellore district (formerly part of North Arcot district) in Tamil Nadu. Three villages were selected in consultation with the NGO, which is active in two of them (Sabthalipuram and Mottupalyam), but not the third (Melvallam).

The case of SHARE is appropriate for the purpose of analysing the role of NGOs in enabling the poor to gain political space for poverty reduction. There are a number of reasons for this. As we shall see below, the objectives of SHARE suggest that the NGO is interested not in 'projectism' but in initiating a process towards empowerment of the poor. Second, the NGO seeks to provide information and knowledge and other resources for their empowerment.

Historical Analysis of Poverty in the Selected Villages

What have been the processes that have generated poverty in the selected villages? Were there changes in the socio-economic status of the different sections in the villages? If yes, what are they, and how did they occur? Were there any changes in the magnitude and condition of poverty? An analysis of these questions is important because it suggests that local organizations should recognize the need for new and innovative intervention strategies, provide ideas relating to the need for a particular resource or opportunity for the poor, and enable the poor to see the root causes of their local problems in macro-policies and programmes. This will, in turn, help them to influence the policies and programmes conceived and implemented by the state.

This section therefore analyses changes in the socio-economic status of the different sections in the villages and processes that generate poverty in the study area. Time-related mapping[5] was carried out in all the villages to trace important socio-economic changes. The work undertaken was similar to surveys conducted in eleven villages very close to the selected villages. The first survey was conducted by Cambridge University, UK and Madras University, Madras, in 1973–74, and the results were published in Farmer (1977). Ten years later, a second survey (Hazell and Ramasamy 1993) was carried out by the International Food Policy Research Institute (IFPRI) and Tamil Nadu Agricultural University (TNAU). The third survey was conducted as part of a research project entitled *Adjustment and Development: Agrarian Change, Markets and Social Welfare in South India, 1973–93*. An article on important findings was published by Harriss-White and Janakarajan (1997).

In the 1950s, the agricultural population in these villages protected themselves against scanty and uncertain rainfall and droughts with tank irrigation. In all the villages, tanks were collectively maintained and were used to recharge wells. Fields were irrigated through water drawn from wells either through human (*etram*) or animal (*kavalai*) power.[6] Much of the area was irrigated by tanks and wells. All the land in the villages was cultivated, the important crops being paddy, *ragi* (a grain) and groundnuts. Agriculture was the main source of employment, as water-raising and cultivation were done using human and animal power. The wages paid were low, around 2 rupees per day, but agricultural labourers led a comfortable life. Purchasing power was high and health status good, as the diet consisted of locally grown staple food grains and pulses. In all the villages, the main caste groups were Vanniyars and scheduled castes (SCs, granted special concessions and formerly considered untouchable), although there were also Mudaliars in Melvallam, potters in Mottupalyam and Muslims in Sabthalipuram. The SC households lived in their own hamlet away from the main village, and caste discrimination was prevalent.

From the late 1950s and 1960s, farmers started constructing wells in the command[7] (and also non-command) area of tanks, following a widespread drought in the early 1960s. The number of wells in the district increased from 1.5 lakhs in 1950 to 1.75 lakhs in 1960 (1 lakh = 100,000). Subsequently, well irrigation gained prominence at the expense of tank irrigation, and the number of diesel engines increased. This, however, did not have any dramatic impact on employment because the growth of diesel engines was slow, and water-raising and cultivation were still done using human and animal labour. Employment opportunities improved as the growth in well irrigation increased cropping intensity and production. Employment opportunities were also stated to be better because of quarrying and the establishment of a sugar mill in the area.

Striking changes began to occur from the late 1960s with the adoption of new agricultural technology in the district. This technology package included the supply of high yielding varieties (HYV) of seeds and support towards the purchase of other inputs, namely credit and fertilizers. The area under HYV paddy increased rapidly in the1960s.[8] The results of the first survey (Farmer 1977) indicate that transplanting and manure use were widespread, fertilizers and manures were widely used, yield rates had gone up and the cultivation of paddy had become profitable. The main constraints for the non- (or limited) adoption of HYVs were inadequate credit facilities and water (Chinnappa 1977).

Farmers interested in adopting HYVs sought to solve the 'water problem' by expanding well irrigation and purchasing electric pumpsets. The total number of wells in the district increased from 0.5 lakhs in 1905 to 1.51 lakhs in 1950, 1.75 lakhs in 1961 and 2.29 lakhs in 1971. In order to improve the efficiency of the water-raising, the number of electric pumpsets increased from 20,000 in 1960 to 1.20 lakhs in 1973-74 (Bandara 1977: 325) – over 50 per cent of the wells in the district. The main reasons were the increased profits from cultivation, not least due to the subsidized loans and electricity provided by the government (B. Harris 1977).

Notwithstanding the reduced employment opportunities from powered irrigation, the money wages for male farm labourers increased from 2 rupees (with food) in the late 1950s to 15 rupees (with food) in the 1970s. The corresponding figures for female agricultural labourers were 0.5 rupees and 6 rupees respectively. There was upward mobility for a few SC households in a position to adopt the HYV technology, and improved work opportunities for agricultural labourers with the increased production.

By the 1980s, there was a rapid rise in the area under HYV cultivation and in the consumption of fertilizers and pesticides. Real incomes from the cultivation of paddy and groundnut increased (Hazell and Ramasamy 1993), but the well irrigation began to have adverse consequences. Between 1971 and 1982, 71,722 wells were dug in the district, taking the total number to over 300,000. The villagers reported the drying up of tanks and lakes due to the groundwater level falling. This necessitated large investments in deepening of wells and purchasing electric pumpsets with a higher lifting power. Small farmers could not make such a high investment, and turned to less water-intensive crops such as groundnut and banana (Hazell and Ramasamy 1993: 34). Thus, although 'water problems' were solved, constraints of a new type emerged.

The impact of the new agricultural technology on employment was becoming negative. Villagers reported that employment opportunities had been reduced due to increased mechanization and the introduction of less labour-intensive crops. By the mid-1970s, the mechanized ploughing of dry land had become much more extensive and mechanical threshing had become quite common amongst the wealthier farmers with access to bank credit (J. Harris 1977: 141). Hazell and Ramasamy (1993: 240) noted that total employment in crop production declined by 4 per cent per paddy farm in the re-survey villages between 1973–74 and 1983–84. Furthermore, the use of family labour increased on both small and large farms between

1973–74 and 1983–84, hence the brunt of decline in total employment was borne by the hired workers. Yet real wage rates modestly increased 'because of a decline in the amount of hired labour supplied by farms operating with more than one hectare of land, and because of competing employment opportunities in dairying and non-farm activities' (ibid.). This is supported by the mapping exercise in the selected villages, which also showed that the greatest reduction of work opportunities in agriculture was for *dalit* labourers.

By the 1990s, low rainfall, reductions in the groundwater table and the drying up of tanks resulted in a reduction of irrigated area and a growth of cultivable wastes in the villages. Government rules on the spacing of tubewells have not been observed. Although the construction of new wells has slowed down, about 5,000 to 7,000 wells in the district were energized per year in the 1980s. The rate at which wells were abandoned also increased. With the collapse of traditional water-management practices on tanks and tank water becoming polluted with agro-chemical effluent, the tank in Sabthalipuram is now able to supply only silt for making bricks. The villages are completely dependent on well irrigation, but with the competitive deepening of wells leading to a high failure rate, agricultural yields are becoming affected. The paddy yield rate declined from 3.5 tons per hectare in 1973–74 to 3.2 tons per hectare in 1993–94. Groundnut yields also declined, from 1.4 tons per hectare to 1.0 ton per hectare during the same period (Harriss-White and Janakarajan 1997).

The problems associated with well irrigation affected the small and marginal farmers most severely. They neither had sufficient capital to deepen the well, nor could they bear the risk of it subsequently failing. Second, with the deepening of wells, the energy consumed per well increased from 2,501 units in 1980–81 to 3,897 units in 1992–3. This increased the cost of cultivation. Third, power cuts often made it difficult to maintain the irrigation required for crops such as paddy. These factors resulted in cropping pattern changes, especially among small farmers. The re-surveys in 1993–94 revealed that the bulk of the area owned by small peasants was cultivated with groundnut, while rich peasants continued to grow paddy on a large proportion of the area (Harriss-White and Jana-karajan 1997: 1473).

Employment opportunities in both villages declined due to: (i) the decline in well-irrigated areas; (ii) the decline in yields and production; (iii) the growth in the number of marginal farmers (due to a combination of sale and partition[9]) and the consequent reduction in employment, as these tend to be family operated; and (iv) farm mechanization. Farm mechanization was a recurring theme in all the surveys. All apart from the first survey confirmed the growth in farm mechanization and the shift to less labour-intensive (and income-elastic) crops of bananas, vegetables, and so on. The mapping exercises revealed a rapid rise in agricultural money wages in the 1980s and 1990s, which is confirmed by the re-surveys. The paradox of widespread agricultural unemployment coexisting with rising wages could be explained by the growth of non-farm employment opportunities in the villages. Quarrying, bidi (cigarette) rolling, construction, commuting to Vellore town to work in the urban informal sector, trades and services have become important non-agricultural employment avenues in Sabthalipuram, while construction, leather-tanning, trades and services and head-load work are important in Mottupalyam and Melvallam. Both pull and push factors operated: the pull factor was higher wages in the non-farm sector, while the push factor was the worsening of employment opportunities within agriculture and low wages.

The time-related mapping also shows the qualitative changes that have taken place in the villages. With an improvement in educational facilities and the introduction of a midday meal scheme in schools, educational levels in the villages have in general improved. Health appears to have declined with changes in consumption patterns and problems of sanitation (poor drainage in both villages is leading to a proliferation of mosquitoes), notwithstanding improved medical facilities. The surveys of nutritional status revealed that while nutritional intake among better-off households vastly improved between 1973–74 and 1983–84, there was a 70 per cent shortfall in the case of landless households (Andersen and Jaramillo 1993). By the 1990s, the households with nutritional stress were estimated to be between 17 and 35 per cent among poor peasant and landless households (Harriss–White and Janakarajan 1997: 1474).

The social status of the depressed castes improved due to their upward mobility (stemming from the adoption of HYVs and the general improvement in employment opportunities outside agriculture). An active *dalit* movement against untouchability and temple-entry restrictions in northern Tamil Nadu also contributed. Now there is free mixing of people belonging to the upper and lower castes. Upper-caste persons go to the houses of depressed castes and attend marriages, but do not eat food there. Harris (1993) and Harriss–White and Janakarajan (1997) point to a different dimension of discrimination when they note that there are social restrictions of entry into highly capital-intensive and profitable non-farm activities, which is again confirmed by our mapping.

The foregoing discussion suggests that the changes in lift-irrigation technology and new agricultural technology led to intended consequences such as growth in the area cultivated with HYVs, increased yields, double-cropping, rising wages and the adoption of new agricultural technology by small and marginal farmers (including those belonging to SC households).

On the other hand, the changes in cropping pattern in favour of less labour-intensive crops and an overall decline in agricultural employment opportunities due to mechanization were unintended consequences. The political space for the poor was influenced by both the intended and the unintended consequences. The problem of unemployment was due to government subsidy-oriented policies aimed at lift-irrigation and mechanization within agriculture. Yet the poor cannot see this as the reason for widespread unemployment. The fact that the new agricultural technology enabled some of the poor to become better-off through individual-based entrepreneurial strategies made the others blame themselves for their poverty rather than pointing their fingers at the deep-rooted structural factors and government policies as the root causes. The analysis also shows that poverty has become more diverse and complex and that it is interlinked with the processes of agricultural growth and change and with access to resources. This may have hindered the establishment of a discourse in which poverty and poverty reduction were significant issues.

The Condition and Severity of Poverty in the Selected Villages

Wealth-ranking exercises in the selected villages provide a distribution of households by wealth categories (Table 8.1). The criteria adopted by the people in the wealth ranking were broad[10] and varied between Vanniyar, Muslim and SC localities, meaning that the very poor in the SC locality are different from the same category in the Vanniyar locality. For this reason, poverty levels in one locality cannot be compared with those in another. Table 8.1 suggests that, in all the villages, a larger proportion of SC households belong to the categories of 'very poor' and 'poor'. In one village, most of the Muslim households are poor.

The criteria adopted also show that the very poor are characterized by material deprivation, a lack of assets, unemployment, the casual wage labour, a higher dependency ratio, a high incidence of child labour, poor access to educational and health facilities, and dependence on employers for consumption credit. The poor have similar characteristics, but the main difference between poor and very poor is that the former have a relatively lower dependency ratio and more family members of working age, and are better able to access employment opportunities. In addition, although the poor suffer from uncertain employment in the rainy season, they are able to draw upon savings from peak season earnings. The well-off and better-off households not only possess productive assets and are involved in non-farm activities, but also have better access to government services and often have household members with salaried employment. The well-off among SC households are characterized by members with salaried employment,

TABLE 8.1 Distribution of households by wealth categories in the selected villages (%)

Categories	Colonies of Sabthalipuram			Colonies of Mottupalyam			Colonies of Melvallam	
	Vanniyars	Cobblers	Muslims	Vanniyars	Cobblers	SCs	Vanniyars	SCs
Very poor	8.7	27.5	14.9	17.8	51.5	22.4	10.5	59.1
Poor	19.6	57.5	44.7	15.1	39.4	44.7	12.9	13.6
Better-off	21.7	15.0	27.6	32.9	9.1	7.9	64.3	11.4
Well-off	50.0	0.0	12.8	34.2	0.0	25.0	12.3	15.9
Total	100.0	100.0	100.0	100.0	100.0	100.0	100.0	100.0
	(92)	(40)	(47)	(73)	(33)	(76)	(171)	(44)

Note: Figures in parentheses denote the total number of households in each colony.

better educational levels, participation in local decentralized government, and good networks with government institutions.

Seasonality mapping and focus group interviews with the poor and poorest in three localities of each village, and open-ended interviews with 10 per cent of the very poor and poor households, provide the data for the following discussion on the severity of poverty.

First, there are differences across villages in type of employment. In Sabthalipuram, non-farm activities form an important source of employment and livelihood, while agriculture is the important source of employment in Mottupalyam and Melvallam. Since agricultural employment tends to be seasonal, there are fewer work opportunities in Mottupalyam and Melvallam, where male workers have full employment in four months, 25 per cent employment in four months and occasional employment in the remaining months. In contrast, male workers in Sabthalipuram have full employment in five months, 50 per cent employment in two months and 25 per cent employment in five months.

There are also gender differences here. In Sabthalipuram, while male workers find non-farm employment in quarrying, construction and brick factories in the vicinity of the village and informal sector in Vellore town, women are involved in both non-farm (*bidi*-rolling and NGO craft centre) and farm activities. In Mottupalyam, while most of the men are involved in non-farm activities in construction, leather work, and small business, female workers are mainly involved in agriculture. The pattern in Melvallam is similar to that in Mottupalyam, except that some of the women in the latter village work in the NGO craft centre. This has implications as far as the availability of employment for men and women is concerned. Male workers have better employment opportunities in Sabthalipuram. In Mottupalyam and Melvallam, female workers have employment all through the year, while male workers have very little employment in four months. But employment opportunities, which are highly seasonal, reach the peak in both agriculture and non-agriculture during the harvesting season, and are very low during the rainy and summer seasons. Quarrying comes to a halt during the rainy season, as do work in the craft centre and *bidi*-rolling, as the quality of the work is affected by the dampness of palm and *bidi* leaves.

Wage rates also vary depending on type of employment. Daily wage rates are 25–30 rupees for men and 20 rupees for women (without food) for agricultural work during the peak season. During the slack season, wage rates do not decline, but the number of working hours seem to be longer. In quarrying, men receive 60 rupees per day, while women receive 30 rupees per day. *Bidi* workers earn 30 rupees for rolling 1,000 *bidis*. In construction, daily wage rates go up to 80 rupees.

Wage rates are thus high for quarrying and construction. Yet not all workers can participate in these activities. Quarrying in Sabthalipuram is mostly confined to men from Muslim and SC households because this work involves the loading and unloading of the trucks. Hence women (especially Muslim women) prefer not to participate. There is also the fear of a high accident rate. In Sabthalipuram, earning members from three poor households became physically disabled in accidents, as a result of which these households slid into the category of the poorest. Similarly, *bidi*-rolling is almost restricted to the households of physically weak men and Muslims.

There is also a gender division as far as work opportunities are concerned. A large proportion of the women are engaged in agriculture for two reasons: landlords prefer women workers, as wage rates are lower, and men prefer to work in highly paid non-farm activities. Due to *purdah*,[11] unmarried girls and young women do not take part in agricultural work. Hence they are mainly involved in *bidi*-rolling, the craft centre, and so on. The poor households belonging to non-SC communities perceive that work in the craft centre is of low status. All these factors constrain women's access to highly paid non-farm employment, and force them to take up disease-inducing *bidi*-rolling and low-paid agricultural work.

The high incidence of common diseases leading to higher expenditure on health during the rainy season results in increased food shortages during this season. The Muslims also face difficulties during Ramadan, as expenditure goes up[12] and the ability to work declines due to fasting. Non-Muslims also face shortages during these festivals, which occur during the off-season. In both the rainy season and festival months, the poorest meet their basic needs through loans borrowed from moneylenders at high interest rates. These accumulate if households are unable to clear them in the peak season because of illness, sudden loss of employment opportunities due to drought and similar problems. In this respect, the poor are less vulnerable due to a lower dependency ratio of consumers to workers, which enables them to save during periods of employment and reduce their dependence on moneylenders.

Because there are fewer employment opportunities during the rainy season, many of the poorest households can afford only two meals a day. Food shortages are most acute in female-headed households, and in households headed by a physically disabled person. When there is a shortage of food, men and boys are given priority. In Muslim households, there is no discrimination against the aged and girl children. In SC households, the aged are discriminated against in food allocation. In all localities, it is the women who have the lowest priority during periods of food shortage.

In focus group interviews conducted in seven localities across the selected villages, the poor and poorest households were asked to list and rank the causes of poverty. Causes and symptoms of poverty were often mixed together. Sen's approach to poverty (1981) is useful in this context. Building upon his concept of entitlements, it can be noted that failures relating to endowment (a lack of assets, physical weakness and a lack of citizenship), production (asset quality, a lack of education and skills and a lack of government help) and exchange (produce prices, unemployment and wages) result in poverty. Kabeer (1994) includes consumption failures (intra-household inequality, vices such as drinking, higher dependency ratios, and so on) as another cause of poverty.

Table 8.2 shows that a higher dependency ratio (that of consumers to workers) was cited as the cause in all the localities, while lack of assets, unemployment and vices were cited as causes in six out of seven localities. Physical weakness and a lack of education and skills were cited in five out of seven localities. As most of the very poor and poor households do not have land or other productive assets, they have to hire themselves out in agricultural or non-agricultural employment. Unemployment was cited as a cause of poverty in six out of seven localities. The lack of employment opportunities, especially in the non-farm sector, was perceived to be due to a lack of education and skills. Physical weakness, mainly due to illness or a poor diet, produced an inability to take employment when it was available. Even if the poorest had employment, the wage income was insufficient because of the higher dependency ratio. 'Vices' such as drinking were cited as a cause for poverty in six localities (mostly SC and Muslim) as male workers spent most of their earnings on drinking, exacerbating consumption failures within their households.

TABLE 8.2 Causes of poverty in the selected villages

Causes of poverty	Number of localities where the cause is cited
Lack of assets	6
Unemployment	6
Physical weakness	5
Lack of education and skills	5
Higher dependency ratio	7
Vices (drinking, etc.)	6
Lack of help from the government	3
Low wages	2
Female-headed households	3

The analysis of the condition and severity of poverty, together with historical processes generating poverty, suggest that relative poverty between the poor and the well-off, and also within SC households, has increased. Given the nature of the poverty and the processes behind it described above, which intervention strategy was adopted by the NGO?

SHARE's Intervention Strategy

In the late 1970s, the Christian Medical College (a well-known hospital located in Vellore town) found that the poor in the hinterland were not able to access the hospital's medical facilities because of their acute poverty, while the better-off from distant places were able to do so. To fulfil its moral responsibility to the local population, it facilitated the formation of a few organizations in the locality to work for the economic development of the poor so that they could access health facilities.

One of these organizations became registered as an NGO in 1992 under the name SHARE. It now works with about 4,000 women belonging to landless and marginal farmer families. Its aim is to enable poor women to undertake income-generating activities through skill upgrades, marketing and raw materials. To achieve this, SHARE has initiated income-earning opportunities such as palm-leaf craft, sisal-fibre craft and *korai* mat-weaving. In 27 villages, craft centres were started for this purpose. SHARE provides raw materials and sells the finished products in the national and international markets. In 1995–96, products worth 30.53 lakhs were sold, of which 99 per cent was sold in the international market (Rajamma and Nadarajan 1997).

In Sabthalipuram and Mottupalyam, the total number of women and young girls belonging to Muslim and SC communities and working in craft centres was 60 in 1994–95, declining to 37 in 1998–99.[13] SHARE provides training to women in making palm-leaf products, supplies them with raw materials and markets the products abroad. After deducting the cost of raw materials, monthly wages are paid to the women. Between 1994–95 and 1998–99, the average annual income of a craft worker increased from 2,727 rupees to 5,370 rupees in Mottupalyam, and in Sabthalipuram from 1,764 rupees to 4,917 rupees in the same period. The income varied among members and at different times in a year due to factors such as the season (in the rainy season, production cannot take place due to dampness, which spoils the leaves), domestic demands, and alternative possibilities of employment. To reduce the work burden on women members, SHARE provides education and support services (evening study centres for school students, child-care centres and drinking water facilities) for the poor and their children.

Even though income from craft activities appears to be low, it plays an important role for the poorest. One member, a widow living with her deserted daughter, stated that the craft centre income, together with subsidized food grains supplied by the Public Distribution System (PDS), enabled her household to survive. According to her, 'because there is PDS, we are able to purchase food grains at a low price. But without the craft income, we would not have been in a position to purchase.' Another woman earns 600 rupees per month, which constitutes only a small proportion of the total income of the household (with her husband's business income forming the bulk), but this 'gives her a personal freedom she never had before'. In the case of 15 out of 31 craft workers in these villages, the income from craft activity formed more than 40 per cent of their total household income. The positive impact of this income is seen in increased expenditure on food, clothing, health and education.

However, SHARE realized the limitations of working only in income generation. For a number of reasons it was not able to include many of the poor in this activity. First, it was costly to provide training in palm-leaf production and in supplying raw materials. Second, older women, who have experience of agricultural work, prefer to work as agricultural labourers. Third, craft activity is assigned a low status by some. Finally, poor women from higher castes do not like to work in the production centre alongside women from the depressed castes.

More significantly, SHARE began to discuss the importance of structural factors that constrain women from playing an active role in decision-making within the community and wider arena and the role SHARE should play here (Murugesan 1999: 155–6). The organization decided to undertake more activities with the aim of empowering women.

The first activity was the formation of self-help groups (SHGs) from 1995 onwards. When SHARE obtained funding support from a donor in 1994, it liked the idea of self-help promotion proposed by the donor. Subsequently, SHARE formed SHGs for both craft members and other poor in the villages. The aim now was: i) to cover a large number of poor in the villages where it was working; ii) to provide opportunities for women to undertake income-generating activities; and iii) to create a forum where women could come together to discuss their problems and take collective action.

The organization also started two SHGs for women in Sabthalipuram and Mottupalyam villages. One of the groups in each village consists of craft members, while the second is formed with other poor women. An animator appointed by SHARE took the lead in the formation and strengthening of groups; subsequently, group leaders took an active part in the management of the group. The members in the four groups in these villages contribute savings regularly. Between 25 and 60 per cent of members took loans from SHGs, which were used for consumption as well as production, although the proportion of women starting their own business with SHG loans was low in both the villages.

A further set of activities aim to bring about social change. These include awareness programmes on matters relating to the development of women, equality of women, women's rights in family and society, and so on, together with training programmes on the development of leadership skills and personality improvement. The aim is to help the women to move forward on the road to empowerment (Murugesan 1999)

The third activity was resource mobilization from the government and banks by the women. The organization provides information on various government programmes that are meant for the poor and help members in accessing them. A significant proportion of the members of the craft centres and SHGs now possess a good knowledge about various government schemes, and some of them avail themselves of them.

The fourth activity was enabling target-group members to contest *gram panchayat* elections. Awareness and training programmes in women's rights and the new and old systems of local decentralized government were organized for both animators and women members in 1995. Of 13 women who contested ward positions, 5 won, though none of the 3 women contesting for the presidency won (Murugesan 1999).

Attempts at Poverty Reduction by Local Organizations

Line departments Line departments and ministries at central, state, district and lower levels undertake agricultural and rural development programmes to address the problems of the poor – lack of assets, unemployment, poverty and inability to meet basic needs.

Most of the people in the selected villages are aware of programmes relating to basic needs. All the sample households use the PDS to obtain rice and other essential provisions. Most of them have availed themselves of housing facilities from the government. They are aware of pensions given to the old and widows, and also of the procedures involved; a significant proportion of them have even obtained them. Another government programme that is often used is assistance provided to educate girl children. In addition, most of the sample households use health and educational facilities within the villages. However, one significant aspect is that there is no difference in utilization patterns between the NGO villages and Melvallam. Some of the difficulties faced by the poor in obtaining benefits from the government are discussed below.

'Corruption' in the line departments is an often-cited factor. Even those poor who have obtained benefits have had to bribe the officials concerned. For instance, one widow obtains 150 rupees as a pension every month. She had to spend an amount almost equivalent to six months' pension as bribes to doctors and officials in the line department and for travel and documentation in order to obtain the pension.

The demand for housing is quite high in the selected villages. The government has been providing housing for the last 15 years. Nowadays, it has become difficult to mobilize assistance for housing because of a widespread perception among government officials that this need has already been met. To some extent this view has been strengthened by incidents of the following type. About 20 per cent of our sample households, which have already obtained housing from the government, either do not stay in these houses (they rent them out) or sell them on, as they already have their own houses. In a few cases, the 'request' for housing comes from those households which want an additional house for the future requirements of an unmarried son in the household.

Realizing that obtaining assistance towards housing is becoming difficult, 40 SC households in Sabthalipuram joined together to approach government officials and undertake a collective follow-up. They contributed money towards expenditure on travel and the other expenses of three representatives. After five years, a few of the households obtained benefits. While the experience suggests that collective action could work with respect to some types of government assistance, especially if a cross-section of poor households is involved, it also points to the critical role of the representatives with respect to their accountability to others. This includes both accountability to the group and, in the case of a bank loan or similar, accountability for the group. Few felt that the latter was realistic.

Some of the households could not use government schemes and programmes because of cultural values. One member of a craft centre would not approach officials to obtain an old age pension for her father-in-law as it would reflect poorly on the family. Others stated that corruption, cumbersome procedures and bureaucratic delays frequently stood in the way of obtaining benefits.

The poor generally see the line departments as being not particularly pro-poor, and inefficient in the selection of the needy and in the provision of benefits. They also state that government officials are corrupt and insist on countless procedures. The perception among government officials is that the very poor are not organized to obtain enduring benefits from the government and there are too many difficulties in reaching them. Thus, while vast sums of money are spent on rural development and poverty alleviation, the very poor rarely benefit.

Banks and cooperatives The Formal Rural Banking System (FRBS)[14] has experienced a phenomenal expansion in the number of bank branches, deposits and number of advances. In order to improve access to credit for the rural poor, commercial banks were asked to play a social role and to target credit through a number of subsidized credit programmes. The FRBS was also made responsible for disbursing loans to beneficiaries of the Integrated Rural Development Programme (IRDP) and the Development of Women and Children in Rural Areas (DWCRA) programme in collaboration with line departments and the elected leaders of *gram panchayats*. The IRDP was initiated on a nationwide basis in the early 1980s to increase the income-generating assets of the poor directly through a mixture of subsidies and credit. Under the DWCRA programme, government staff in a village would set up a 15-member women's group, which, after regular savings of 30 rupees by each of the members for six months, would be eligible for an interest-free loan from a local formal bank. The number of DWCRA groups has increased phenomenally in recent years (Rajakutty 1997: 91).

All three villages are served by commercial banks and cooperatives. Each of the commercial banks in these villages has mobilized 15–20 million rupees as deposits and lent about 10–12 million rupees as credit. In each of the credit cooperatives, the proportion of borrowing members is less than 50 per cent, and the share capital forms only a small proportion of the total lending. Hence they depend on an apex cooperative bank for onward lending. The credit cooperatives have mobilized 3.5–6 million rupees as deposits and have lent 2–8 million rupees for rural lending.

From the official standpoint, these financial institutions have been doing very well. It is to be noted that the FRBS was in crisis during the 1980s, with mounting overdues (largely due to managerial and political factors) and recurring losses. As part of the ongoing financial reforms (linked to structural adjustment policies), banks are being asked to follow strict credit norms and to earn profits every year. In the past, the performance of the branch manager was evaluated on the basis of deposits. Now the criteria are lending, recovery and profits in addition to deposit mobilization. The managers of the commercial banks and credit cooperatives in the selected villages have fulfilled the criteria and are in the good books of their own management. This is incredible because, among other things, in the past losses were attributed to priority sector lending.[15] Information from banks in the selected villages shows that they provide over 80 per cent of the credit to the priority sector and still earn profits. How is this possible?

The answer to this lies in the lending portfolio. The distribution of total advances shows that most loans (90 per cent in the case of cooperatives and 75 per cent in the case of commercial banks) go to crop production, which falls under the priority sector. However, an analysis of the amount lent for crop production shows that most loans are against jewellery and existing deposits. A significant proportion was given for sugar-cane cultivation, with security provided by the local sugar factory. The rest was given directly to farmers, of whom 70 per cent are regular borrowers.

Given that the poor and poorest in the selected villages do not have assets in land, jewellery or deposits, it is obvious that much of the credit from FRBS is going to the more affluent and has little to do with poverty alleviation.

The financial institutions in the village provide only 5 to 10 per cent of the total advances in a year to the IRDP, employment generation and the DWCRA. The reasons given for the lower allocation of funds for poverty alleviation are the following. First, such loans suffer from problems of selection, monitoring and repayment. Second, the beneficiaries are selected by line departments and elected leaders of *gram panchayat*s where patronage is the most important factor. Hence lists sent in by line departments and local, decentralized government institutions are regarded with suspicion, and financial institutions consequently reject a large number of applications. Third, branch managers are advised by their regional offices to go slow as far as lending for poverty alleviation is concerned and not to lend any amount more than a pre-arranged target.

The manager of the local bank in Mottupalyam acknowledged that they are not doing anything for poverty alleviation, let alone poverty reduction. He noted that if the banks are to play a significant role in poverty alleviation, there needs to be appropriate legal provisions to recover the loans and the selection of borrowers should be left to the banks. If the latter is not possible, the line departments and elected members of *gram panchayats* should also be involved in recovery. He concluded that these conditions are difficult to achieve in the short run. Hence NGOs may have to shoulder a greater responsibility for poverty alleviation.

The widespread perception is that banks do not lend to the poor or to women, insist on countless procedural formalities, ask for collateral security, and generally lend only to regular customers and account holders. Unless one is recommended by an influential person, it is therefore difficult to obtain credit from banks.

Decentralized government In 1993 the Indian government brought in the 73rd constitutional amendment, which made key changes in the rules relating to decentralized government[16] and gave priority to decentralization, people's participation and democracy at the local level. The amendment adopted a three-tier model, with democratically elected governments at the village, *taluk* or *mandal* and district levels. The *gram sabha* (people's assembly), consisting of all voters in a *gram panchayat* area, was to be convened at least twice a year at ward level to incorporate people's views into planning and implementation.

Tamil Nadu state did not hold elections to *gram panchayats* for a long time. Under the 73rd constitutional amendment, the state government had to conduct the elections in 1996. The target group of SHARE did not contest any of the seats in Sabthalipuram and Mottupalyam. In all three villages, *gram panchayats* have been constituted and functioning since 1996.

The president of the *gram panchayat* of which Sabthalipuram is a part was elected from six candidates in 1995. She is a graduate and belongs to the Vanniyar caste. When asked to describe Sabthalipuram, she noted that 'the village predominantly consists of Vanniyars who solidly stood behind me in the election'. Interestingly, she does not refer to silted tanks, poor sanitation, or the fact that over 50 per cent of the village are poor and unemployed. When asked what has been done for the poor in the village, she looked very baffled, asking in return: 'What has the *gram panchayat* to do with poverty?'

This question naturally surprised us, but it provided answers to several questions. The 73rd constitutional amendment may have provided a political opportunity, but it has not succeeded in providing the poor with political agency, or in raising poverty as a central concern. Many people regard the *gram panchayat* as an elected executive to implement public works. It is not perceived as an organization enabling the participation of the poor so that they can access and contest policy formulation and implementation.

This is corroborated by an analysis of the income and expenditure of *gram panchayats* in the selected villages, which shows that most of the expenditure incurred in the last two years went on the protected water supply, road construction and providing streetlights. The *gram sabhas* were not held even once to ascertain the views of the people in the planning, implementation and monitoring of the programmes. It is generally noted that the presidents of *gram panchayats* are kept busy recovering the vast sums spent during the elections by awarding contracts to those offering bribes and to those who have supported them in the elections. The ward members belonging to political parties other than those to which the presidents belong complain about the corrupt practices of presidents. Yet, to date, they have done nothing to raise these issues in *gram panchayat* meetings, except questioning the choice of person to whom the contract is awarded.

Some poverty alleviation is achieved by *gram panchayats*. Works relating to protected water supplies and sanitation contribute to the improvement of health status. They participate in the selection of beneficiaries for the IRDP, widows' pension schemes, incentives for female education, and so on. While the presidents complain about the lack of absolute powers in the selection, the people see the selection as based on political considerations and corruption. The presidents rejected the allegations by stating that they went strictly by the list of the poor prepared in each village. When a copy of the list was requested, it was stated that the list was not readily available and it has not been available during subsequent visits.

To conclude, the 73rd amendment's stated objective was for the poor to occupy executive positions in the local decentralized government and to participate in policy formulation and implementation. Among both the elected leaders and the poor in the research villages, the work of local decentralized government is seen to implement public works rather than to engage explicitly in poverty reduction.

Conclusions

In the organizational mapping conducted in Sabthalipuram and Mottu-palyam, the people rated the PDS, protected water supplies (through the *panchayat*) and schools (with a meal provided) as the most important local organizations with respect to their poverty condition. After these came SHARE, while banks and cooperatives come a distant fifth. *Gram panchayat* and line departments were rated last, and spatially presented as being very, very removed from the poor. The pattern was similar in Melvallam, except that SHARE was not in the picture. This suggests that the presence of an NGO has had little impact on the functioning of local organizations, notwithstanding the fact that it has sought to facilitate new ways by which the poor can represent their interests. What are the factors contributing to this failure?

First, the basis for the intervention strategy of SHARE was not rooted in the poverty condition and processes of the local area. The historical analysis of processes generating poverty showed that new agricultural technology and lift irrigation, together with changes in cropping patterns, resulted in widespread unemployment and livelihood problems for the poor. However, SHARE did not initiate work around the poor's engagement in the local labour market – for example, on their rights relating to employ-ment and wages. Instead, the organization began with income-generation activity. One might argue that this also addresses the problem of un-employment. But, as the research shows, unemployment continues to be an important problem for the poor, even after nearly fourteen years of work by SHARE in income generation.

Second, even if the organization wanted to represent the interests of the poor in the labour market, one wonders whether this would have been possible. This is because, as the discussion of historical changes in the socio-economic status of the different sections showed, livelihoods of some of the SC households improved through their entrepreneurship. The fact that historically the poor have had little success in promoting their interests in local political forums only serves to confirm the notion that only individual efforts can lead to improvement. This was repeatedly revealed in discussions with poor households. It is certainly not conducive for an NGO that seeks to pursue poverty reduction through empowerment.

Third, the institutional channels that the NGO sought to create with which the poor's interests could be projected need to be examined as to whether they could serve that purpose in practice. The SHGs are not homogeneous and consist of the poorest, the poor and others. In one of the SHGs in Sabthalipuram, a woman belonging to the 'well-off' category managed to join the group and functioned as its leader until recently. When asked about the poverty-alleviation strategies that the poor should be following, she noted that individual strategies are the best. When asked about collective struggles to secure the rights of the poor in the labour market, she stated that she was not in favour of them, as the reason for being poor is not low wages, but laziness. While I do not wish to generalize on the basis of this case, it does suggest that such heterogeneity may hinder the process of generating and facilitating the possibilities for the poor to exert an influence on the political and economic process.

As the discussion on the condition and severity of poverty reveals, poverty is complex and its nature varies between villages and the caste groups within a village. In such a situation, one wonders whether the formation of organizations such as SHGs and craft centres, with almost identical functions and activities, will help the poor to access and contest policy formulation and implementation.

The ability of these organisations to help the poor obtain opportunities for poverty reduction also needs to be questioned. Asked about what is discussed in the meetings of craft centres and SHGs, one woman stated that 'we discuss personal problems'. Another woman gave an example of an issue relating to domestic violence that was discussed in the craft centre; in this instance the other members counselled her to be patient, saying that things would sort themselves out on their own. But a significant proportion of members stated that they are so preoccupied with the production of palm-leaf products that they talk only about orders, production, quality and meeting deadlines. The monthly meetings of SHGs are used mainly for savings collection and to arrive at lending decisions. Very little time is spent in discussing issues relating to the community or to their poverty. For instance, although the mandatory *gram sabha* meetings have not been held in the village for two years, women members have not discussed this issue, let alone pressed the *gram panchayat* to hold such a meeting.

The organizations also seem to be inadequate for the purpose of providing opportunities for the poor to influence political processes. For instance, there is no forum at either village or *gram panchayat* level where members of SHGs and craft centres can meet and exert any influence on political and economic processes. Similarly, there is no federation of SHGs at the project level. As a membership-based organization, SHARE could be considered a federation. But it is not always clear whether this is an NGO facilitating social change at the local level or a federation representing the interests of its member organizations at higher levels.

SHARE is part of only one NGO network that markets products in the international market. Although it makes efforts to enable the poor to access the resources of the government and banks by empowering them, the main strategy used is to mobilize the resources for its target group on its own. The organization believes that it has been able to achieve success in resource mobilization because of: i) the image that SHARE is a sincere, transparent, democratic and accountable organization; ii) the networks that the organization has built up with the officials and bankers in the district; and iii) the representative status accorded to some of the office-bearers of SHARE in various decision-making committees at district level. So far, the priority given to building up or becoming part of NGO networks designed to represent the interests of the poor in policy formulation and implementation has been low.

Fourth, the existence of poverty at the local level is recognized, and the poor are aware and capable of discussing many of its causes. At the same time, their view that it is best to bring about change through individual strategies suggests that the politicization of poverty has yet to take place and that poverty is not part of a broader political discourse. It should perhaps not be surprising, therefore, that the target group members of SHARE do not discuss the lack of *gram sabha* meetings with reference to poverty reduction.

Both banks and decentralized government could do a lot for poverty reduction. While banks and line departments do little in this locality, decentralized government is failing to apply the resources it has to poverty reduction. Sanitation, protected water supplies and road construction are examples of work that is central to changing poverty. Yet the local *gram panchayats'* work relating to the de-silting of tanks, improving the water table in the locality, providing sanitary facilities for women, undertaking employment-oriented public works for the poor, and so on, is conspicuously absent. And SHARE's target group members fail to challenge the organizations on this failure, expecting little else.

Fifth, the target group members of SHARE constitute an exclusive group separate from the other poor in the villages. For example, in one of the meetings held on organizational mapping, there was a difference of opinion on how to place SHARE. Two of its members wanted to give a higher rating to SHARE on the grounds that the craft centre provides employment almost all the year round, and SHGs provide loans to those who cannot obtain them from the banks and provide supplementary education to children and training on a wide range of issues to women. Others present agreed with the reasoning, but still rejected the rating. Their argument was that these positive things happen only in the case of the 25 or so SHARE members in the village. Since the number of poor is much higher, a higher rating cannot be assigned to SHARE. This suggests that SHARE's work in income generation and welfare may have helped its own target group, but that it has failed to include the other poor in any endeavour to represent the interests of the poor in policy formulation and implementation.

Although SHARE's objective is the empowerment of poor women, and although it has been making sincere efforts to achieve this objective by implementing programmes and activities aimed at livelihood provision and capacity-building, the organization has been facing constraints and obstacles in generating the possibilities for the poor to reduce their poverty. The constraints are deficiencies in its technical and political capacity. The obstacles are wider socio-economic and political processes and a lack of pro-poor attitudes in other local organizations. Given that NGOs alone cannot reduce poverty and that other local organizations are not pro-poor in their nature, poverty reduction remains an outstanding problem.

Notes

1. This chapter immensely benefited from rich discussions and debates within the LORPA programme, and among LORPA researchers. I thank Neil Webster, Lars Engberg-Pedersen and Ole Therkildsen for their comments on an earlier draft of the chapter.

2. There are about 20,000 NGOs registered under the Foreign Contributions Regulation Act (FCRA), 1976. Since educational and charitable institutions are also required to be registered under the FCRA, one can assume that 50 per cent of them are assumed to be active in rural and urban development. There are also NGOs without FCRA registration, which undertake development activities with assistance from the government and local contributions. If we include these organizations, the likely number is around 20,000.

3. The data used in this chapter are part of an ongoing Action Research Project (ARP) on poverty-alleviation strategies initiated jointly by the German Development Corporation/Self-Help Fund (GTZ/SHF) and the Institute for Social and Economic Change (ISEC).

4. A block is an administrative unit comprising about thirty to forty villages.

5. This was done with two to three elders in each of the villages. The yardstick used

to recall the changes was different in each case; some have used important events (such as the birth of a child), some have used their age (i.e. when the person was 15 years old, 25 years old, etc.), and one person used the different political rules (such as Congress rule). In these exercises, PRA techniques were used to facilitate the respondent in recalling the changes and in quantifying their extent.

6. The water in the tanks is often used for irrigation, and the command area is the area that can be covered by the water.

7. Although oil engines began to replace kavalais from the First World War, growth was slow, from twelve in 1915 to 150 in 1947 in the district (Bandara 1977: 326).

8. The proportion of land under HYV cultivation to total area under paddy cultivation increased from 0.2 per cent in 1967–68 to 56.5 per cent in 1970–71. The area under HYV cultivation and improved varieties to total area under groundnut cultivation increased from 7.4 to 81 per cent during the same period (Chinnappa 1977: 94).

9. See J. Harris 1993 and Harriss-White and Janakarajan 1997 for more details.

10. The criteria developed with the villagers included the following: i) basic needs (food, clothing, shelter, dependency ratio within the households and income); ii) assets (land, cattle, savings and jewellery); iii) well-being (ability to access and utilize the school and hospital facilities); iv) employment [type of employment (farm or non-farm, casual or permanent), unemployment and child labour]; v) isolation [female-headed households, help (or lack of it) from the government and community]; and, vi) dependency (borrowing, etc.).

11. Cultural norms stipulate that Muslim women should veil their faces and stay within their homes.

12. Even the poorest household has to give gifts and other alms to relatives and the needy.

13. The number declined because craft activity is preferred by the households with young and unmarried girls.

14. Commercial banks, Regional Rural Banks and cooperatives.

15. The FRBS has stipulated since the mid-1980s that 40 per cent of total advances made by commercial banks, RRBs and cooperatives should go for agriculture, small manufacturing, trades and services. This is referred to as priority sector lending.

16. The amendment included: i) regular elections to PRIs; ii) reservation of seats for women, *dalits* and Adivasis at all levels; iii) elections every five years; iv) a Finance Commission every five years to review finances, taxation and funding allocations to the panchayats; v) PRIs to be responsible for government schemes and programmes aimed at economic development and social justice in rural areas; and vi) *panchayats* to be responsible for collecting certain taxes.

Bibliography

Aziz, Abdul (1993) *Decentralized Planning: The Karnataka Experiment*, New Delhi: Sage.

Andersen, Per Pinstrup and Mauricio Jaramillo (1993) 'The impact of technological change on food consumption and nutrition', in Peter B. R. Hazell and C. Ramasamy (eds), 1993.

Bandara, C. M. Madduma (1977) 'Hydrological consequences of agrarian change', in B. H. Farmer (ed.), 1977.

Chinnappa, B. N. (1977) 'Adoption of the new technology in North Arcot District, in B. H. Farmer (ed.), 1977.

Engberg-Pedersen, Lars (1998) 'Studying poverty – concepts and approach', in Neil Webster (ed.), *In Search of Alternatives: Poverty, the Poor and Local Organizations*, CDR Working Paper No. 98.10, Copenhagen: Centre for Development Research.

Farmer, B. H. (ed.) (1977) *Green Revolution*, London: Macmillan.

Harris, B. (1977) 'Rural electrification and the diffusion of electric water-lifting technology in North Arcot District, India', in B. H. Farmer (ed.), 1977.

Harris, J. (1977) 'The limitations of HYV technology in North Arcot District: the view from a village', in B. H. Farmer (ed.), 1977.

— (1993) 'The Green Revolution in North Arcot: economic trends, household mobility, and the politics of an "awkward class"', in Peter B. R. Hazell and C. Ramasamy (eds), 1993.

Harriss-White, Barbara and S. Janakarajan, S. (1997) 'From green revolution to rural industrial revolution in South India', *Economic and Political Weekly*, 21 June.

Hazell, Peter B. R. and C. Ramasamy (eds) (1993) *The Green Revolution Reconsidered: The Impact of High Yielding Rice Varieties in South India*, New Delhi: OUP.

Kabeer, N. (1994) *Reversed Realities: Gender Hierarchies in Development Thought*, London and New York: Verso.

Murugesan, K. (1999) 'Experiences of "SHARE" in its attempt at ensuring participation of women in the election to local administration', in D. Rajasekhar (ed.), *Decentralized Government and NGOs: Issues, Strategies and Ways Forward*, New Delhi: Concept.

Rajakutty, S. (1997) 'Development of women and children in rural areas (DWCRA): are we on the right course?', *Journal of Rural Development*, 16, 1.

Rajamma, G. and V. C. Nadarajan (1997) 'Mid-Term Review of SHARE's Activities, Vellore: SHARE, mimeo.

Rajasekhar, D. and Namerta (1994) 'Wage labour in the agricultural sector', in Sarath Davala (ed.), *Unprotected Labour in India: Issues and Concerns*, New Delhi: FES.

Rajasekhar, D. and N. L. Narasimha Reddy (1997) *Local Development Programmes and NGOs: A Guide on Local Government Programmes for Field Workers*, Bangalore: BCO and NOVIB.

Reddy, N. L. Narasimha and D. Rajasekhar (1996) *Development Programmes and NGOs: A Guide on Central Government Programmes for NGOs in India*, Bangalore: BCO and NOVIB.

Sen, A. K. (1981) *Poverty and Famines: An Essay on Entitlement and Deprivation*, Oxford: Oxford University Press.

9

Local Institutions in Bangladesh: An Analysis of Civil Society and Local Elections

Kirsten Westergaard and Abul Hossain

Bangladesh has a long tradition of devolution, as local government dates back to the 1880s, when the Local Self Government Act was passed during the British period. Since independence in 1971 Bangladesh has also had numerous non-state institutions, not least in the form of non-governmental organizations (NGOs), most of which are donor-financed. The main purpose of this chapter is to explore and discuss the extent to which the more recent decentralization has benefited the poor economically as well as politically. Another purpose is to explore the nature of civil society and political space, and to examine whether political space in Bangladesh allows the poor and/or local organizations to pursue successful strategies in terms of poverty reduction and democratization.

The State, Civil Society and Political Space

In analysing the nature of the state in Bangladesh as well as the potential for poverty reduction through devolution and NGO strategies, we shall as a first step use Mouzelis' conceptual framework of a 'mode of domination'.[1] It is concerned with the level of the polity, and the concept of 'the relations of domination' points to the manner in which politico–military technologies, that is, the institutionalized ways of regulating the distribution of political power between dominant and dominated groups, are controlled (Mouzelis 1990: 66).

The distribution of power in part depends on the process of inclusion – that is, the way in which the majority of people are brought into the national centre in the process of creating national arenas on the economic, political and cultural levels. Mouzelis argues that in late-developing societies the process of inclusion or 'opening-up process took place in a pre-industrial context, where the industrial classes were weak in terms of both numbers and organization, and where an overall weak civil society was unable to check the state's patrimonial-despotic features' (1990: 140). The result is that, in such societies relations of domination are characterized by incorporative modes (1990: 73–7; 1996: 57–62). One mode is '*clientelism* through the use of vertical networks of patron–client relationships for bringing the lower-class strata into national politics. The basic effect of clientelism is the maintenance of the status quo where fundamental class issues are systematically displaced by personalistic squabbles over the distribution of spoils.'

Another mode is '*populism* which mobilizes newcomers into active politics via the masses' attachment to a leader whose charisma becomes the major source of legitimation'.

The process of inclusion thus took a vertical, authoritarian turn, and the distribution of political, civil and socio-economic rights was uneven and restricted: 'the lower classes, although brought into the national centre, were left out as far as basic rights were concerned, rights guaranteeing them a reasonable share in the distribution of political power, wealth and social prestige' (Mouzelis 1996: 53).

In Mouzelis' approach, therefore, the process of inclusion in late-developing countries takes place in a societal context where civil society is weak. This is the case in Bangladesh, which is characterized by an absence of strongly organized trade unions, peasant organizations and other non-state interest groups.

We are well aware that the concept of civil society is highly contested and that there is no consensus on the meaning of the concept. For us *civil society* is a certain arena of society: the public space between the household and the state, where groups (social actors)[2] interact with each other and with the state. It is an arena within which normative struggles are fought out. It is primarily a *relational* concept. Struggles (or dialogue) within civil society and between civil society and the state define rules shaping interactions and power balances between society and government. The outcome of the struggles influences the *political space*.

A further dimension should be added to the interactions and power balances between state and society: international structures of power increasingly influence the nature of the state and of civil society, as well as their interaction.[3] With its great dependence on foreign aid, this dimension is very important in the Bangladesh case. To us, therefore, analysing civil society involves the exploration of struggles and power relations.

The nature of the state in Bangladesh Bangladesh became an independent nation in 1971 following a war of liberation from Pakistan. Politically, it has alternated between coercive and incorporative modes of domination. Martial law governments and coercive relations of domination prevailed between 1975 and 1990. As one of us has argued elsewhere (Westergaard 1996a), during the parliamentary periods relations of domination have been characterized by incorporation, in its populist as well as its clientelist forms. Economically, the regime of Hussain Mohammed Ershad (1982–1990) was characterized by the introduction of structural adjustment policies, including privatization and a greater reliance on NGOs in service delivery, as advocated by the international aid community. With Ershad's overthrow following a popular uprising in late 1990, economic policies did not undergo great changes, but the re-introduction of a parliamentary form of government turned the political situation into what may be described as a transition to democracy. This created a political opportunity structure[4] and, as described below, this opportunity was exploited by some advocacy NGOs.

In analysing the populist mode of domination it is useful to draw upon Laclau's (1977) discussion of the role of ideology to interpellate – or constitute – individuals as subjects. He points out that in populist ideological discourse, individuals are interpellated with reference to 'the people', or other similar non-class references.

Historically, the people of Bangladesh have been interpellated as religious, Bengali and Bangladeshi subjects.[5] During the anti-colonial movement against the British, the population was mobilized primarily as religious subjects in the movement for a Muslim homeland, Pakistan. Later, during the liberation struggle against Pakistan they were interpellated as Bengali subjects, where the ideology was based on Bengali culture and language as well as secularism. After the overthrow of the Awami League government in 1975, the territorial aspect of the national identity was stressed in the ideology of the martial law governments, and the people became mobilized as Bangladeshi Muslim subjects. This ideological discourse has an anti-Indian as well as an anti-Hindu flavour, thus giving communal overtones to the national ideology.

Today, people in Bangladesh remain divided on the issue of national identity, an issue that is reflected in the ideology of the two major parties: the ruling Awami League, stressing the cultural Bengali heritage and the legacy of the Liberation struggle; and the main opposition party, the Bangladesh Nationalist Party, stressing the territorial aspect of Bangladesh ('Bangladeshi'). The issue of ideology and national identity is also reflected in the struggles within civil society. As we shall show below, while many NGOs have mobilized the poor and women to fight for their economic, political and cultural emancipation, fundamentalist groups are opposing these strategies. There are reports of mullahs refusing to officiate at funerals for families associated with NGOs, and many NGO-run non-formal schools have been vandalized and burned by religious groups. The resurgence of the Jama´at-i-Islam party has undoubtedly been a central factor in this.

The populistic/ideological discourse is interwoven with the clientelist mode of domination through the predomination of personalist politics. This is exemplified by the two major parties, where the leader of the ruling Awami League is the daughter of 'the Father of the Nation', Sheikh Mujib, who led the independence movement and was assassinated in 1975; while the leader of the Bangladesh Nationalist Party is the widow of a former president (Ziaur Rahman, known as Zia), who was assassinated in 1981. In the political speeches of the two women, mutual personal attacks are frequent, and repeated references are made to the legacy of the deceased father and husband, respectively.

It is the clientelist form of incorporative relations of domination that pervades Bangladesh. This is shown not least through patronage, which is a salient feature and which at the national level is exacerbated by foreign aid. As Sobhan (1993: 246) has pointed out:

> For those who control the dispensation of public resources access to aid is a source of patronage. It increases the command over jobs and resources. It follows that for any government in Bangladesh aid is political power. The more aid at the disposal of the government the more patronage it commands. The provision of jobs, the scope for commissions and peculation are matched by the election gains from being able to locate an aided project in a particular area.

Power relations in rural areas: the case of Boringram Historically, relations of domination in Bangladesh have been exercised through multiple networks of patron–client relations (Wood 1992). In the rural areas the major asset is land, and those with surplus land exercise control over others through quasi-monopolistic employment, usurious money-lending, and the allocation of land for tenancy. During the elections to the local councils, vertical patron–client relationships have worked, by and large, in favour of getting the local patrons into office; that is, the incorporative-clientelist mode of domination is repeated at the local level.

At the same time, power relations at the local and the national levels interact. Those in power at the national level have attempted, usually successfully, to build up a rural power base by aligning themselves with local power-holders. On their part, leaders of local councils have tended to associate themselves with the party of the government in power, many changing party affiliation with successive changes of government.

Boringram is a pseudonym for a village in the northern part of Bangla-desh. Literally it means 'red soil village', implying that the village is located in the Barid tract, which is characterized by red clay of old alluvium. In 1975–76 Westergaard (1980) undertook an economic and social study of the village.

> Traditionally, the most important social institution in rural Muslim Bengali society is the *samaj*, meaning community, a symbolic and institutional reference for the political and religious community. It is led by a council of elders who have the function of moral arbiters in community life and play an important role in dispute settlements at informal village courts (*shalish*). Looking at the institution of the *samaj*, Bertocci (1980: 114) has argued that 'as a *cultural* model of solidarity [it] takes concrete shape in rural Bangladesh as the expression of the power domains of the economically and politically dominant families and their members'.

Major religious functions are observed within the *samaj*. It may be coterminous with a village or extend it. Until some thirty years ago, the *samaj* in Boringram was coterminous with the village and was under the leadership of the village headman, who was the head of the richest household in the village. This person was also powerful outside the village and had been chairman of the local government at union level during the British period. His second son had been a member in the Pakistan period, and his third son was chairman of the union *parishad* from 1973 to 1977, at the time of the original village study (the third son will be referred to as the 'Boringram chairman').

After the death of the old headman, there was a fight over land as well as a fight for power between his two oldest sons, and the *samaj* split into three, two factions being headed by the two rival brothers and the third by an influential person who was not related to the old headman and who wanted to set up his own *samaj*, rather than join any of the brothers.

At the time of the 1975–76 study, the village was divided into the three *samaj*, but we would argue that although village unity was broken and joint undertakings made difficult, the *samaj* system still functioned. One reason is that religious ceremonies and disputes settlement continued within the individual *samaj*. Another is that the villagers considered themselves as belonging to a *samaj*. On the other hand, it could be argued that factionalism had superseded the community unity implied in the notion of *samaj*.

Economic and social changes At the time of the 1975–76 study, agricultural production was more or less stagnant, and the situation corresponded quite well to Bhaduri's (1973) 'A study in agricultural backwardness under semi-feudalism'. There was little investment in agriculture, and agricultural wages were way below the minimum wage.

In the mid-1970s a shortage of employment in the farm and non-farm sectors and low agricultural wages meant that the landless and land-poor faced severe poverty. The data showed that about 36 per cent of the 122 households in the village, including most of the landless, were unable to provide their families with rice throughout the year. These were defined as living below the poverty line. Most of these families would often starve, while some managed to eat one meal a day through the help of relatives or by borrowing. In a few of the better-off households sons with an education were employed as teachers, and some of the rich households had also diversified into trading in buffaloes and rice. A few households were engaged in petty trade, and there were two tailors and two carpenters in the village. Labour migration was very limited. Most of the landless and land-poor were dependent on the landowners for employment, and the majority remained unemployed outside the peak agricultural season. The social structure was characterized by the patron–client relationships described in the introduction.

Irrigation picked up in the early 1980s. Farmers now use high-yielding seed varieties of paddy, and since the mid-1970s average yields have more than doubled.

By the mid-1990s, the situation had completely changed due to capitalist investment in agriculture. Although the data on land-holding shows that there has been an overall trend towards smaller holdings in 1995–96, cultivators are better off, due to the increase in agricultural production mentioned above.

The improved agricultural practices have benefited not only the cultivators but also the agricultural labourers, as the adoption of higher yielding varieties has increased the demand for labour, which in turn has influenced daily wage rates. While the daily wage for agricultural labour was slightly below two-thirds of the minimum wage in 1975-76, today it is considerably above.

Besides the development in the agricultural sector, other developments have taken place in the area. Boringram is located about three miles from a *thana* headquarters. During the 1980s the government of Bangladesh spent huge amounts of money upgrading the *thanas*, which resulted in a lot of construction and the rise of a small-town, semi-urban middle class. These developments in turn resulted in an emergent service sector, including trade and transportation.[6] In the 1990s over half of the present 245 households were involved in the non-agricultural sector.[7] The importance of income from this sector is especially important for the landless, many of whom are involved in the informal sector, where daily incomes are almost twice as high as the salary for agricultural labour.

The improved economic situation of the landless has had an impact on the traditional power structure: Until 1979–80 there were no further splits within the three *samaj*. At that time the government introduced a village-level government (*gram sarkar*), and the son of the first son of the old village headman was elected secretary (he will be referred to as the 'grandson'), while the son of the leader of the outside faction was elected president (both their fathers had died). Because of a change in government policy (the then president had been killed), the *gram sarkar* system lasted for less than a year, but during this short period the 'grandson' emerged as a village leader. At the same time, the three *samaj* started to split up for various reasons, including not obeying the *samaj* rule of not taking meals in households outside one's own *samaj*, quarrels over the distribution of meat, moral misbehaviour, and so on.

In the late 1990s there were ten *samaj* in the village, many of them consisting of a few related households who celebrated religious functions together. Until 1995 the biggest *samaj* in the village was headed by two schoolteachers, one being the son of the original *samaj* leader outside the old headman's family. It had 64 members and functioned as a *samaj* for religious purposes; but at the time of the *Kurbani Eid* (a Muslim festival involving animal sacrifice) in 1996 they could not agree, and the *samaj* became dysfunctional. The members were dissatisfied that there were no longer any *shalish* within the *samaj*, not least because the two leaders are rivals. At times one of the two leaders may try to settle a dispute, but this is no longer satisfactory.

The breakdown of the biggest *samaj* is a challenge to the system, and the villagers talk about the breakdown of the *samaj* system. Many interviews revealed that the ordinary villagers no longer trust the leaders. We are inclined to relate this breakdown to economic developments. As mentioned, the *samaj* is led by elders who also happen to belong to the group of influential landowners; and its institutional function in the political and religious sphere parallels the institution of patron–client relationships in the economic sphere. In both the institution of the *samaj* and within the patron–client relationship, there is an implicit reciprocity, often between the same sets of persons: in the religious sphere the rich households are supposed to share their meat with the poor at the time of the *Kurbani Eid*, while in the economic sphere they are supposed to help their clients in times of need.

Economic development in Boringram has meant that the poor are no longer in a dependency relation to the landowners for work, as there is an excess demand for their labour. They are also no longer dependent on the landowners for credit, partly because of their improved earning capacity, and partly because of the availability of loans from three credit NGOs. At the time of the 1975–76 study, however, the villagers had been dependent on the big landowners, and they took their leadership for granted. This does not imply that they trusted their leaders, but means only that they were not in a position to dispute their power. Since the breakdown of the patron–client relationship they no longer see their advantage in blindly following the leaders, many of whom are involved in factional disputes.

Looking at the *samaj* as a cultural model, Bertocci has speculated on a possible breakdown in a different way, stressing the notion of legitimacy:

> [W]hen the powerful conduct themselves in manners which betray the traditional bases of their legitimacy as leaders, they expose themselves to resistance which is predicated on that very same moral order, around which deeply held notions, involving justice itself, the powerless may mobilize and formulate a vocabulary of resistance in their own manner ... Should *samaj*-driven notions of solidarity take hold and coalesce around groups pushed by material conditions into heightened class-consciousness, one outcome could be abolition of *samaj* as an organizational form itself. (Bertocci 1980: 121)

It is not possible to judge whether the present leaders conduct themselves in a manner that betrays the moral code more than the leaders of one or several generations ago, but certainly their legitimacy is highly questioned. The powerless in Boringram have not developed a high degree of class-consciousness; their resistance is more in the form of passivity in not following the leaders, but no alternative leadership has developed.

With the incipient breakdown of the *samaj* system, the village as a community is in an anomalous situation. On the one hand village disputes are in most cases settled within the village. This is possible because the 'grandson' is still symbolically regarded as a village leader, despite the fact that he has moved to the nearby town, where he works as a schoolteacher. He is often called in as a *salishker* or 'arbitrator' to arbitrate in the village, both by individual *samaj* and for dispute settlements between one or more *samaj*. He is well respected because of his skills as a *salishker* and because he is known not to take bribes. We would argue that his relationship to the villagers constitutes a kind of informal governance of the village community. The villagers are very concerned that dispute settlements should take place within the village and not be referred to the police, as they are known to take bribes.

On the other hand, factionalism is very much part of village life, and the rivalry between the descendants of the two sons of the old village headman still continues. With the migration of several educated and influential persons to the nearby small towns, power struggles increasingly take place beyond the village.

Union politics During the Pakistani period and since independence in 1971, local government systems have come and gone, following the changes in government at the national level. None of the systems introduced since independence has been allowed to function long enough to become consolidated, and over the years a number of acts and amendments have been introduced (Siddiqui 1994; Westergaard and Alam 1995).

TABLE 9.1 Administrative structure in Bangladesh

Administrative unit	Numbers
division	5
district	64
thana (upazila)	489
union	4,460
gram parishad (village)	c. 83,000

For most of the time the union parishads have been the most important representative bodies, and the law rests on two amendments to the Local Government Act, which were passed in 1993 and 1997. A union parishad consists of a chairman, elected throughout the union, and twelve members, nine of whom are elected from each of nine wards, and three female members directly elected from each of the three zones (each consisting of three wards).

The union parishads being the most recurrent local government bodies, it is at this level that local politics beyond the village level take place. In the union to which Boringram belongs there are three influential families who have for decades competed for the chairmanship of the union parishad. One is the family of the old village headman of Boringram. As already mentioned, he was chairman of the union board/council during the British and Pakistani periods, and his third son (the 'Boringram chairman') has been chairman twice since independence. He was an unsuccessful chairman candidate in the previous (1992) union parishad election. In addition, one of the chairmen during the Pakistani period is related to the old headman's family by marriage.

A second family is that of the incumbent union parishad chairman at the time of the 1997 election. His father had been a member of the union council in the Pakistani period. The third family has also held the chairmanship for two generations, in the Pakistan period as well as in independent Bangladesh.

In the 1970s the legacy of the liberation struggle also played a prominent role at the local level. Although this has diminished, the political affiliation of the various candidates does enter into the power struggle. The

'Boringram chairman's' family remained loyal to Pakistan during the liberation struggle and is now affiliated with the Bangladesh National Party (BNP) which was formed in 1978 by the then President Zia (whose widow is now the leader of the BNP). The incumbent chairman at the time of the election was an influential Awami League member who was active in the liberation struggle and is now commander of the *thana* Freedom Fighters Association as well as a member of the *thana* Awami League committee. He is also chairman of the high school committee located at the union level. The headmaster of the high school used to belong to the *samaj* in Boringram that supports the Awami League. He now lives outside the village, but remains respected in Boringram and is sometimes called in to settle disputes in the village. The third influential family in the union joined the Awami League during the liberation struggle, and the head of the family was appointed relief chairman just after independence. His son has been elected chairman since independence, but he does not belong to any political party.

During the December 1997 election there were eight candidates for the post of union *parishad* chairman, almost all from the landed or well-to-do section of the population. They included the incumbent chairman, one person from the third traditional chairman family, and a newcomer who had a lot of money.

The 1997 election process in Boringram[8]

Choosing candidates During our visit to Boringram in February 1997, the villagers were already discussing who should be their candidate for union *parishad* chairman. At that time the villagers in general showed no great enthusiasm for any of the possible candidates. When we asked why they did not try to find a good candidate, a common answer was that: 'No good persons are interested in standing for election to union *parishad*.' One of the possible candidates was the son of the old village headman, the 'Boringram chairman', who had declared his candidacy. Although he was not generally liked in the village, many villagers supported his candidacy. There were no other candidates from the village, and by and large villagers prefer a union *parishad* chairman from their own village, not least because this means that development funds are more likely to come their way. The main opposition to his candidacy came from his nephew (the 'grandson' and leader of the rival family faction turned *salishker*), who openly argued against him. When the 'Boringram chairman' toured the union, he realized that he was unlikely to get major support, and just prior to the filing of nomination papers decided not to run for chairman. Meanwhile Nabi, who comes from a landed family in a neighbouring village, decided to run as a candidate for the chairmanship. He had been a chairman candidate several times before, but had been defeated. Early on, many people from the study village were in favour of him, as they considered him a 'regional' candidate. Nabi is a distant relative of the old village headman's family. While they support the Bangladesh National Party (BNP), Nabi had participated in the liberation war and was supported by the *thana*-level Awami League leadership, which had decided not to support the incumbent chairman, although he was a member of the *thana*-level Awami League committee.

Three people in the village had filed nomination papers to run as member candidates for the union *parishad*. As Boringram is the largest village in the ward, the villagers stand a good chance of getting one person elected (one person has been elected from the village in most union *parishad* elections, including the previous election in 1992). The villagers were interested in getting a Boringram person elected as member, but they were afraid that their votes might be split among the three candidates and that none of them would be elected. Therefore a meeting was called on the premises of the large mosque in the village, and, in the presence of the various *samaj* leaders, they decided to select one member candidate only. The other two candidates withdrew their nominations, and the selected candidate was asked to refund the campaign expenditures of one of the other candidates, who was a poor person.

The person selected at the meeting was Abu, a son of the 'Boringram chairman' who had decided to withdraw his candidature for chairman. Although Abu was selected as 'the village candidate' at the meeting, not all villagers were in favour of him. As was the case in his opposition to the 'Boringram chairman's' candidature, the 'grandson' opposed Abu's candidature, and his son openly campaigned for another candidate. Various persons interviewed estimated that around 60 per cent of the voters in the village were in favour of Abu.

Although Abu and his family support the BNP, an influential Awami League member in the *thana* who used to live in the study village strongly supported Abu, as he felt it was important for the village to get a member elected. He told us that the party inclination of the members did not matter: 'We [the Awami League] are in power, and we can manage them.'

Altogether there were four member candidates from Ward 2, to which the study village belongs. Abu and two other candidates were from landed, well-to-do families, while the fourth was a lower-middle-class person.

There were four women candidates for the one seat in Wards 1, 2 and 3. Three different groups from the village worked in favour of three of the women candidates. However, as there was no woman candidate from the village, the people were not very interested in the election of the female member. We interpret this as reflecting not a lack of interest in women union *parishad* members as such, but rather the villagers' preoccupation with their 'village candidate' for member and their 'regional candidate' for chairman.

The election Election campaigning started in the union and the village more than a month before the election date. The candidates and their workers put up posters and visited voters from door to door, often at night. They entertained villagers with *bidi* (local cigarettes), tea and biscuits in the village shops and the bazaars. There are two shops in the village, and their sales increased considerably during the campaign.

Apart from entertaining, all the candidates spent a lot of money in order to secure the 664 votes controlled by the inhabitants of Boringram.[9] On the basis of numerous interviews we estimated that the 'regional' chairman candidate (Nabi) spent approximately 10,000 takas;[10] the 'village' candidate for member around 35,000 takas; and the winning woman candidate 15,000 takas.[11] The money was spent on various purposes. Thus the 'village' member candidate spent around 8,500 takas repairing a mud road running through the village. Several candidates donated money to the village *madrasah*, or Islamic primary school, as well as to two small mosques used for daily prayers. Finally, the buying of individual and collective votes was widespread.

The combined primary and high school at the entrance to the village was used as the polling centre for Ward 2, to which the village belongs. At about noon the grounds were filled with voters. The campaign workers of the various candidates were still trying to buy votes.

As already mentioned, there are five villages in Ward 2, Boringram being the largest. People came from all five villages, and the turnout was high: at 97 per cent in Boringram and an average of 95 per cent in the other four villages.

Most people in the village were very happy with the election results. Abu, the 'village' candidate for member, won the seat in Ward 2. The chairman candidate who was favoured by most of the people in the village – Nabi, their 'regional' candidate – also won and became chairman of the union *parishad*.

The woman who was elected in the zone comprising Wards 1, 2 and 3 was the candidate who had spent the most money.

Challenges to the Traditional Power Structure

With the breakdown of the *samaj* system a political space emerged, which was, however, not exploited by the villagers. There was no attempt to build up an alternative leadership to challenge the clientelist mode of domination, neither in Boringram nor at the union level. When it came to selecting candidates for (male and female) members and the chairman of the union *parishad*, representatives from the traditional landed classes were chosen. When discussing the selection of candidates, we referred to the villagers' general lack of enthusiasm for available candidates. Nevertheless, the study revealed a lot of interest in the election and the voter turnout was very high.

It is difficult to determine which factors caused this interest. One factor could be the union *parishads'* access to development funds. Whether they like their candidate or not, the villagers know that development funds are more likely to come their way if they have a union *parishad* member from their village and a chairman who is at least from their vicinity (or 'region'). It is well known that members' own returns from investments in election campaigns are very high. As is the case at the national level, for those who control the dispensation of public resources, there is wide scope for commission and speculation.

In our conceptual framework, an alternative leadership is needed to challenge the incorporative mode of domination and thus the traditional power structure. As, by and large, the major political parties in Bangladesh do not have a political agenda for dominated groups, we need to look for other actors within civil society.[12] In the Bangladesh context, we consider NGOs and politically mobilized groups of poor as the major social actors in civil society that are advocating for the rights of the poor.

NGOs emerged on a large scale in Bangladesh during and after the liberation war in 1971, and since the late 1970s many of them have initiated new participatory development strategies focusing on the rural poor and women. There are two overlapping debates on the role of NGOs in the development process in Bangladesh. NGOs activities are often regarded as alternatives to official programmes and one debate thus concerns the record of NGOs with respect to service delivery to the poor. The other debate concerns the role of NGOs in the process of democratization. In their role in advocacy, many NGOs use the concept of empowerment in their strategies. To us 'empowerment' is concerned with enabling poor people to decide upon the actions which they believe are essential to their development, not least structural causes of poverty and political marginalization.[13] In other words, the strategy aims at challenging the clientelist mode of political inclusion.

Most development NGOs in Bangladesh pursue a dual strategy of credit provision and service delivery programmes together with empowerment. A few focus solely on conscientization and empowerment. Below we shall discuss two development NGOs, one a strict advocacy NGO focusing on self-reliance, the other pursuing the more prevalent dual strategy. The analysis of the former case is based primarily on the 1992 union *parishad* election, that of the latter primarily on the 1997 election. The 1992 union *parishad* elections took place about one year after the popular uprising against the military rule of Ershad. Albeit at a late stage, many NGOs had participated in the movement, and this created an opportunity for them in the new political climate. The 1997 union *parishad* elections took place two years after the Awami League returned to power. During the 1996 parliamentary election, several NGO leaders more or less openly supported the Awami League, and the subsequent period has been characterized by good relationships between NGOs and the government.

Nijera Kori Nijera Kori[14] started working in the development and social areas in the early 1980s. It operates in all five divisions of Bangladesh. It is one of the few NGOs that remains firm in not going in for credit programmes. Rather the emphasis is on self-reliance, and the objective is to organize groups of poor people by making them conscious so that they may assert their rights and discharge responsibilities.[15]

Prior to group formation, information is collected and analysed on various forms of corruption and exploitation prevailing in a particular area. Nijera Kori operates a number of special programmes, including: Legal Aid Support (between mid-1996 and mid-1997 they supported approximately one hundred cases involving illegal possession of *khas* (government-owned) land, killing, oppression of women and environmental issues), Education, Women in Development, Human Rights, and Environment, which includes a movement against shrimp cultivation in South Khulna, where the case study is located.

This particular union was chosen for study because the Nijera Kori groups appeared highly mobilized and politically conscious there. This was due to severe conflicts in the area, especially as regards shrimp cultivation within the polders (land reclaimed from the sea). The Dutch Development Agency and the World Bank each had a major development project in the area, and they have opposing policies regarding shrimp cultivation.

The World Bank is in favour of shrimp cultivation inside the polders, and it stresses the economic gains to cultivators and the export earnings to the country. Because of the high incomes to be earned shrimp cultivation is very attractive, and many individuals from outside the area have invested in its production. In order to keep out absentee shrimp cultivators, the World Bank is encouraging the formation of cooperatives for the controlled and integrated rearing of shrimps, and one NGO, Caritas, is in charge of organizing local shrimp farmers in World Bank areas. However, non-resident shrimp cultivators continue to be active in the project area.

Because of the many side effects, especially for the rural poor (such as the salinization of fresh water sources affecting the health situation and homestead garden production), the Dutch Development Agency is opposed to shrimp cultivation in its project area.[16] The main purpose of the project is to improve internal water management, and the project has several social components, in which Nijera Kori was involved at the time of the study.

The landless groups organized by Nijera Kori in the Dutch development area are also strongly opposed to shrimp cultivation, and when a very influential outsider tried to introduce it in 1990, they, along with many other residents of the area, organized a demonstration. During the course of the demonstration gunfire took place, one woman being killed and several landless group members injured. This incident was followed by a number of court cases filed by both sides.

The conflicts over shrimp cultivation, coupled with over a decade of group mobilization and conscientization, have resulted in a high level of awareness among the members of the Nijera Kori groups. This came to light in both interviews with local level groups and the union *parishad* election of 1992.

In one of the villages adjacent to the confrontation over shrimp cultivation, interviews were conducted with members of some of the Nijera Kori groups. They listed a number of benefits following group organization. The first thing mentioned was that, due to their strength, they had been able to establish the rights of local people against shrimp cultivation. Second, the society had established a primary school in the village. Further, within the union they had arranged about twenty marriages without dowry, and they had also taken part in arbitration or *shalish* among themselves.

On the economic side, groups of landless women had obtained employment in maintaining the embankment. The women worked in shifts of two to three months each in order that all the needy women would benefit from the employment. The landless male groups had obtained a lease on *khas* land from the Bangladesh Water Development Board. This had not been an easy process, as the wealthy of the area, as well as outsiders, used to be given the lease and tried to prevent the landless from cultivating the land. With the help of the Dutch project and Nijera Kori, the landless groups finally obtained the lease and cultivated the land jointly, setting aside 20 per cent of their earnings for a fund administered by the society, the rest being distributed among the members.

Because of the special political situation in the area, Nijera Kori had encouraged group members to put up candidates for election. Several interconnected factors influenced the election alliances, the campaign and the outcome of the union *parishad* election of 1992. One important factor was the attitude towards shrimp cultivation, another was the attitude towards the Nijera Kori groups, and a third was the attitude towards the incumbent union *parishad* chairman, who also won the election for chairman in 1992. The chairman is a middle peasant who is opposed to shrimp cultivation in the area and supports the landless. According to him, the role of the middle peasants is to mediate between the rich and the poor, and he in fact sees himself as a leader of the landless.

At the time of the 1992 union *parishad* election, the unions were divided into three wards, three members being elected from each ward.[17] The area of the union studied covered three different areas. Thus Ward 1 was located within the World Bank project; Ward 2 was divided between the Dutch pilot project and an outside area, and Ward 3 was completely within the Dutch project. During the 1992 election campaign, the chairman decided to enter into alliances with a number of the member candidates, including the two candidates belonging to the Nijera Kori groups.

The campaign alliance had the greatest success in Ward 2, to which the chairman belongs. Here the Nijera Kori groups had put up a member candidate who had entered into an alliance with two middle peasants. All three candidates belonged to the chairman's alliance, and all three got elected. In the ward about one-third of the middle peasants were in favour of shrimp cultivation; one of them contested the election, but was defeated.

In Ward 3 the situation was more complicated. The Nijera Kori groups had also put up a candidate in this ward. He was supported by the chairman, who had furthermore entered into an alliance with two other middle peasant candidates, one of whom was actually opposed to the Nijera Kori groups and in favour of shrimp cultivation. According to one of his opponents, the member had supported the chairman and his alliance with the poor, as he realized that the poor were strong and he wanted to be on the winning side. Also in this ward all the member candidates belonging to the chairman's alliance got elected to the union *parishad*.

As mentioned above, Ward 1 was located within the World Bank project area. Nijera Kori is not active in this area, and no landless groups had put up candidates for the union *parishad* election. In this ward the chairman had entered into an alliance with one of the member candidates who got elected, partly on the votes of the poor in the area. The other two member candidates who got elected were middle peasants who were opposed to shrimp cultivation but also very much opposed to the chairman, especially his system of mobilizing group votes.

The outcome of the union *parishad* election was very successful for the Nijera Kori groups as well as for the chairman. The former had nominated two members to fight the election in the name of the groups, and all group members had contributed 10 takas for the election campaign. Their success was not limited to their winning two seats in the union *parishad*, but should also be measured by the fact that the chairman and many of the middle peasants were in fact supporting them through election alliances. Of course, the chairman and the middle peasants also benefited from these alliances. The fact that the middle-class candidates sought the alliances of the poor groups' members is one indication that the poor had become a local power factor to be reckoned with. It was not a question of who was using whom, but rather an alliance to their mutual advantage – to use the chairman's expression, 'politics is tactics'.

The Rangpur Dinajpur Rural Service Programme (RDRS) The RDRS started during the war of liberation in 1971, working among refugees in India. It operates in 28 *thanas* in the six northern districts comprising the greater Rangpur-Dinajpur area, which is one of the poorest areas of Bangladesh. Over the years the focus has shifted from rehabilitation to long-term development, and in 1989 its core project, the Comprehensive Project (CP), was set up. A key component within the CP is the development of people's organizations at two levels: 1) the sub-village level or neighbourhood level, through the formation of male and female Primary Groups, and 2) the union level, through the federation of Primary Groups within the union.

From the outset the RDRS has stressed both service delivery (especially training) and awareness. Initially loans were financed through group savings, but in 1995 the RDRS started a big credit programme funded through a foundation sponsored by the World Bank. At around the same time, it started building up the federations financially. Once established, the federations receive a grant to construct a federation centre, and they also receive interest-free loans for investment in income-generating activities. In addition, they may borrow money from the RDRS at 14 per cent interest.

Unlike most NGOs, which have more or less turned into credit organizations or quasi-banks, the RDRS is primarily concerned with institution-building. However, the credit programme takes up a lot of staff time, and some within the RDRS find this detrimental to the institution-building process.[18]

An evaluation undertaken in 1994 of income-generating and employment activities showed that many members had improved their economic situation, as a result being no longer economically dependent on the money-lenders-cum-rich farmers for usurious credit and employment. We also found that, through their strength in numbers, some federations had put pressure on the union *parishad* chairman to obtain a lease on roads for tree-planting (retaining 60 per cent of the profit after the trees or their fruit had been sold). Others had obtained leases on ponds from the union *parishad*. In one instance the federation had put pressure on the union *parishad* chairman to secure compensation for a female primary group chairwoman who had been raped by an influential person. Some federation members had also been elected to the local union *parishad*s.(Westergaard 1996b: 36–8).

Such cases have multiplied in the intervening years. The most noticeable evidence of strength in numbers was witnessed during the 1997 union *parishad* election. In one of the districts we visited, 113 male and 72 female federation members had contested the election. Of these, 94 (three chairmen, 66 ordinary members and 25 female members) won the election. A calculation made by the RDRS indicates that areas with a high percentage of population with RDRS members as well as of large amounts of credit disbursed had the highest number of federation members elected to the union *parishad*s. It is, however, also noteworthy that the areas with the highest number of elected federation members are also the areas where the Bangladesh Communist Party has been strongest, implying *inter alia* areas with a tradition for organizing people.

One of the union Federations visited is located in such an area. It was started in 1991 with two male and three female groups. At that time it had savings amounting to 1,000 takas. At the time of our visit (February 1998) it had 20 male and 22 female primary groups. Economically, it has done very well, making its first investment from its own money in 1993. In 1995 it bought land for the federation centre, after which the centre was constructed with money from RDRS as well as its own money. In 1996 it invested in the lease of two *hat*s (local markets), 50,000 takas coming from its own money, the other 50,000 takas being seed money. Subsequently it has invested in a host of different business ventures, the most expensive being the construction of a *godown* (warehouse).

The members of the federation have done very well economically. This was revealed through interviews with three of the leaders who had all joined the RDRS in 1987.[19] At the time the chairperson was a ferryman and possessed only his homestead land; now he owns three acres of land and has a small hardware shop. The vice-chairperson (a woman) was working on tree plantations at the roadside leased by the RDRS; now she works in the federation's farm. When she joined the RDRS the family had a homestead only; now they have one acre and a tree nursery. The secretary had half an acre when he joined the RDRS; he has since been trained as a veterinary assistant by the organization and now owns just under three acres.

In terms of empowerment, the federation has also done well, with four male and one woman member of the federation being elected to the union *parishad*. The woman member is the vice-chairperson of the federation, while the others are not on the executive committee. They were all given about 1,000 takas from the federation for entertaining voters. The rest of the expenditure they managed through friends and their own money. It is interesting to note that three of the five members spent much less during the campaign than did their competitors: the woman member spent 6,500 takas, while the runner-up candidate spent 70,000 takas.

As mentioned, the federation is located in an area where the Communist Party of Bangladesh (CPB) has been strong. Three of the four federation male members elected to the union *parishad* used to be members of the CPB, but they have all joined the Awami League (AL). (It should be pointed out that the CPB leader from the area has joined the AL and many have followed him.) Most of the members of the executive committee of the federation are AL, and we were told that 75 per cent of federation members support the AL. The chairperson, however, has no political allegiance.

Discussion Our presentation of the two NGO case studies shows that they have benefited the poor economically. However, this does not amount to a challenge to the power structure. When it comes to political empowerment, it is implicitly assumed in the discussion that getting elected to the union *parishad*s constitutes a challenge to the local power structure. We would argue that this is often the case, but it depends on the degree of politicization of the groups of poor, and whether mobilized groups of poor are in fact getting their own candidate elected and whether this person will act on the part of the poor and not for his or her own benefit.

In the South Khulna case, the Nijera Kori groups were politicized, not least because of the violence that had taken place over the issue of shrimp cultivation. In this case, it is a question of how far the middle peasants will go in aligning themselves with the poor. In an interview with the union *parishad* chairman following the 1992 election, he indicated that it would be a problem if the poor got five seats or more (that is, over half). The result of the 1997 election shows that the alliance was not sustainable.

During our 1998 fieldwork we came across a number of Nijera Kori groups that had got their members elected to union *parishad*s in 1997. One group had fought for access to *khas* land since 1986 and was very politically conscious. Six males and one female had been elected to the union *parishad*, and they regarded Nijera Kori as their 'party'. It remains to be seen whether members from this group will be re-elected in the next election.[20]

With regard to the RDRS, we do have some negative evidence from another RDRS group visited after the 1992 election. Here the chairman of the federation had been elected member of the union *parishad* with the highest number of votes in the whole union, and we were told that the federation planned to have him stand for election to chairman in 1998. The vice-chairperson was a woman who was very active and had done a lot for a primary group. On our return visit in 1998 we found out that the woman's group no longer functioned, as she had used the credit given to the group for her own purposes; and the federation chairman had not been re-elected, as he had benefited himself and not the federation members during his term as union *parishad* member. This case reinforces earlier observations regarding the lack of long-term heterogeneity of the groups (Westergaard 1996b: 52). It seems that in some of the groups an elite is developing, which in some case succumbs to clientelist politics through personal squabbles over the distribution of spoils.

It is difficult to interpret the change in political affiliation on the part of the RDRS group. The primary reason is probably the change made by their political leader from the area. This could be interpreted as an opportunistic move, not unlike the pattern followed by many union *parishad* chairmen, who often change their party affiliation to whichever party is in power.

While quite a few members of groups of mobilized poor people were elected to union *parishad*s in 1992, the numbers elected in 1997 were much greater, from Nijera Kori and RDRS, as well as from other NGOs. With the introduction of elected women members, many women belonging to groups organized by various NGOs were elected to the union *parishad*s in 1997. A research question for the future will be to analyae whether the male and female representatives of the poor – or some of them – will fight for pro-poor policies and thus constitute a real challenge to the traditional power structure.

Conclusions

This chapter has explored two different strategies through which the economic situation of the poor has improved. In both cases the traditional power structure has changed although for different reasons and with different results.

In the Boringram case, the economic situation of the villagers, including the poor, has improved following the increased productivity of the land. This improvement is due to neither local government nor NGO activities,[21] but rather to the availability of irrigation following the privatization of shallow tubewells. Although many poor households had lost whatever land they used to possess, quite a few had exploited the economic opportunities by entering the informal sector. Others had benefited from increased wages for labour following the rise in demand.

We have argued that the breakdown of the traditional social system (the *samaj* community) was caused by the change in the economic structure, as the poor were no longer in a dependency situation *vis-à-vis* the powerful landowners. We further argued that this process had created a political space, but the poor did not exploit it. No alternative leadership had developed to challenge the mode of domination, as witnessed during the 1997 election to the union *parishad*.

One possible explanation for this is provided by McAdam et al. (1996: 5): 'At a minimum, people need to feel both aggrieved about some aspect of their lives and optimistic that, acting collectively, they can redress the problem. Lacking either one or both of these perceptions, it is highly unlikely that people will mobilize even when afforded the opportunity to do so.'

Our analysis of the changes in Boringram shows that, although there are still considerable economic disparities, the poor have no clear reason to feel aggrieved, their economic situation having improved considerably during the past couple of decades. It is also important to note that, unlike South Khulna and the northern part of Bangladesh, the Boringram area has no tradition of radical politics, and no NGOs have mobilized the poor politically in the area.

The two NGO cases discussed are located in areas that have experienced little increase in productivity and no general economic improvement. Here, as our case studies show, NGOs have been instrumental in improving the economic situation of the poor. We have argued that being elected to local government bodies constitutes an important element in the political participation and political empowerment of the poor. Our case studies also show that the strategies have been successful politically.

In our discussion we showed that, following the downfall of the Ershad regime, the 'political opportunity' structure was such that political space was available for NGOs (and other social actors) to mobilize the poor and to improve their economic and to some extent political conditions. We would also venture the argument that some advocacy NGOs have been instrumental in shaping the political space in which they operate. We would further venture the proposition that the nature of the political space is influenced by donor policies stressing democracy and poverty reduction as well as the donors' substantial funding of NGO activities. Or to put it more strongly, through their support of advocacy NGOs with regard to poverty reduction, women's empowerment and legal and human rights, the donors indirectly become social actors in civil society.

However, it is an open question what NGO activities mean in the long run, and how wide the political space actually is. With regard to the latter, one case from the 1992 union *parishad* election shows that, as far as local politics are concerned, the political space has its limits. In five unions in the north, groups of very poor day-labourers mobilized by an advocacy

NGO (not included in our study) had put up candidates for all nine member posts as well as for chairman. Elections took place on different days, and on the first voting date the respective group won the chairmanship as well as the majority of the member seats in the union. Following this, all the dominant and competing factions in the five unions felt that their power was threatened and they joined together. With the help of armed men they ensured that NGO members could not vote in the remaining four unions. They also initiated acts of terror, including burning NGO schools and beating up NGO members. The local administration and the deputy commissioner sided with the local elite, and charges were filed against the NGO fieldworkers.[22] The case also reveals the difficulties of challenging the system: once the union *parishad* was constituted with the elected poor members, the local administration sabotaged its pro-poor policies.

With regard to longer-term developments, it remains to be seen whether the poor will remain dependent on the NGOs or whether they will become a 'political' force in their own right. Another aspect concerns the relationship between NGOs and the donors, not least because most NGOs are dependent on donor funding.[23] The donor community more or less competes in channelling funds to the NGOs. With the donor stress on 'democracy building', this policy has increased in recent years and is likely to continue in the foreseeable future. This dependency on foreign funding implies that NGOs are not free agents, a fact that may be detrimental to their advocacy role in the long term.

To conclude, we have shown that in the 1990s the nature of the Bangladesh state was characterized by the incorporative mode of domination. Although we have argued that relations of domination at the national and local levels interact, our focus on local-level political processes has shown that these possess their own dynamic. In our case studies, clientelist relations of domination have weakened and the political space has broadened. In the Boringram case, the weakening of the clientelist relations of domination was caused by changing economic structures. The poor did not exploit the emerging political space, not least because of the lack of a radical political tradition. In the two NGO examples, clientelist relations of domination were weakened following the exploitation of the political space by advocacy NGOs and the emergent political agency of mobilized groups of the poor.

Despite the somewhat autonomous nature of the political processes at the local level, we would argue that substantial changes in the relations of domination at the local level are unlikely to take place as long as the incorporative mode of domination prevails at the national level.

Notes

1. The concept is developed and discussed in several publications. See Mouzelis 1986, 1990, 1996.

2. The notion is based on Long's (1992) concept of social actors, that is, social entities to which are attributed the power of agency.

3. See also Huber et al. 1993, p. 73.

4. For a discussion of 'political opportunity structure' see McAdam 1996.

5. For more details, see Westergaard 1985.

6. In 1975–76 the *thana* town had a number of tea-stalls. In the late 1990s there were three restaurants, which were fully occupied most of the day, catering also to the through traffic between northern Bangladesh and Dhaka. Several modern shops (for shoes, stationery, bicycles, and so on) are also located in the town. Service and trade activities predominate over production activities, which are negligible. For further details, see Westergaard and Hossain 2000a.

7. For details on employment in the non-agricultural sector, see Westergaard and Hossain 1998.

8. For further details, see Hossain and Westergaard 1998.

9. There is a total of 1,664 votes in Ward 2, to which Boringram belongs.

10. US$1 equals approximately 45 takas.

11. These estimates are only for money spent in the village. The chairmen candidates campaign in all villages of the nine wards of the union, and many informants estimated that the 'regional' candidate spent 3 to 3.5 lakh takas (the highest was 6 to 6.5 lakhs). Candidates for union *parishad* member campaign in all villages in one ward, and our informants estimated that the 'village' candidate spent 65,000 takas (the highest was 1.4 lakhs). The women candidates campaign in three wards, and their estimated expenditures were given as follows: the winning candidate 60,000 takas and the other two women candidates between 15,000 and 30,000 takas each (1 lakh equals 100,000).

12. Like Mouzelis (1996: 53), we consider political parties to be part of civil society. This approach is followed by some but by no means all theorists.

13. See Oakley et al. 1991: 9 and Pearse and Stiefel 1979: 8.

14. Literally 'we can manage ourselves'.

15. This and the following description is taken from Nijera Kori's *Annual Report 1996–97*.

16. For details of the problems associated with shrimp cultivation, see Datta 1994.

17. The number of wards was changed by the Local Government (union *parishad*s) (Amendment Act), 1993.

18. For further discussion of this point, see Benini and Benini (1997), who provide a good analysis of the sometimes-contradictory goals of the RDRS.

19. The 1998 study of the RDRS is based on a survey of several federations. Methodologically, it has the weakness that short periods of time were spent in each federation, and there was no time to conduct interviews with the ordinary members, as was the case in 1994.

20. For further details, see Westergaard and Hossain 2000b.

21. As mentioned in the main text, three NGOs are active in Boringram with credit

programmes for poor women. While these programmes are not completely negligible, our interviews show that by and large they have had little effect on household income.

22. For details, see Hashemi 1992.

23. In order to receive foreign funds, foreign and national NGOs have to register with the NGO Affairs Bureau. In 1997, 1,152 NGOs were registered, of which 136 were foreign.

Bibliography

Benini, Aldo A. and Janet K. Benini (1997) *Federations – A Shelter for the Poor? The Experience of RDRS Bangladesh.* A Report for the Rangpur Dinajpur Rural Service (RDRS), Dhaka, December.

Bertocci, Peter J. (1980) 'Models of solidarity, structures of power: the politics of community in rural Bangladesh', in Myron J. Aronoff (ed.), *Ideology and Interest: The Dialectics of Politics* (Political Anthropology Yearbook I), New Brunswick, NJ: Transaction Books, pp. 97–125.

Bhaduri, A. (1973) 'A study in agricultural backwardness under semi-feudalism', *Economic Journal*, 83: 329.

Datta, Anjan (1994) 'Expanded shrimp culture in Bangladesh. A note on socio-ecological costs', paper prepared for the 4th European Network of Bangladesh Studies Workshop, Amsterdam, 25–27 August, pp. 25–7.

Denconsult (1994) *Rangpur Dinajpur Rural Service Programme (RDRS)*, Copenhagen: Evaluation Report Prepared for the Danish Ministry of Foreign Affairs, Danida.

Hashemi, Syed (1992) 'State and NGO networks in rural Bangladesh: conflicts and coalitions for control', paper presented to the Seminar on State and Non-State Provision of Services in Eastern Africa and South Asia, Centre for Development Research, Copenhagen, June.

Hossain, Abul and Kirsten Westergaard (1998) 'The union parishad election in Bangladesh. A case study of a village in Bogra', paper (draft) presented at the European Network of Bangladesh Studies, Bath, UK, April.

Huber, Evelyne, Dietrich Rueschemeyer and John D. Stephens (1993) 'The impact of economic development on democracy', *Journal of Economic Perspectives*, 7, 3: 71–86.

Laclau, E. (1977) 'Fascism and ideology' and 'Towards a theory on populism', in Ernesto Laclau (ed.), *Politics and Ideology in Marxist Theory*, London: New Left Books.

Long, Norman (1992) 'From paradigm lost to paradigm regained? The case for an actor-oriented sociology of development', in Norman Long and Ann Long (eds), *Battlefields of Knowledge*, London: Routledge.

McAdam, Doug, John D. McCarthy and Mayer Zaid (eds) (1996) *Comparative Perspectives on Social Movements: Political Opportunities, Mobilizing Structures, and Cultural Framings*, Cambridge: Cambridge University Press.

Mouzelis, Nicos P. (1986) *Politics in the Semi-Periphery: Early Parliamentarism and Late Industrialisation in the Balkans and Latin America*, London: Macmillan.

— (1990) *Post-Marxist Alternatives: The Construction of Social Orders*, London: Macmillan.

— (1996) 'Modernity, late development and civil society', in Lars Rudebeck and Olle Törnquist (eds), *Democratization in the Third World. Concrete Cases in Comparative and Theoretical Perspective*, Uppsala: Uppsala University.

Nijera Kori (1997) *Annual Report 1996–97*, Dhaka.

Oakley, Peter et al. (1991) *Projects with People: The Practice of Participation in Rural Development*, Geneva: International Labour Organization, p. 9.

Pearse, Andrew and Matthias Stiefel (1979) *UNRISD Popular Participation Programme: Inquiry into Participation – A Research Approach*, Geneva: UNRISD.

Rudebeck, Lars and Olle Törnquist with Virgilio Rojas (eds) (1998) *Concrete Cases in Comparative and Theoretical Perspective*, London: Macmillan.

Siddiqui, Kamal (ed.) (1994) *Local Government in Bangladesh*, Dhaka: University Press.

Sobhan, Rehman (1993) *Bangladesh: Problems of Governance*, Dhaka: University Press, chapter 5, p. 246 and chapter 6, pp. 287–9.

Westergaard, Kirsten (1980) *Boringram: An Economic and Social Analysis of a Village in Bangladesh*, Bogra, Bangladesh: Rural Development Academy.

— (1985) *State and Rural Society in Bangladesh: A Study in Relationship*, London: Curzon Press.

— (1996a) 'Decentralisation, NGOs and democratization in Bangladesh', in Lars Rudebeck and Olle Törnquist (eds), *Democratization in the Third World: Concrete Cases in Comparative and Theoretical Perspective*, Uppsala: Uppsala University.

— (1996b) 'People's empowerment in Bangladesh: NGO strategies', *Journal of Social Studies* (Dhaka), 72: 27–57.

Westergaard, Kirsten and Mustafa Alam (1995) 'Local government in Bangladesh: past experiences and yet another try', *World Development*, 23, 4: 679–90.

Westergaard, Kirsten and Abul Hossain (1998) 'The Green Revolution and the growth of the informal sector in Bangladesh', *Journal of Social Studies* (Dhaka), 79, January: 29–48.

— (1999) 'Local government in Bangladesh', *Sociologus* 49, 2.

— (2000a) 'Boringram: A restudy of a village. How to live better on less land', in Rounaq Jahan (ed.), *Bangladesh: Identity, Politics, and Economy*, London: Zed Books.

Wood, Geoffrey D. (1992) 'Introduction' in Bosse Kramsjo and G. D. Wood, *Breaking the Chains: Collective Action for Social Justice among the Rural Poor in Bangladesh*, Dhaka: University Press.

10

Local Organizations and Political Space in the Forests of West Bengal

Neil Webster

Democracy and democratization have become priorities in aid and development circles over the past ten years or so. The need to bring about a transition to democracy or a consolidation of democracy is seen as central to development that is successful, sustainable, empowering, poverty-reducing, and much more. While few today would disagree with the argument that there is a relationship between democracy and development, there is little agreement as to what that relationship is and how it can be used to promote development.

The attempt to define democracy, to identify the processes central to democratization, and to design policies and aid programmes to facilitate the transition to and consolidation of democracy have remained inconclusive. Contested issues include the compatibility of democracy and development, the type of democratic system most suited to development, the impact of previous political regimes on the transition to and sustainability of democracy, the benefits stemming from popular participation on the design and implementation of public policy, and whether development is best served by democratization at the local or the national level, to name but a few.

Discussions have not been helped by the fact that ideological as much as development and analytical needs have informed much that has been written. The collapse of the Soviet Union and the retreat from the state-planned economies, the failings of structural adjustment and the calls for democratization, and the move towards empowerment and self-help have all served to reinvigorate calls for democracy and democratization programmes. Not least they have served to elevate expectations as to what greater political participation can bring.

Ideological and analytical differences notwithstanding, there is a strong case for suggesting that democratic politics can provide the room for socially and economically marginalized groups to organize and act. If such organization and action can be directed towards affecting public policy, then democracy can become be a vehicle not only for development, but for poverty reduction as well. The political agency of the poor can affect the design and implementation of public policy.

This is a seductive and consequently popular argument in current development thinking and policy, an argument that runs directly counter to the thinking that dominated the 1960s, 1970s and early 1980s, in which strong government rather than democratic government was held to be the key to successful economic development and social change. It is also an argument that lies directly behind the advocacy for democratization and the aid policies that seek to support it.

There is a high degree of instrumentality to this thinking. Popular participation is held to be the key to better development outcomes, whether at the level of national economic and social policy or at the local level of projects. Better identification and design, better implementation, more sustainable outcomes and greater local ownership are among the gains to be made. In political terms we can talk of greater legitimacy, transparency, accountability and responsibility to others, some of the key requisites for 'good governance'. But the potential to achieve political participation is highly conditional upon the political environment. From a political standpoint this is usually seen in terms of the nature of the democratic regime, the checks and balances on power in the system, and the depth of democracy present. But it is also dependent upon the socio-economic condition of the population. History has repeatedly shown that the condition of poverty is not conducive to democracy. For some, the chronology of poverty reduction and democracy is important. Leftwich (1993: 13) argues that: 'If the primary developmental objective is the defeat of poverty and misery, then liberal or pluralist democracy may also not be what many Third World or Eastern European countries need or can sustain in their present conditions.'

Others suggest that where widespread poverty is present, it is best that democracy be pursued at the local level through strategies based upon grassroots organizations and community-based groups. Liberal democracy at the national level is seen to offer little to aid development, in particular pro-poor development (see Landell-Mills 1992). In many countries it is the case that elites can quite easily support a constitutional democracy while giving very little away to the population in terms of participation in public policy, resource allocation or programme implementation (see Slater 1989). Democratization at the local level through creating elected de-centralized government, the development of a dynamic civil society and the acceptance of the rights and responsibilities of citizenship can help to contest the authoritarian nature of central government and its policies.

The decentralization of government and the use of local NGOs in development have emerged as two important institutional means to support the transition to democracy. Elected local authorities are seen as an institutional means for situating policy formulation, resource allocation and programme implementation at local levels, to which interest groups lacking national presence or representation can gain access. It is also hoped that this can bring public policy within the reach of the poor. For their part local organizations and associations, facilitated by NGOs, are seen as a means by which to secure representation and access to local government and local administration. With institutional innovation it is thereby hoped that the poor can begin to access, participate in and influence public policy to their benefit.

While government and donor agency interventions can help shape the context in which local development processes take place, they are not in a position to direct the actions and responses of local actors. Outcomes are more often than not unintended rather than those planned by the government, donor agency or other exogenous actors. The bad news in this for governments and donors is that development through local democratization is unpredictable. The good news is that there are examples showing that institutional innovation can work for poverty reduction, but in a manner that is more dialectical than causal in terms of the interactions involved.

In order to understand the complexity of the processes leading to a positive outcome, we need to analyse the relationship between local development and national development and the key institutions and organizations involved. We also need to explore the more complex side of poverty at the local level, and the strategies pursued by the poor to contest their condition. The trajectory of public policy, development programmes and reform at the national level then needs to be related to the strategies of the poor (and non-poor) at the local level. In this way the range of possible outcomes can be better understood and poverty reduction better facilitated.

Political space has been argued to be more than political and institutional context (see Chapter 1). The three dimensions proposed, namely institutional channels, poverty discourse and the organizing practices of the poor, can be enlarged upon to embrace the following:

- Decentralization of government whereby powers, responsibilities and resources have been devolved to locally elected authorities.
- Local NGOs with a pro-poor agenda that is permitted by the state and present at the local level.
- Recognition by the poor of their poverty as reflected in their poverty discourse, and their possession of organizing practices with which to cope or challenge it.

- A local tradition of association or community-based organization along lines similar to Putnam's concept of social capital (Putnam et al. 1993).
- A pro-poor orientation to the policies of the government, that is, at the national level, with the interests of the poor being organized and represented to some extent at the local level, through political parties and/or local NGOs.

These assumptions can be said to present a situation in which there is a political space for advocating and pursuing a strong pro-poor orientation to development through linking the poor to the process of governance. In each of the above, different institutional actors are present. The second assumption is that by their nature, or due to forces and mechanisms acting upon them, they will incorporate the interests of the poor into their policies and actions.

However, as poverty is rooted in the politics of power and interest, the interests of the poor will be contested by definition. Even democracy cannot ensure the pursuit of poverty reduction, as a coalition of interests can seek to overthrow the democratic process itself if they feel that their interests are unjustifiably threatened. The issue of poverty might be a political force in a democracy at the national level, but the reality for the poor at the local level is that few have political patrons and that they are often viewed as political liabilities. Somewhat ironically, decentralization with local democracy can undermine the ability of the state to reach the local poor. It is in this context, very much the Indian context, that, I suggest, local-level non-state organizations can play a central role in poverty reduction at the local level.

The Indian Context

Indian democracy is based upon a Western political system and philosophy that have been exported to India. While there is a strong constitutional basis for democracy in India, there has also been a vernacularization of democracy during the transition. Today there is a clear tendency towards a 'majoritist' democracy whereby democratic rule is achieved at the expense of minority groups. Democracy is a means of promoting political exclusion, contrary to Western liberal democratic ideals. Thus it is that the commitment to democratic rule expressed by elite groups at the national level tends not to extend to support for participation and influence among the general population. Political exclusion continues to be widespread, affecting women and low-caste and tribal groups in particular. The two factors combine and complement one another to reproduce a democracy that has a history of addressing poverty through policies at the national level for electoral interests, while the poor remain marginalized and excluded at the local level. The political will to challenge the roots of poverty has been largely absent. Testimony to the failure lies in the marked polarization between the wealthy and the poor in India and the fact that more than 400 million people (40 per cent of the population) are estimated to survive below the official poverty line.

The decentralization of government or *panchayati raj* that was reintroduced with the 73rd and 74th Amendments to the Constitution in 1993 was an attempt to bring about greater participation in development at the local level. Only in a few states can it be said to have had any real consequence for poverty reduction and the poor. Once more the political will necessary to carry through such reforms has been lacking, this time on the part of the state governments. Nor have political parties been willing to use the opportunity to act as local organizers and mediators on behalf of the majority of the population in order to press for implementation and greater representation.

With respect to the democratic system as a whole, it can be argued that political parties have largely failed to provide representation for the majority of the population. While the population might be enfranchised in electoral terms, the majority remain disconnected from the process of governance, and in particular from influence over public policy, resource allocation and development programmes.

Perhaps partly as a consequence of the failings of political parties the 1970s and 1980s have witnessed a rapid growth in NGOs seeking to make cause with the poor. Subsequently the 1990s have seen NGOs being increasingly incorporated into the development programmes of the national and federal states mirroring the pro-NGO trends in international development policy and assistance. NGOs' registration for the receipt of government and foreign funds, the growing number of international and national programmes with funds available for Indian NGOs, and similar developments have led to a formalization of their relationship to the state. One consequence of this acceptance and funding is they are increasingly being (re-)constituted through the policies of the government and of donor agencies, thereby increasing their exogenous status to the local.

If NGOs have become accepted as important institutional means for supporting development in India, the development status of local associations and people's organizations is less apparent. These range from caste-based associations of agricultural labourers and irrigation user groups to people's organizations such as environmental and farmers' social movements. While often accepted for the manner in which they are seen as reflecting popular interest and thus offering sustainability to development interventions, they can also be rejected when they are seen to challenge the authority and wider development interests of the state and the national economy.

Local government, local NGOs and local associations are all actors that are used in interventions designed to enhance popular participation in development. Yet this role is often perceived in terms of their formal status as state or non-state organizations, and in the space or at the level where they act there is little that explicitly raises the question of their political agency. To understand better the dynamic processes involved, in this particular case the question as to how the rural poor have impacted upon the politics and practice of policy at different levels and the consequences of their engagement – both the intended and unintended – requires a more detailed exploration. Not least it requires that the relationship between local and the macro processes involving these institutional actors and the poor be analysed to understand the role of political agency in the formulation and practice of public policy.

These processes are well illustrated by the experiences of Adivasi (tribal) women in south-west Bankura District in the state of West Bengal, where a pro-poor government has been in power for more than twenty years.

The Left Front Government and People's Democracy

The Left Front government (LFG) was elected as the state government of West Bengal in 1977 on the basis of support from the rural poor majority and it established the new system of decentralized government known as *panchayati raj* in 1978, . This was not a revolutionary movement, despite its clear class dimensions, but it did enable the LFG to set about implementing a range of radical agrarian policies that characterized the period 1977–83.

In this early period it was an agrarian politics that was conflictual and often violent, involving personal revenge against oppressive local landlords, moneylenders, local bureaucrats and administrators. But it was also a time in which local politics was constituted in broad-based movements such as 'Operation Barga' (registration of sharecroppers), in the implementation of minimum wages and in the breaking or weakening of many of the hidden forms of dependency and subordinating practices prevalent in local agrarian relations. These movements sought to break the structural relations that gave rise to widespread forms of poverty present in the rural sector. The *panchayati raj* was introduced as an institutional means to implement the agrarian strategy. It is now widely recognized that this strategy has been effective in politically and economically empowering the poor and the more marginal sections of the agrarian social formation (see Rogaly et al. 1999).

The period from 1983 to 1985 was a turning point in the political direction of the LFG's agrarian politics. In 1983 the local *panchayats* proved themselves to be extremely effective in drought relief operations, and in 1985 they were formally brought into the process of development planning. Now one could talk of a genuine degree of local participation, popular accountability and greater effectiveness in the implementation of development programmes at the local level.

From this point the politics of the LFG and its dominant coalition member, the Communist Party of India (Marxist), CPI(M), increasingly focused upon its electoral sustainability at the federal state level. Sustainability at the local level through the involvement and mobilization of the poor in a wide range of local institutions beyond the *panchayats* began to be of secondary concern compared to the electoral support required by the party. The political strategies pursued in order to secure the party's electoral needs both reflected and reinfo: ed the democratic centralism that characterized the internal organization of the CPI(M).

It is not necessarily paradoxical that a strong party and a strong state go hand in hand with the successful decentralization of government. The CPI(M) argues that *panchayati raj* is a 'people's democracy', by which one should understand a pro-poor democracy. Linking poverty with democracy has significant consequences, not least the existence of a strong political will to carry through the tenancy reforms of Operation Barga; to seize and redistribute land over the land ceilings; to pass and push for the implementation of minimum agricultural wages; and to secure access to formal credit and undermine private moneylenders. These are reforms that challenge existing socio-economic relations and the power of local elites. It has also required a strong political will to counter entrenched vested interests in the state and to secure accountable, transparent and effective government.

The CPI(M) party structure has been used to monitor and direct the activities of the local *panchayats* in order to prevent corruption and mismanagement, but also to secure the effective implementation of poverty reduction programmes and their pro-poor agrarian strategy.[1] The CPI(M) has also successfully pushed the local *panchayats* into playing a vital role in local conflict resolution and in establishing a rule of law at the local level that has clearly benefited the poor and marginal groups.

At the same time, successful re-election in four state elections and four sets of *panchayat* elections has seen the emergence of a new leadership accustomed to government. Changes in the nature of the leadership, the rise of a new generation of local political leaders and the development of a tradition of government and administration replacing a tradition of social movements, have brought changes in the perception of political agency in development. If the LFG began by stressing the agency of the poor in terms of their need to mobilize and act in order to implement the structural reforms, today the tendency is to stress the role of the LFG in guiding and administering development for all, including the poor. Explicit in the latter is the idea that development and therefore political agency are best left in their hands.

One of the key areas in which change is being pursued in West Bengal at present concerns forestry and forest management in particular, which, in line with policy in India as a whole, is being pursued in a participatory and decentralized form. This is having direct consequences for Adivasis in the western areas of West Bengal, including Bankura District.

The extract below is taken from the discussion of the new forest policy in the *Economic Review* prepared annually by the state government of West Bengal:

> [The] mere raising of tree cover is not enough, if the raised plantations are not protected. The [West Bengal] State Government through a sustained campaign in cooperation with the *panchayats* has been able to make the poor common people in rural areas aware of the importance of trees. This awareness has facilitated the voluntary involvement of the common people through the *panchayats* in protecting existing forests and the new plantations that are being raised. More formally, common people living in fringe areas of forests have been inducted into Forest Protection Committees (FPC) which also include government officials. In order to encourage the participation of common people in these FPCs, the State Government allows members of FPCs a share of usufruct from the forests. As an instance, in sal forests, 25 percent of the revenue generated through resuscitated sal forests is shared out among the members of the Forest Protection Committees. During 1994–95, 510 FPCs were raised providing protection to 1.45 lakh hectares of forest area. Till March, 1995, 2,745 Forest Protection Committees were operating in the State, protecting 4.24 lakh hectares of forest area.[2]

The language is important both for what it tells us in the text and for what it tells us when we link the text to the author. Forest management is returning to the people, the poor common people. Through institutional means indigenous knowledge and needs are being translated into development, a pro-poor development, for which the West Bengal government is taking the major part of the responsibility, and presumably the plaudits. For the CPI(M)-led LFG, it is a development that reflects one more step in the direction of decentralized and devolved government and development administration in which the state and the villagers combine in their strategies to bring about a pro-poor development at the local level.

However, the text reveals the top-down determination to development based upon institutional innovation discussed in the opening section of this chapter, with the same suggestion of causality between the process of intervention and the ensuing changes that occur. It is an argument that tends to negate the role of the local social actors: the rural poor are 'made aware', 'inducted' and 'encouraged' to participate by being 'allowed' a share of usufruct from the forests.

If political agency on the part of the poor majority was instrumental in first bringing the LFG to power and was reflected in the early reforms that were introduced, are we now to understand that the poor have ceased to possess agency? The case of Adivasi women in south-west Bankura shows that the poor can organize and act in the political space that 'their government' has created for them, but which it fails to acknowledge or appreciate.

Local Change in Bankura District

The area covered by Ranibandh Police Station in Bankura District is for the most part dry, hilly, 'jungle' land. Pockets of irrigated land have developed over the past two decades with the introduction of canals from the immense Kangsabhati reservoir constructed in the 1950s, but much of the water passes through the hills to other areas, and this area is far removed from the lush cultivation of the *namal* or plains further to the east. Most of the land is given over to forests or forest wastelands and remains under the control of the forestry department.

In this area 49 per cent of the population are scheduled tribals and 11 per cent are scheduled castes (1981 Census). The former are mainly Santal and Bhumij. There is also a small number of Mohatos who, though close to Santal in many of their ritual and ceremonial practices (such as the mortuary rituals and the payment of brideprice), are not listed as a scheduled tribe.

In understanding the shaping of political agency in the area, it is important to understand the boundaries that shape the social and political life. In particular, what does it mean to be a 'tribal'? How have they been historically constituted at the macro level through discourse and policy and what has been their response? The Santal 'may be described as naturally a brave but shy child of the jungle – simple, truthful, honest and industrious – before he is brought into contact with alien influences and taught to cheat, lie and steal' (O'Malley 1908: 58, 72). But Santal are also 'the natural enemies of jungle' (Mitra 1953: 156). The Bhumij, literally 'sons of the soil', were once the rulers of Bankura until subjection to colonial rule and the Bengali Hindu domination reduced the majority to landless labourers, tenant cultivators and marginal farmers. The tribals as a whole were characterized as *chuar* or 'unclean jungle robber'. The post-independence continuation of listing certain groups as scheduled tribes, ostensibly to promote their development through positive discrimination, has secured their social, political and economic marginalization from the mainstream. Their 'backward' condition remains 'natural': it is the norm that guides social and political practice and reinforces economic deprivation for 'tribals' as a community. The collective identity imposed by the title of 'tribal' has in turn been rejected by many when identifying themselves against the other, the non-tribal. Instead they have taken the collective name of Adivasi while still retaining their separate identities as Bhumij, Santal, and so on.

Adivasi from south-west Bankura and the neighbouring district of Purulia have long served as a labour reserve for others' development, first in the late nineteenth century, in the coalfields of Bihar and West Bengal, then much later, in the Green Revolution rice fields in the Gangetic plains to the east. As they became increasingly excluded from the forests, and as their lands failed to provide either work or production enough to support their households, the need to realize their principal remaining asset, their labour led to seasonal migration to these fields as an important coping strategy by which the Adivasi households could remain and survive in the villages in south-west Bankura and the surrounding areas.

The migration was seasonal. In the case of the coalfields, the fact that the labourers periodically returned to the villages, particularly at times of intensive agricultural activity, soon led to labour being imported from further afield and a reduction on the reliance on more local labour re-sources. Later, the shift to the double-cropping of rice in the irrigated districts to the east during the late 1960s led to the rise of labour gangs recruited in the villages of south-west Bankura and Purulia Districts. They would travel to the *namal* four times a year, harvesting and transplanting rice crops for Bengali Hindu farmers for periods of up to six weeks. Sometimes just labour-active women and men would travel from the house-hold, leaving their children and lands in the care of parents or relatives, while sometimes whole families would migrate. They would live in straw shelters next to the landowners' courtyards, be paid in kind and cash, and return to their own villages when the work was finished. A few would settle permanently if a landowner was willing to provide land for house construction, but such resettlement is unusual. Santal *paras* (neighbour-hoods) in Burdwan, Midnapur and other districts are usually to be found outside the village perimeter, a spatial representation of the social and cultural exclusion of the 'unclean' tribal, an exclusion practised from the Brahman down to the poorest scheduled caste.

For the Santal and the Bhumij, the forest remains their home. To leave is to leave the principal point through which much of the physical and social world is negotiated. Despite their progressive exclusion from the forest lands (as the 'natural enemy of the forest'), and the means of production they provide the forest remains central to their physical reproduction, providing food, firewood and income-generating production, and to their identity. The forest is the physical embodiment of their knowledge and the central point of reference in their cultural and social practices. As such, it has become a point of resistance and of political action.

The context for political action is quite specific. At the macro-level there is the state, in this case the West Bengal state government. Alongside the state is the Indian Forestry Department operating under the central government. At the mezo-level are the *panchayati raj* institutions of local government, the lower tiers of administrative departments and the NGOs, while at the local level are the Adivasi and their indigenous organizations.

Three specific fields of development practice provide the context for the discussion of the process of democratic development under way. The first is the implementation of structural reforms and decentralized government by the Left Front government in West Bengal, discussed above. The second is the emergence of women's cooperatives in south-west Bankura. The third is the policy of joint forestry management embodied in the National Forest Policy introduced in 1988 by the Indian central government.

Adivasi Women's Cooperatives as Collective Action[3]

In south-west Bankura District Santal and Bhumij women have been keeping plantations of *arjun* and *asan* trees on which they rear silkworms to produce and sell the cocoons for more than a decade in some instances. The village-based cooperatives are each responsible for their own operations, but they are all linked under an apex body, the Nari Bikash Samiti (NBS).

The cooperatives sprang from the women's desire to reduce their reliance on migration to the *namal* and to improve their socio-economic resource base within their own villages. The problems they faced in making the seasonal migrations and the means by which they set about establishing the cooperatives as a form of alternative have been written about elsewhere.[4]

From its beginnings in the early 1980s, the silkworm cooperative movement in the locality has expanded so that in 1997 there were 22 cooperatives functioning in the area, 21 of which were formally registered and all under the apex body, NBS. The extent to which the cooperatives can be described as having been an economic success is debatable. Most are cultivating three

TABLE 10.1 Action and agency in the silkworm cooperatives

Social actor	Socio-economic basis for action	Role (political agency)
Women	Adivasi (non-Hindu). Gender. Economically poor. Labour migrants. Politically marginalized.	Articulating demands for local-based development activities. Organizing on the basis of collective identities. Local assertion of women's and community's interests and rights. Daily organization of work: tree-planting, egg-hatching, worm-rearing, cocoon-collection.
NBS	As above. (character: elected apex body, participatory)	To organise and articulate the needs and demands of the women and the co-operatives: selling cocoons, purchasing eggs, working with government officials, 'spreading the story', and networking with other organizations.
CWDS	Academics with an ideological commitment to being pro-women, pro-poor, and pro-collective action. Not ideologically 'anti-state'. Combination of government and donor funding (character: locally based although offices are in New Delhi; donor-funded).	Facilitation of organization formation and economic activities. Technical and organizational assistance and general logistical support. Raising funds and accessing development programmes from state or donor agencies.
Panchayats	CPI(M) dominated, but with a Jharkhand presence (i.e. demand for an independent tribal state). Ideologically pro-poor. Adivasi and women representatives. Dependent upon electoral support.	Passive support and a minimal engagement.

Local administration	Elitist hierarchically structured line ministries, but with partial integration with local government. Mainly male, Hindu, educated staff.		Partial development support, e.g. by way of development programmes.
Forestry Department	As with the local administration, but located under a central government ministry with only a partial responsibility to the state government.	Long tradition of anti-people forest management and a long history of conflict with villagers at the local level. Currently a passive tolerance of the cooperatives with some individual officials being positive.	Support on the part of key individuals (land minister).
State (West Bengal LFG)	Ideologically pro-poor but not from the poor. Bengali, male, higher caste, educated leadership. Electoral dependence on Bengali heartland. (note: strong hierarchical party structure)	Passive opposition in terms of local electoral politics and the acceptance of local prejudices.	The establishment of some local rights for women. Facilitation of the work of the NGO. 'Coercion' of the forestry department to release land for the cooperatives. 'Coercion' of local government/party and local administration to help the cooperatives.

crops of silk worms annually, with the final crop being the principal commercial crop (the earlier crops produce the eggs necessary for the final crop of silk cocoons). In 1997 most of the women were earning the equivalent of 20 to 30 days' employment during the year, but it varied considerably according to the number of eggs successfully hatched, climatic conditions and similar factors. Market factors play an important role so that the poor harvest in 1995 which resulted in only 227 *cahuns* (1,280 cocoons) of cocoons as opposed to the 400 originally expected, was partially compensated for by the higher price paid due to the general drop in production.[5]

For many of the women, the income had been sufficient to reduce the number of seasonal migrations, frequently from four to two annually, as well as reducing the number of family members going. This is indicative of the wider political and social gains that have directly resulted from the cooperatives. These are well illustrated by the attitude of village men. In 1991 men in the villages visited during fieldwork tended to be extremely negative towards the cooperatives, arguing that they would not last, they were of little economic benefit, and so on. The land registered in the women's names was often stated by men to be in fact owned by men, but on loan to the women. The problem of the younger trees in the plantations being eaten by grazing cattle was another demonstration of the men's dismissal of the cooperatives' work. The women would drive the cattle away and tell off the boys in charge, but the failure of men to take the matter up meant that the women had to be present to guard the trees.

In 1997 the attitude of the majority of men had changed quite radically. Now they regarded the cooperatives in a far more positive light. There had been some economic return and some reduction in labour migration, but in addition the women's organization had secured benefits from government development programmes such as child care centres and health and literacy programmes. They had drawn attention to the area as the story of the 'Bankura experiment' spread and the accompanying kudos that it brought. They shared experiences through NGO networks and other fora, travelling nationally and internationally to discuss, share experiences and learn.

The result has been that the women of the cooperatives have begun to assert a presence beyond the local that in turn has impacted upon the local. They have become an organized presence recognized by others ranging from party officials and development officers at the local level, through to ministers of the state government, and on to academics and development practitioners in the international arena of development studies. Such recognition serves to reconstitute that organized presence and to enhance further the activities undertaken. The women's impact on the villages has therefore been both considerable and dramatic in local terms, and the village men, albeit reluctantly at times, acknowledge the fact.

It is in this sense that the growth of the cooperatives can be described as being not merely the generation of cooperative institutions on the basis of the women organizing collectively, but a social movement aimed at political agency. Today the women strongly identify with the cooperatives in terms of it having been their actions that brought them about, their labour, their lands on which they grow the tree plantations, and their representatives on the NBS who project their interests at all levels. Even the Centre for Women in Development Studies (CWDS) is talked of as being 'their NGO', with its workers being their 'brothers and sisters'. With each of these statements goes the belief, openly articulated, that it has been an achievement by them against others – men in the household, men in the village, forestry officials, government officers, party representatives, Hindu farmers in the *namal* upon whom they are no longer so dependent for work, and so on. Furthermore it is not only a sense of belonging that is embodied in the women's discourse, but also a sense of future achievements that have yet to be made, but are felt to be realizable given their successes so far.

To understand the process of development further, it is useful to look at the roles played by the different social actors involved at the different levels. Those most central to the process are the women, the cooperative organizations, Nari Bikash Samiti (the NGO involved), the CWDS, the local state in the form of the *panchayati raj* institutions and local administrative departments, the Forestry Department and the state in the form of the Left Front government.

Table 10.1 seeks to identify the basis for organizing and thus for the political agency involved for these actors in the processes that have brought about the cooperatives.

Joint Forest Management and Forest Protection Committees

On to this field of development activity has been laid a third significant development in the area, the formation locally of Forest Protection Committees. The macro-policies of the Left Front government created the political space for the Adivasi women to use their resources in forming and running the cooperatives facilitated by the work of CWDS. Now a new set of macro-policy initiatives, grounded in another discourse and another perception of the local emanating from the central Indian government, has been placed over the existing context.

Post-independence forest policy in India as embodied in the National Forest Policy of 1952 was an extension of the colonial practice of scientific forest management, centrally and expertly controlled, with a strong commercial logic to its policies. Forest protection and forest production was the domain of the state. Prior to the Forestry Act of 1927, Adivasis had retained some traditional rights with respect to access to the forests and to its produce. While the 1927 Act seriously eroded these rights, the 1952 policy renamed them concessions. In 1978 the 42nd Amendment to the Constitution placed forest land on the Concurrent List, thereby reducing the powers of state governments and increasing those of the Union government. The policy of centralizing control was taken further with the Forest Conservation Act of 1980 and the Amendment of 1988, the former removing from the states' powers the right to 'de-reserve' forest lands or to permit forest lands to be used for non-forest purposes.

The pro-poor aspects of this forestry policy are hard to locate. If overall economic development, financed by revenues generated by forest production, can be said to be pro-poor, then one might indirectly speak of pro-poor forestry. Yet for the local communities that have been marginalized and excluded from their traditional major sources of income, there was little pro-poor orientation in the programme. In 1976 the National Commission on Agriculture advocated the introduction of social forestry, and many schemes and projects were subsequently launched, but these covered non-forest lands for the most part and were of no help to the villagers in forest regions. It was only in 1988 that a new National Forest Policy to replace that of 1952 began to develop the idea that local livelihoods were integral to local forest management and not its 'natural enemy'. In 1990 the Ministry of Environment and Forestry issued a circular on 'Joint Forest Management' containing guidelines for the establishment of local organizations that were to have responsibility for local forest protection and management. The Forestry Department was to be the implementing body, and representatives from local government were to be included.

In south-west Bankura District, since around mid-1993, 68 local Forest Protection Committees have been established in the Ranibandh range. Each *mouza* (smallest administrative land unit roughly corresponding to the lands of a village) has been encouraged to form a Forestry Protection Committee (FPC) comprising one (usually male) representative from each household in the *mouza*. Thereafter, an executive committee has been formed with six annually elected members plus one appointed by the Forestry Department, one appointed by the local *panchayat samiti* and one from the local *gram panchayat* (the middle and lowest tiers of local government).

The main work of the FPC is to organize the protection of the village forests from illegal felling, firewood collection, and so on, and to carry out work under various Forestry Department programmes including the rehabilitation of degraded forest land, cutting of multiple shoots, thinning cover and other programme-funded work such as digging drinking wells, building check dams for run-off water, and some minor road construction.

Training programmes are also organized, such as bee-keeping, pisciculture and sericulture.

The FPCs have no funds of their own and village collection is the one way by which funds can be generated in the short term, although only three of the FPCs in the area appeared to have ever raised funds in this way. Otherwise the fines levied for the illegal collection of firewood can provide funds, but these are rare. First-time offenders appear to be punished with a warning and the confiscation of the bundles collected. The fact that it is common knowledge what people are up to and that wood is popularly perceived as a common village property has resulted in fines rarely being used. In the longer term the FPCs are entitled to 25 per cent of the net return from the sale of timber in their forest area, but it will be at least ten to twelve years before any such return can begin to materialize.

The Adivasi women have been active participants in the local FPCs from the outset. They began by insisting that one-third of the executive committee's six village members should be women. This demand was based upon the argument that it was women who worked most with forest products and who possessed a better knowledge than the men of the full range of forest resources. They were therefore central to any sustainable management of local forest areas. The argument was presented from a collective standpoint through the representatives and members of the cooperatives. Village men, local government and forestry officials accepted the argument – the cooperatives had been working for more than ten years at this point – and one-third female representation on the executive committees became policy at Bankura District level, that is, well beyond the area covered by the cooperatives.

The attitude of the Forestry Department was the most negative factor. The traditional ideas that they had been the protectors of the forest, that they possessed the expert knowledge necessary for forest management, remained. Alongside these attitude problems remained the more personal antagonisms between villagers and local forestry officials rooted in cultural hierarchies, rent-seeking activities by officials (bribes for permitting women to collect firewood, deals with local timber merchants for the felling of certain trees), inflexible application of laws and fines, and much more.

The Forestry Department faced pressure from the demand for policy change from above, pressure from local government and political parties, and the problem of a shortage of resources at the local level. The Ranibandh Forest range has a staff of 54 and some 7,000 hectares of forest land to administer. As the FPCs took on their new formal status, the forestry department found that their own importance at village level began to decline. At the same time, FPCs were only village-level bodies, which did not possess the weight and political resources of a bureaucracy. When some of the FPCs began to demand that their share of the tree harvest should be 50 per cent and not 25 per cent, this was easily rejected by reference to official policy. When it was pointed out that the section of the Forestry Department responsible for selling the wood was not seeking out lucrative markets further afield, but selling at prices well below the market level to established customers (for example, mines, plywood manufacturers), thereby reducing the return to the FPCs, the criticism was ignored.

At the local level, both villagers and committee members in the FPCs argue that they have gained considerably. Yet there is an interesting dimension to their argument, namely that the FPCs were already in existence in most villages prior to their formal recognition in mid-1993 and that the difference today essentially is that the Forestry Department and local government are now working with them.

The villagers say that formal recognition of their responsibility for local forests has reduced the conflicts with local forest officials, has enabled them to cooperate with neighbouring villages who have their own forest areas, and has given them the recourse to authority necessary to prevent illegal felling. As for the programmes that come through the Forestry Department, these are discussed in terms of how they have enhanced their existing use of the forest rather than radically changing their engagement with it.

The fact that this view of the FPCs places a somewhat different emphasis as to who is the prime mover in bringing about sustainable forest management from that presented by the government of West Bengal illustrated in the quotation from the *Economic Review* is important. From the local perspective, one can say that, through their policies, the state government and the central government have opened up certain opportunities at the local level. Furthermore, through its earlier reform programme, the state government facilitated a greater political space for local political activity through policies such as decentralization, land reform and minimum wages. But one cannot argue that these macro-interventions foresaw the outcomes that have emerged.

Certainly the Adivasi women do not believe this to be the case. In 1996 they sought to bring their political engagement in the field of forestry into the higher levels of policy and planning by bringing all 68 local FPCs in Ranibandh Range into a collective organization with an elected executive body to represent their needs and interests. With the help of the CWDS an extensive campaign has been launched to establish the body. By spring 1996, 75 per cent of the FPCs had agreed to join in forming the apex body, and a provisional election date had been set. Again, the rule that at least one-third of its elected members should be women is one of the central principles of its constitution. Following the election, the apex body has registered under the Friendly Societies Act in order to achieve formal recognition. The response of the Forestry Department at the local level has been to refuse to talk to this new body, as there is no provision for its involvement under the guidelines and requirements of the community forestry policy. The local *panchayats* adopted a less rigid and more pragmatic position, possibly influenced by the elections at national, State Assembly and *panchayat* levels due in 1998. Among the villagers as a whole, there is general support for the body. The previous successes gained through local political agency are well recognized.

Political Agency and Poverty Reduction in Local Development

Two key, but different dimensions stand out in the above. One is the different levels at which development activities and interventions are occurring and their interdependence. The second is the juxtaposition between structure and agency that is occurring, primarily at the local level, but which can also be observed at the levels of regional and state politics and policy when these are included in the picture.

In presenting the emergence of the women's cooperatives, I have focused upon the actors at different levels who have been central to their formation and functioning. In this sense they could be described as stakeholders in the politics of their formation and its consequences, and in the realization of their productive potential. By using the term actor I am stating that they possess a potential political agency in the development process. I am also suggesting that the actions of organizations and institutions more directly involved in policies possess agency in terms of the interests they serve, and that this is also central to that same development process.

However, political agency also has to be understood as being rooted in the underlying relations that give rise to certain actions and not others. Here we must recognize the dynamic nature of the process that is under way. On the one hand we have seen the interaction between the macro and the local levels whereby reform policies emerging from another set of political processes can facilitate change. In the above this resulted in Adivasi women being accepted as stakeholders or social actors within the economic and political life of the household, the village, the district, and so on. To some extent this could be described as an intended outcome of the reform process. The pro-poor orientation of the Left Front government, articulated through its reform programme as described above, created the political opportunity for the emergence of the Adivasi women's cooperatives in Bankura.

Next we come to the area of unintended consequences, where the experiences of one socio-economic field are transferred into the actors' engagement in another. In this case it is in the manner in which the relationship between women, Adivasi, the poor and their counterparts (men, caste Hindus and the wealthy) changed on the basis of their engagement in the cooperative production of silk cocoons. The experience of these changes then became the basis for challenges to policies in other resource arenas. Political agency moved from Adivasi women in cooperatives to Adivasi villagers in Forest Protection Committees. Local organizations of the poor rooted in one set of poverty dynamics served to generate local organizations of the poor in another linked, but still separate, set of poverty processes.

This is the local dynamic of development, the study of actors moving in time and space. Here time can be understood in terms of the accumulation of knowledge in the form of tactics and strategies for coping with one set of poverty conditions, and space is to be the frame in which this knowledge is utilized. Movement between spaces is then understood as the transfer of this knowledge into another defined set of conditions, another context or frame. In reality it is a continual process, and the distinctions of time and space serves only to delineate key points in the process, particular points where there is a crossing of contextual boundaries.

In general terms this can be described as a process in which the local engages with the macro and vice versa. At the local level it is experienced and articulated as decisive breakthroughs in the local actors' relationship to the macro, from passive recipients to active participants, in clear 'victories' in the form of gains and concessions won from traditionally dominant actors in different arenas of markets, government services, administrative officialdom, and so on. It is the classic transition from interests to rights, but this time on the part of the poor.

From a developmental perspective, we would describe this process as being the democratization of the local that enables its (re-)constitution by local actors previously marginalized or excluded from the development process, both economically and politically. If the LFG has legislated for rights for these women, then it is their own local organization that has implemented those rights. In turn, it is the women's interpretation of their rights that has been directed through political action back at the macro-level through both their own practice and through lobbying and advocacy and the general 'spreading of their message'. It is by tracing this engagement in the politics of development that we can see the way in which interests can become translated into rights through the political actions of local organizations based upon the rural poor. This is the political agency of the poor affecting public policy. It also illustrates how rights, as legislated for by the state, have to be contested and won at the local level if they are to be genuinely pro-poor in their outcomes.

Here democracy is linked with development in which the poor are central actors in affecting the nature of outcomes. This takes place not within a framework based upon a logical causality, but within one that searches for the explanation at both the level of action and the level of structure. Structure lies in the relations that structure the actors' engagement and perceptions of each other. In the case of Adivasi women, social and economic relations have been central to structuring their entitlements and in shaping their responses to interests that emerge out of the inequalities that arose.

This chapter has also sought to demonstrate how actors at other levels are involved in both shaping and changing these relations, not directly, as they would perhaps have us believe, but indirectly, through the impact that policies and reforms have had in shaping the political space for Adivasi women's actions. This is to argue that effective public policy for poverty reduction cannot be achieved through innovative institutional mechanisms for securing popular participation alone. Political agency cannot be left to actors outside the local, for this will only exclude the poor. While a pro-poor government can effect structural changes that might improve the condition of the poor and create institutions in which it is intended that the poor should participate or be represented, these are not enough. One must wager on the poor as well and open up to their political actions and agency.

Notes

1. The 1980s saw West Bengal's annual rate of growth of food grains production increase from an average of 0.6 per cent from 1969–70 to 1981–82, to 6.5 per cent from 1981–82 to 1991–92. This placed it among the fastest-growing states in India. While technology, particularly concerning irrigation, has played a significant role, political interventions that have preserved and often improved participation of the rural poor in production have been central to both the growth in production and the rural poor's economic improvement.

2. *Economic Review 1995–96*, West Bengal State Planning Board, pp. 30–1.

3. Special thanks are due to the women of the Jhillimilli cooperatives and the workers of the Centre for Women's Development Studies, both in New Delhi and in Jhillimilli, Bankura District, and to Narayan Banerjee in particular. The research could not have been undertaken without the assistance provided by Asis Das and Bela Bandyopadhyaya.

4. See Webster 1994.

5. In 1995, 197 *cahuns* were sold to the government-promoted Khadi Industries Marketing Board at prices of 1,175 rupees for good quality and 600–1,100 rupees for poorer-quality, i.e. broken, cocoons. Thirty *cahuns* were sold to private traders at 1,200 rupees, since they will take only cocoons of good quality. Fifty *cahuns* remained unsold at the beginning of 1996, of which 30 were of poorer quality and 20 of good quality. These were also expected to be sold to the Khadi Industries.

Bibliography

Government of West Bengal (1996) *Economic Review 1995–96*, Calcutta.

Landell-Mills, P. (1992) *Governance, Civil Society and Empowerment in Sub-Saharan Africa: Building the Institutional Basis for Sustainable Development*, Washington, DC: World Bank.

Leftwich, A. (1993) 'Voting can damage your health', *Times Higher Educational Supplement*, 13 August, pp. 11–13.

Mitra, A. (1953) *An Account of Land Management in West Bengal 1870–1950*, Alipore: West Bengal Government Press.

O'Malley, D. S. E. (1908) *Bankura*, Calcutta: Bengal District Gazetteers, The Bengal Secretariat Book Department.

Putnam R. with R. Leonardi and R. Nanetti (1993) *Making Demoncracy Work: Civic Traditions in Modern Italy*, Princeton, NJ: Princeton University Press.

Rogaly, B., S. Bose and B. Harriss-White (eds) (1999) *Sonar Bangla? Agricultural Growth and Agrarian Change in West Bengal and Bangladesh*, New Delhi: Sage.

Slater, D. (1989) 'Territorial power and the peripheral state: the issue of decentralization', *Development and Change*, 20, 3: 501–31.

Webster, N. (1994) 'Tribal Women's Co-operatives in Bankura, West Bengal', *European Journal of Development Studies*, 6, 2: 95–103.

11

Political Agencies and Spaces

Lars Engberg-Pedersen and Neil Webster

The poor are not victims, but active agents in securing their own livelihoods. They exploit whatever economic opportunities are available in order
to survive and to improve their condition. They pursue strategies designed
to legitimize claims, to place others under moral obligations to provide
benefits, to accumulate for investment, to draw on family, friends and
acquaintances, to manipulate discourses to their own advantage, to side
with leaders and organizations who may turn out to be useful, to gain
access to resources whose ownership is disputed, and so on. In short, the
poor are constantly seeking to manoeuvre within given conditions and to
generate room for profitable activities.

The political is not excluded from this manoeuvring. It is clear from
the contributions to this volume that poor groups often seek to influence
political processes in the broad sense. Basing their actions upon a long
history of opposition to the state, groups of rural poor have seized the
opportunity in Bolivia to access and control the newly created municipalities. This is far from being an unambiguous process, since suspicion of
the purposes and implications of the Law of Popular Participation of 1994
is widespread. In Bangladesh, which has a much longer, albeit inconsistent,
history of decentralization and local government, some rural poor have
run for Union elections. This is not a countrywide phenomenon, but it
appears to be heavily dependent upon the support of NGOs and on local
histories of struggle around resources and livelihoods on the part of the
poor. Another problem is that the poor's representatives sometimes pursue
individual strategies of enrichment to the detriment of their constituencies.
Nevertheless, the poor have actively organized or used existing organizations to try to exercise pressure on policy-making and the distribution
of public funds.

Evidently, the political is not confined to discussions in elected bodies.
Struggles over natural resources and access to government programmes
are examples of areas in which the actions of the poor are more often than

not using social practices of manoeuvring and alliance in order to secure gains and win favours. The poor appear to have little faith in and low estimates of success concerning the formal procedures and processes of administrative and elected institutions. In these respects, the poor are no less enterprising. In Mexico, diverse groups nurture good relations with officials in both local and national government in order to obtain resources from the National Funds in support of Social Enterprises. Among the Mexican poor there are those who are adept at exploiting the rivalries of different departments and different levels of the state, revealing the latter to be less monolithic than often believed. Similarly, Adivasi women, who belong to some of the most deprived groups in West Bengal, have been able to draw on their experiences in organizing silkworm cooperatives in their interaction with the Forestry Department, not only securing better representation within the Forest Protection Committees, but also linking many of these committees under an apex body in order to assert pressure for change in forest policy and its administration at different levels.

Turning to the crucial issue of land, evidence from Mozambique and Zimbabwe documents that poor people are ready to fight for their cause and to use a wide range of tactics in pursuing their objectives. Where there is no effective state but strong competition for land, the poor have sought other actors that could legitimize and authorize their claims. The chiefs have come to occupy this position in Mozambique, and poor people involved in land disputes have not been slow to exploit the chiefs' concern for peace in their constituencies. Although land disputes decided in the chief courts do not always benefit the poorer parties to the dispute, a significant number of them have been able to present and win their case in this 'traditional' institution setting. Contemporary rural Zimbabwe is characterized by the grabbing of land by different groups in anticipation of land reform and growing pressure from the commercialization of land. The national political regime has, to put it mildly, expressed itself rather inconsistently on these issues. This has not prevented groups of landless people from invading large-scale commercial farms or claiming land in Communal Areas. The resulting violence and evictions have often served only to produce more organized and determined actions by the landless in order to gain land.

Thus poor groups in many situations are trying to manoeuvre within the political sphere as a way of reducing their vulnerabilities and improving their living conditions. But politics is dangerous. Entering into processes and relations in which power is an intrinsic feature involves risk, particularly for the powerless and vulnerable. There is little doubt that fear arising from this danger is a formidable barrier in the realization of the political agency of the poor. It is therefore not surprising that marginalized groups tend to support existing political regimes. As Karsten Paerregaard notes, concerning a Peruvian community leader: '[H]is continuous drifting in and out of offices according to the shifting political environment reflects a highly pragmatic notion of politics among Alto Cunas peasants who tend to identify with rather than contest the existing power hierarchy' (see Chapter 3). In Burkina Faso, a similar tendency to avoid outspoken opposition can be determined. Parts of the rural population pursue a strategy of evasion in relation to politics and government intervention, and many Burkinabè NGOs have an ambivalent and uneasy relationship with political parties, local governments and the state.

While the political agency of the poor in some cases remains only potential, its presence and role is sufficiently documented in this volume for it to be recognized as a central element in processes of poverty reduction. It is also evident that the notion of political agency on the part of the poor needs to be qualified in a number of ways. First, the poor constitute a very heterogeneous category, only in extremely rare cases acting in a collective and coordinated manner. The political actions of marginalized groups may have indifferent or even detrimental consequences for other poor people, due to the highly structured world of poverty. While some unions of coca leaf producers and other organizations of poor people have been able to access and control the new local government institutions in Bolivia, a concomitant increase in the marginalization of women appears to have taken place. In the Zimbabwean case study, the contest over land has led to antagonisms between old and new immigrants concerning land despite the fact that both groups face similar degrees of deprivation. In Mexico, some poor people have been able to access the government support programme, whereas others have not, allegedly because they did not side with the 'proper' organization. Second, the notion of political agency on the part of the poor does not presuppose high levels of mobilization and organization. It is quite often individualized in nature, frequently informal, and nearly always aimed at short-term economic gain. It is reflected in daily actions and negotiations in response to new opportunities or deteriorating conditions.

Notwithstanding the state's lack of resources in many countries, it is frequently the state that is the focal point for struggle. This can be a direct consequence of government policies and programmes, but it can also be a reaction to the power it wields, for example in dictating solutions to social conflicts. Even in the study from Mozambique, where the state is rather distanced from the settlement of land disputes, the possibility of taking a case to the *posto administrativo* or higher-level state authorities still exists and influences litigants' strategies in land conflicts. The informal, elusive, sometimes questionable nature of the poor's political agency also comes out clearly in the same study, as land disputes are not only taken to various authorities for settlement, but are also characterized by violence, poisoning and witchcraft accusations.

Given that the political agency of the poor remains only potential in some situations and possesses such diversity of expression and form in others, a most pertinent question concerns the conditions under which marginalized groups and poor people choose to act politically to improve their livelihoods. Why should they seek to mobilize and influence government policy or participate in programme implementation?

Several of the studies indicate that organizational experience (West Bengal, Bolivia and Mexico), support from NGOs (Karnataka, Bangladesh and Zimbabwe) and government decentralization (West Bengal and Bolivia) are among the factors that contribute to the poor's realization of their political agency. What they all demonstrate is the importance of the local context. It is at this level that the poor subsist and where immediate gains are likely to be secured. It is the local that possesses the greatest detail in the cognitive maps of the poor and where they feel most capable of assessing the utility of political struggle against other activities that might yield a more immediate return. Thus a wide range of economic, social and organizational issues in the locality may influence poor people's decisions concerning whether to undertake political actions and the form these should take. However, a central conclusion running through all these studies is the significance of national politics in a broad sense.

National Politics and Poverty Reduction

The general political environment, the attitude of the government, and the dominant political discourses have a strong bearing on the poor's political strategies. The specific policies and programmes of the national government are, of course, of direct importance, as the studies from Mexico and Bolivia document. In the wake of structural adjustment policies, the Mexican government has organized social compensation programmes, albeit in the context of general cuts in social welfare and public services. These programmes have become the object of intense competition, and not only among the poor, since in Villarreal's words (see Chapter 4) 'rural livelihoods have come to depend on aid policies and government social programmes in a large way'. Institutional reform in Bolivia is also significant to the poor, for while it opens up new possibilities for access and influence, it closes off existing ways of exerting pressure on political processes. While the local government system within the framework of the state has been democratized to the advantage of some marginalized groups, the national unions that have traditionally spoken on the part of the poor appear to have lost influence. This is due to the institutional reform being based upon territorial representation, with no formal role for professional organizations.

Government policies are, however, far from the only ones to be important. The general concern with poverty in national political discussions and struggles is just as important. The Left Front government that has led West Bengal since 1977 was from the outset very concerned about the rural poor and carried through significant initiatives in the areas of decentralization and land reform. This pro-poor atmosphere was conducive to the mobilization and organization of marginalized groups such as the Adivasi women, who have overcome much local resistance, not the least because of state-wide discourses stressing poverty reduction and the political agency of the poor. Another vivid example of the importance of national political processes and struggles is provided in the Peruvian study of the coping strategies of peasants during three decades of change. From pro-poor land reforms through a devastating civil war to a neo-liberal political regime, the rural people have sought to make a living, and although they have not been passive victims of the various ideological and violent fashions, peasants have sometimes experienced extremely limited opportunities both politically and in general. Links between national and local levels are also emphasized in Burkina Faso. Most local political issues are heavily controlled by the national regime, and this centralized nature of policy-making rules out any concern for the political agency of marginalized groups, despite the contemporary period of democratization. Similarly, the clientelist nature of many political processes at both local and national levels in Bangladesh seems to prevent marginalized groups from influencing policies because there is a tendency among the leaders of poor people's organizations to 'succumb to clientelist politics through personalistic squabbles over the distribution of spoils' (see Chapter 9) whenever they come into power.

Government policies, like national politics, are, accordingly, of great importance when it comes to realizing the political agency of the poor. During the 1980s it was repeatedly argued that the state has not been very effective in initiating economic growth in many African, Latin American and South Asian countries. State-led development was discredited and neo-liberal market-based solutions were also promoted in relation to poverty (Toye 1987). While it has been recognized during the 1990s that the state has a role to play in both development and poverty reduction (World Bank 1997), we suggest that this role is not peripheral, but rather crucial in providing the conditions under which poor groups may also take up political action to improve their livelihoods. Government policies to support the poor, government rhetoric recognizing the plight of the poor, and administrative practices explicitly considering marginalized groups can all effect the general political environment as well as the particular social struggles in which poor people are involved. The possibility of legitimizing claims by referring to official statements or bureaucratic procedures is a strong asset for the poor. This is particularly clear from studies on Zimbabwe, where marginalized groups base their occupation of land on President Mugabe's speeches, and on West Bengal, where the Forestry Department increasingly, though somewhat reluctantly, includes poor users in the management of forest lands.

However, if we take a sweeping look at the studies presented here, the role of the state seems in most cases to be somewhat ambiguous. Notably in countries like Burkina Faso, Peru, Mexico and Bangladesh, the state has done very little to support the political agency of the poor. The governments of these countries have not sought to promote a political discourse on poverty reduction, or to influence national politics in a pro–poor direction. Whatever advantages marginalized groups have been able to seize, has been through their own efforts, often circumventing official channels. In other countries, such as Bolivia, Zimbabwe and Mozambique, the role of the state is less clear, possibly because it is weaker. While some initiatives acknowledge the poor and their political rights, others appear to have more to do with nation-building and state control. In West Bengal it appears to be a changing role: 'If the Left Front government (LFG) began by stressing the agency of the poor in terms of their need to mobilize and act to implement the structural reforms, today the tendency is to stress the role of the LFG in guiding and administering development for all, including the poor' (see Chapter 10).

This does not mean that national politics generally have become harsher to the poor. On the contrary, the 1990s have probably witnessed a heightened concern for the political rights of citizens, including marginalized groups, as part of the post–Cold War enlightenment and the general shift towards democracy, good governance and human rights. Whatever one thinks about this change and its consequences in terms of the transition towards democracy by a growing number of countries, it is certainly the case that groups of poor people have greater opportunities to organize and act politically today than was the case one or two decades ago. Neo–liberal criticism of the state's role in development must take some of the credit for this. Today it is no longer possible for governments and state officials to assert an exclusive or superior responsibility for all development activities within a society. On the other hand, the fundamental ideological struggles that have characterized recent politics in many countries have seriously affected the living conditions and opportunities of the poor. Although Marxist-inspired movements have emphasized the plight of the deprived, their methods and the implications of their struggles have often worsened poor people's livelihoods. This is most evident in Peru and Mozambique, which have both suffered from prolonged civil wars, but it is also the case in other countries in which 'the communist threat' has been used to control and suppress the mobilization and organization of marginalized groups. From this point of view, the retreat from fierce ideological conflicts must be welcomed.

Institutional reform, notably decentralization and democratization, has constituted the most popular way of seeking to integrate the poor into politics in recent years. We see, however, three substantial limits to these institutional measures. First, the initiatives taken are often limited to a particular sphere (for example, decentralization) or even to a restricted part of this sphere (for example, administrative decentralization). There is little understanding of the need for complementary institutional reforms that simultaneously address the social, economic and political factors constraining the political agency of the poor. The example of West Bengal is again a case in point because the state government there introduced a number of measures (land reform, decentralization, minimum wages) that combined to reduce the dependencies and vulnerabilities of marginalized groups. However, programmes and policies in one sphere often counteract initiatives in another. Such inconsistencies are illustrated by the example of the Bolivian government, whose initiatives in support of public participation and the indigenous population go hand in hand with the repression of demonstrations, the arrest of union leaders and a campaign by state-supported paramilitaries against coca leaf producers.

Second, institutional reforms are sometimes carried out in a half-hearted fashion, either being rendered ineffective from the outset, such as devolving authority without resources, or else being diluted through the implementation process, as is often the case with land reforms. The decentralization process in Burkina Faso suffers from a number of shortcomings. Only candidates from the national political parties can run for the municipal councils, resulting in local politics being controlled by the needs of actors at the national level. Also, the relationship between the municipalities and the local administrative offices of state ministries has not been adequately defined, and it remains uncertain what form decentralization will take in the rural areas. Zimbabwe is haunted by similar inconsistencies, as seen in the ambiguities in government policies with respect to the Communal Lands, the Rural District Councils and the 'traditional' chiefs. While marginalized groups may find it advantageous to manoeuvre in situations of fluidity and ambiguity, the outcomes in the longer term do not often benefit the poor.

Third, when institutional reforms are planned and implemented carefully, their success may be limited if they are undertaken in a political, social and economic environment that runs counter to the needs of the poor. This is illustrated by the study of local elections in Bangladesh, where the dominant factions, supported by armed men and the use of terror, have prevented groups of poor day-labourers from having their own candidates elected. In other places, marginalized groups did not seek to influence the elections due to the clientelist nature of local politics. In Tamil Nadu, Rajasekhar has noted that the poor do not view the local government as accessible. The *gram panchayat* is regarded as 'an elected executive to implement public works' not 'an organization that would enable the participation of the poor so that they can access, control and contest policy formulation and implementation' (see Chapter 8). Although the context is not specifically anti-poor, the state initiatives to create decentralized government institutions and a rural banking system have not proved successful in terms of supporting marginalized groups. To understand this, it is necessary to look beyond institutional reform and to search for other crucial factors affecting or preventing the political agency of the poor.

The Bewildering Richness of Local Actors, Actions and Processes

The interaction of the political agency of the poor with institutional actors in national politics takes place in extremely diverse settings in these case studies. It is not possible to combine this diversity and the range of processes involved into a standard formula of process and action. Our aim is not to identify a set of crucial mechanisms through which the poor are always able to address and influence political processes. It has been demonstrated that these can be formal or informal, at the planning or implementation stage, and nationally or locally specific. Thus the issues raised in the introduction are revealed in quite different manners within and between countries.

However, it is possible and reasonable to identify a number of questions that have been highlighted in the different studies. First, discursive struggles are a fundamental part of the political processes in which poor people are engaged. Because of their situation, marginalized groups do not have many assets to use in their endeavour to influence politics, but prevailing discourses clearly constitute one that they may be able to turn to their advantage with as much skill as other, more affluent groups. Local discourses on poverty and democracy are, for instance, used during land disputes in Angónia, Mozambique, where being poor and needy supports one's case at the chiefly courts. Ongoing discussions of democratization are also used by the poor since 'democracy is perceived as the opportunity to make your own demands and claims' (see Chapter 5). In neighbouring Zimbabwe, we have already noted how people refer to the speeches of President Mugabe in order to obtain land. Also, discourses on historical injustice, 'traditional' rights, sacrifices during the liberation war and opportunities for modernization are variously drawn upon to legitimize claims to land. The significance of a poverty discourse is stressed in the Mexican study, as many draw directly on the terminology of poverty. 'The discursive practices within which interests were articulated all made reference to the poor and poverty alleviation, but the rules of the game were contested, identities redefined and needs "re-invented"' (see Chapter 4). That discourses and identities are far from fixed is clear. Instead, they are being moulded and transformed constantly in order to legitimize the needs and interests of the various actors. In Burkina Faso, a discourse on poverty and poverty reduction is conspicuously absent. While women can increasingly refer to a discourse on their particularly harsh living conditions, other marginalized groups do not have such opportunities. This is partly explained by the fact that poverty is perceived to be degrading and shameful. Rather than being an asset in discursive struggles, being described as poor means incurring further disadvantage.

A question related to the discursive struggles is the practice of naming. In the conflicts studied in Bolivia and in Zimbabwe, the naming of actors has been crucial. In Bolivia, the Law of Popular Participation identified the Territorial Base Organization (OTB) as the focal point for people's influence on local political processes, and the idea was that existing organizations should register as OTBs and thereby become renamed. This provoked a strong response, and peasant leaders argued: 'If they change our name, what they really want to do is to change our organization, and transform it so that it can be managed by the government' (see Chapter 2). This feeling was sufficiently strong to pressure the government into changing its position. In Zimbabwe, the strategy of naming was used by a local government seeking to evict people from a particular tract of land. These people were described not as settlers but as 'squatters', and their presence was termed 'illegal'. The intention was to undermine their claims for land in both legal and 'traditional' terms. Such attempts to define and name particular actors and issues are not mere questions of semantics; they often have profound effects on the way actors perceive conflicts and the issues involved. Naming is central to the manner in which problems are defined, to the power of discourse, and to political struggle.

Second, the role of local organizations is anything but clear in relation to poverty reduction and the facilitation of the political agency of the poor. In the study of a range of local organizations in Tamil Nadu, including banks, local governments and a NGO, the mixed attitude towards marginalized groups is evident, despite the presence of an official discourse on poverty reduction and institutional channels for accessing local political processes. Banks are expected to give loans to poor people, but they insist on collateral; local governments do not see it as their responsibility to deal with poverty reduction; and the local NGO concentrates on short-term poverty alleviation through income-generating activities rather than political mobilization. Although NGO support is extremely important to a large number of poor people, it is interesting to note that the income-generating activities address, in particular, the needs of young, unmarried women from depressed castes. Despite the best intentions, it is unlikely that this support will bring about the political mobilization of significant poor groups or that the NGO will achieve any significant poverty reduction.

In Burkina Faso, people's associations and local NGOs are reluctant to become involved openly in politics, and they seldom advocate the concerns and needs of marginalized groups at the levels of local government or the state. Furthermore, as mentioned previously, there is a lack of recognition of poverty as being a problem in itself. Little is accordingly undertaken to direct activities towards the marginalized groups apart from the women who figure prominently in the rhetoric, at least. Furthermore, leaders of people's associations and NGOs have sufficient leeway to use their organization for individual purposes. Although publicly distancing themselves from politics, many organizational leaders have informal relations with politicians designed to further their political careers, and they may be more concerned about strategic manoeuvring for personal influence than about poverty reduction. This point is supported by the study from Mexico, where local organizations through which poor people can gain access to government funds are caught in a variety of interests and agendas. The concerns of marginalized groups are mixed and blurred with other concerns, and 'the poor's interests' become a highly negotiated and ambiguous matter. The conclusion that arises from this evidence is that any organization claiming to represent the interests of the poor must be viewed with scepticism. This is not least due to the poor being a heterogeneous group, their needs being interwoven with the interests of others and often suppressed due to this interlinkage of interests, and the deeper structural conditions causing their poverty rarely being addressed by such organizations.

Third, when poor people attempt to confront and influence political processes, this often takes place against a background of very mixed sentiments regarding the role of the state. On the one hand, the state is typically expected to deliver social services (Burkina Faso, Tamil Nadu, West Bengal, Bangladesh) and to provide support when living conditions worsen (Mexico, Tamil Nadu, West Bengal). In some cases, marginalized groups long for recognition as 'loyal citizens' and 'faithful subjects' of the state (Peru), and poor people may also look to the authority of the state to prevent illegal acts and to regulate social conflicts (West Bengal, Mozambique). Accordingly, the state is to some extent met with expectations that it should create a safe and supportive environment.

On the other hand, people's experience with the state is generally quite negative. With the partial exception of India, there is a widespread feeling that the contemporary state follows closely in the footsteps of colonial powers in the way in which it seeks to intervene, control and marginalize particular groups. The whole history of suppression is unfolded in a recent political document from a national union of peasants in Bolivia, where a very negative picture of the world outside the peasantry is presented. 'The peasants see themselves as oppressed, dominated and exploited, and in opposition not only to the capitalist society ... but also to the government, the state and most political parties' (see Chapter 2). A similar, though less openly expressed, view of the state and other non-local actors is shared by villagers in Burkina Faso. Confronting, even addressing the state is dangerous, partly because of its powers, and partly because political processes are seen to produce arbitrary results due to constant power struggles and the numerous agendas involved. In Zimbabwe, obtaining land has been a long-term expectation of many groups. Various statements made by the government have fuelled this desire, but the lack of action has undermined people's confidence in the state, and the resulting frustration and impatience have stimulated land invasions. The eviction of settlers or 'squatters' by the Rural District Council has produced a sense of betrayal among the settlers and their supporters, who had expected something different from the state and the council.

Fourth, and linked to the previous point, rural groups often seem to be sceptical of the various attempts by states to organize the rural setting, be it through institutional reforms such as decentralization or direct intervention in people's organizations. The opposition to the state in Bolivia has already been noted, but it has a particular organizational twist to it. People's organizations have long lived a life not just parallel to state structures, but also outside their reach. In many areas, the municipalities have had very little influence on local social processes, whereas community organizations have functioned as *de facto* local governments. One purpose of the Popular Participation Act is to change this situation, and people fear this new imposition of homogeneity and transparency by the state. Also in Mexico, rural groups resist the state's institutional interventions. Since the 1970s the state has sought to organize the rural population in cooperatives and other forms of organization, mainly to people's dissatisfaction. Accordingly, the recent government programme supporting social enterprises has been forced to accept rather informal 'partner' organizations such as kinship networks.

The creation of Forest Protection Committees in West Bengal is another example of an institutional intervention by the state, albeit with different implications for the poor. Chapter 10 shows that poor groups have been able to exploit attempts to organize them giving considerable benefits to the poor Adivasi women involved. However, a significant general point is that institutional reform is a two-edged sword as seen from the perspective of the poor, because while it may provide opportunities for the poor to access and contest political processes, it may also produce greater state control of and interference with social life. Given the rural population's historical and present experience with the state, it is no wonder that people's organizations and marginalized groups may be worried about their autonomy and self-determination when institutional reforms are undertaken.

Fifth, despite the real and potential political agency of the poor investigated in this volume, a theme running through a number of these studies is that the rural population and marginalized groups partly try to seal off themselves from outside powerful actors. Whether deliberately or as an unintended but appreciated consequence of other needs and actions, the peasant community in Peru, the chiefs in Mozambique, the *samaj* in Bangladesh and the leaders of peoples' organizations in Burkina Faso all appear to function as intermediaries between the state and the poor. Peasant communities in Peru have been the primary institution through which villagers have sought to resist the encroachment of their land by neighbouring *haciendas*, and they also constituted the arena mediating the land reform act and the poverty discourse in the 1970s. In the context of an authoritarian political regime and a brutal civil war, chiefs in Mozambique have been regarded by many of the rural poor as the only institution providing some protection against the vagaries of national processes. Although in decline, the *samaj* (a political and religious community institution) in Bangladesh has not only been useful in dispute settlements, religious matters and mutual assistance within its territory, it has also mediated the interaction between the outside world and the villagers, which resembles very much the role of people's organizations in Burkina Faso. Given the numerous interventions from outside with substantial technical and social implications, peasants in this country are anxious that the leaders of their organizations resist the less desired dimensions of state and project activities.

However, it is not only the rural population and marginalized groups who are interested in intermediary institutions: there is little doubt that the state- and national-level actors need such channels when they address the rural population. By definition, therefore, the role of intermediary is important in providing power, and local elites will therefore seek to control the mediating institutions. However, control does not mean absolute power, and the relationship between local elites and marginalized groups remains ambivalent and not just exploitative. For instance, the role of the chiefs in

Mozambique has been a subject of local debate for some time. It has been argued by Frelimo and others that the chiefs represent a feudal, reactionary world order, while others have gone to the other extreme, claiming that the chiefs embody the authentic, original, African culture. From the perspective of the poor, Chapter 5 clearly documents that there are advantages as well as disadvantages in the chieftainship. It is this mixed role of local elites that is important to recognize in the context of poverty-reduction efforts.

Political Space and Poverty Reduction

Given the very diverse histories, trajectories and experiences characterizing the localities and actors studied in the present book, it is not possible to make detailed statements on the specific conditions that are both necessary and sufficient for poverty reduction. We have noted that institutional reforms such as decentralization and state-initiated rural organizations can be double-edged swords from the perspective of the poor. We have also seen that the recourse to political discourses and practices of naming are extremely important in most political struggles, and that marginalized groups may take advantage of such discourses as one of their few assets. However, discourses may also go against interests of the poor by ignoring their needs or addressing the concerns of only a small fraction of the deprived. While the organizational practices of the poor are undoubtedly of importance when they try to assert their rights and vindicate their claims in political arenas, questions as to which practices and how they are best utilized cannot be answered on the evidence here.

We have argued that it can be meaningful to speak of a political space for poverty reduction when all three dimensions (institutional channels, poverty discourses and organizational practices) are present in such a manner that they support the political agency of the poor. Even when this is the case, it will not ensure that poverty reduction does occur. Yet the evidence of these case studies does indicate that this kind of political space, and the consequences it has for government policy and practice, does appear to have impact on poverty. Perhaps the clearest example is provided by the case study in West Bengal. Here all three dimensions are shown to be present, and a group of particularly deprived people, Adivasi women, have succeeded in gaining representation and influence in bodies responsible for policy and programme implementation. Bolivia supplies another example, albeit with a fly in the ointment. Institutional channels have been created, but people regard them with some scepticism. While discourses emphasizing the interests and needs of marginalized groups do exist, and organizational practices of the poor are widespread, the state continues to practise exclusion and to use violence against those it distrusts or opposes. Consequently the political space for poverty reduction, while greater than before the introduction of decentralized government, remains fragile in Bolivia. The climate of mutual suspicion between the rural poor and the state continues to limit the potential of the reforms, and it remains to be seen as to whether there will be any significant increase in the poor's influence.

The remaining case studies have been undertaken in societies where one or more of the dimensions of political space are lacking or where the context denies their potential. The evidence from Mexico gives some ground for optimism, but the organizational practices found to be present in the study are remarkably individualistic and are focused on short-term material gains rather than on achieving any form of collective political influence. In the case of Bangladesh, existing political discourses reveal only a partial concern with issues of poverty and the interests of the poor. In those areas in which there is NGO support for the political mobilization of the poor or where there are experiences of organization and mobilization from earlier independence movements, there has been some success in getting poor candidates elected to local government. Interestingly, the Bangladesh study reveals two issues that go against the political agency of the poor, even in those areas with NGO support. The first is the role of local elites in manipulating the electoral process, and not least in preventing poor people from voting. The second is the clientelist nature of politics, which serves to undermine the consequences of candidates being elected from among the poor, as they are pressured towards the politics of factionalism and self-enrichment. Even if political space were present, influence on and control over political processes would have to be fought for by the poor – they are not gently given or secured.

From the perspective of the household, economic progress and an improvement in its material conditions are perhaps the most significant changes in terms of poverty reduction that can occur. Changes in daily income, in returns to cultivation, in the amount of land owned or accessible for cultivation, or in the amount of employment obtained possess an immediacy and have direct consequences for a household that other changes may not. Changes in legal rights of access to forests, the provision of health services and the decentralization of government are not so immediately associated with improvements in household livelihoods. Yet an increase in female wages or in the number of days in agricultural employment in a year are the outcomes of a range of actions by diverse actors, only a few of which the household can influence, and many of which it might not be aware of. Nevertheless the sustainability of the outcomes often remains dependent upon the continuing actions of these 'more distant' actors as well as upon the actions of the poor themselves. If rights are to be implemented and secured, if the interests of migrant workers and land evictees are to be considered, if gender equality in the case of poor women is to be upheld, the poor must increase their influence over questions of resource distribution and policy-making. To achieve this in turn requires that the institutional channels for engagement in policy and programme fora be present, participatory and informed with an awareness and responsibility for poverty reduction and the poor.

In addition to the presence of informed political institutions through which policies are designed and programmes implemented, there is a need for engagement on the part of the poor. The organizing practices of the poor groups, though present, have more often than not operated in a context in which the political exclusion of the poor has been more evident than their political inclusion. Access to power, to decision-makers, has been negotiated and bought rather than secured as a right. Where the poor have taken overt political action, the threat of such action in the eyes of the state has tended to outweigh a more positive interpretation that stresses the importance of participation and engagement as political processes. Rarely is such action by the poor blamed upon institutional failure or the political exclusion of the poor. Even where it is seen as such, the means are not seen to justify the causes or the ends.

The patron–client relations that have dominated the political practice of poor people have served throughout history to exclude and obscure decision-making processes from the eyes and ears of the poor. In discussing political space, the focus has been on the possibility and potential for bringing the political agency of the poor into the process of governance. In the Introduction to this book it was acknowledged that the discussion of political space is closely linked to, and builds upon, the contemporary interest in democracy, local democracy, and the poverty-reduction potential that the general transition towards democracy can offer. However, the three dimensions discussed as being necessary if poverty reduction is to be a significant reality tend to focus upon the domestic political arena. This is not surprising, as it is the relationship between the local and the macro, between specific groups of the poor and the state, that concerns us. Yet the context for these relations is also being shaped and influenced by international actors and actions. In the case of Peru migration occurred across national boundaries, and in a number of the countries in these case studies international donors agencies are active agents in the constitution of local NGOs and as funding agencies for local projects and programmes.

The recognition of the current role of international actors in shaping and influencing the local and macro arenas of the case studies in this volume takes the discussion back to the point at which much of the contemporary interest in the local begins, namely at the global level. Academics in the North, donor agencies and Northern NGOs have all been instrumental in the elevation of the local in development studies and policies. While the focus upon the local is undoubtedly of considerable importance in the reassessment of approaches to development, development policies and the types of institutional mechanisms used for development interventions, the determination of what constitutes the local remains under-researched. A particular danger is that the local is simply defined as the opposite of the state, as the counter to central planning, as the place where people can secure their own development if permitted to do so. Such an approach to the local tends to make assumptions concerning how groups, including the poor, behave in developmental terms, and to analyse their actions according to abstract concepts.

What the case studies demonstrate is that there is a political agency on the part of the poor that exists at the local level. They also suggest that it does not need to be constructed, isolated or remoulded. Rather than seeking to locate local civicness, social capital or similar 'community phenomena', the need is to study the manifestations of political agency and seek to find ways in which it can be introduced into the broader political processes that guide a country's development trajectory. This will support poverty reduction. At the same time it has been argued that poverty is relational and that it involves power. Logically, the powerful will seek to deny the agency of the poor. It is the reciprocities of the relations involved that render the control of power open to negotiation and contest. Denial, as practised through political exclusion, can be challenged, and it is here that international actors have a central role to play. If donor agencies and other national and international actors can facilitate the connection of the poor to the national processes of politics and decision-making, the interests of the poor can begin to affect the development agenda.

Whether one is seeking to enhance local democracy, promote accountable and transparent decentralized government, secure basic human rights or promote local economic growth, the processes examined in the various case studies contribute to a better understanding as to how these might be pursued. Despite the specificity of the local and country contexts of these case studies, the analyses do support a common approach towards development, an approach that emphasizes processes over procedures, a focus on relations over a focus on individual capacities, and the need to combine strategies and actions at the local level with politics and actions at the national level.

Of the three dimensions necessary to produce a political space conducive to poverty reduction, it is perhaps in the field of support for institutional channels through which the local can be connected to the macro, and support for a better discourse on poverty, that donor agencies and govern-ments can best intervene. Involved here are decentralization, a dynamic civil society, support for the media, the development and dissemination of informed thinking on poverty, knowledge as to the scale and dimension of poverty present in a country, linking poverty to issues of gender, minorities, the environment, age, regional location, elevating poverty into the popular arenas of debate and discussion, and so on. Such measures can serve to change the local and macro contexts in which the poor find themselves. They can help to bring the political agency of the poor into a development trajectory that sees poverty reduction not only as a primary objective, but also as a real possibility.

References

Toye, John (1987) *Dilemmas of Development: Reflections on the Counter-revolution in Dev-elopment Theory and Policy*, Oxford: Oxford Univerity Press.

World Bank (1997) *World Development Report 1997. The State in a Changing World*, Oxford: Oxford Univerity Press.

Index